Stock Selection

Stock Selection

Buying and Selling Stocks Using the IBM PC

Jeremy C. Jenks

Robert W. Jenks

JOHN WILEY & SONS

New York   Chichester   Brisbane   Toronto   Singapore

Library of Congress Cataloging in Publication Data
Jenks, Jeremy C.
    Stock selection.

    Bibliography: p.
    Includes index.
    1. Investments—Data processing. 2. Stocks—Data
processing. 3. IBM Personal Computer. I. Jenks,
Robert W., 1946-   . II. Title.
HG4515.5.J46 1984   332.63′22′02854   83-12394
ISBN 0-471-89476-1

Printed in the United States of America

10 9 8 7 6 5 4 3 2 1

Preface

There are three parts to this guide to *Stock Selection*. The first part explains time-tested methods used by investment professionals in selecting stocks. This section will help you understand the fundamentals of value, such as the growth potential of a business and the quality of a security. The second part of the book explains the Microsoft Basic programs for doing the valuation analysis to select stocks. It was written to be run on the IBM personal computer, and comes with a detailed explanation of how to run the programs. The final part of the book explains how to use the valuations to make good investment decisions by fitting them into the framework of the constantly changing economy and market.

As everyone who has looked at stock tables knows, stocks have violent price fluctuations. For example, IBM was selling at 56 the first trading day of 1982, and closed the year at 96. The surge in the market from mid-August 1982 to the year-end saw some stocks at least double in price. Obviously, if one knew what stocks were worth at any particular time, it would be simple enough to buy the ones that were bargains and avoid those that were not. Stocks rarely sell for what they are worth. They are constantly in the process of going from undervaluation to overvaluation, and then back again; this fluctuation presents great opportunities for the knowledgable investor, yet poses great risk for all investors.

The programs are located in the Appendix. They are well-organized and easy to use, and you have the option of purchasing a diskette which contains all the programs, and comes with actual valuation data on 30 stocks especially selected for their various attractive investment characteristics. The stocks include AT&T, IBM, Johnson & Johnson, Merck, Procter & Gamble, Schlumberger, Texas Instruments, and others, some not so well-known. You can add as many more stocks to the program as you wish.

This is a "how to do it" book. It tells you where to find the information you need, while giving complete and detailed instructions on how to use a computer to select stocks that are undervalued while avoiding those that are overvalued. It explains how to select stocks that will benefit from various economic conditions, and shows you how to recognize when to be an aggressive stock buyer. It points out which indicators will give you early warning that the market may be headed for trouble, and discusses strategies that can improve your market profits. It explains clearly what types of investments are suitable for you and for any kind of investor. It provides you with information that is important to investors in such detail that you will need no other sources. The bibliography lists books that cover pertinent subjects in greater depth if you wish to learn more. The glossary explains the most frequently used financial and accounting terms found in the book.

This guide is well-illustrated with a variety of charts and tables that will help you to understand the matters discussed. The summary valuations on over 200 stocks are classified by industry, according to their sensitivity to various economic conditions.

Both amateur and professional investors can profit from reading this book, whether they have a computer or not, because it provides insights into making sound investments. While portions of our methods are original, they are based on procedures that are widely used and accepted by financial analysts. These methods are useful to anyone with a computer. If you do not yet have a computer, you will probably want to get one and start running the programs.

Can anyone use and profit from the methods described here, or does it require special talents? In all honesty you must be able to follow the described routines carefully and thoughtfully to get the best results. If you decide to type the programs in yourself, be extremely careful to follow them exactly as they appear in Appendix A. However, you do not need any specialized education or exceptional skill. Get your bright teenage children interested in stocks and watch them go. It will surprise you.

Is this book an easy road to riches? Certainly not. There isn't any such thing. But if you want to accumulate a nice nest egg, this book will make it easier, while steering you around a number of the pitfalls that trap many investors. You will also get some surprising insights into what really happens on Wall Street from the distilled knowledge gained in over 40 years of hands-on investment experience.

Good investing!

JEREMY C. JENKS
ROBERT W. JENKS

Islamorada, Florida
September 1983

Contents

1

The Facts of Life on Wall Street

RESULTS OF STOCK INVESTMENT

Even Wall Street professionals have some erroneous ideas about the results that can be achieved from stock investment, so we will briefly review some of the evidence. Some years ago, a well-regarded technical analyst said that his charting methods picked stocks that went up 70% of the time. Is this good? No; based on recent studies this is not exceptional.

A thorough computerized study, covering millions of combinations of stocks and holding periods over a span of years, shows that if stocks are selected completely at random, for example, by throwing darts at the stock tables, 78% of the trades will be profitable. Why is this? The answer is complex, but basically, stock prices have risen over the years because profits have grown along with an expanding economy. A factor to consider has been that corporations pay less than half their earnings in dividends, and reinvest the balance in ways that add to profits. Inflation has also been a major reason, as will be discussed later.

Other studies show that if an investor bought a representative slice of the market in 1926 and reinvested the dividends, the return on the investment would have been about 10% per year, over the fifty-seven years. In comparison with recent high interest rates, 10% is not outstanding. However, if there are no taxes or other offsets, your money will double in a little over seven years. Fifty thousand dollars, invested 30 years ago at 10%, tax free, with the income reinvested, would now be worth over $872,000. Such is the power of compounding.

This, and other evidence, shows that stock investment has been profitable for most investors. In later chapters, such matters as the relative attractiveness of stocks versus bonds or other types of investment are covered. However, the main theme of this book is how to select stocks, not whether bonds, real estate, or gold might be better at some particular time.

THE RANDOM WALK

The anecdote about the chartist is not intended to discredit technical analysis. However, for our purposes, we do not use technical analysis of stock price movements. Instead, we select stocks on the basis of fundamentals such as earnings prospects and growth potential, as will be described.

What makes stocks go up or down? There obviously are a number of influences, but these apparently do not include past price movements. The "Random Walk" theory expresses the opinion that stock price movements are random and that there is no relationship between a stock's past price movement and those of the future. Bringing stock trading volume changes into the analysis does not improve the results; in other words, the combination of price and trading volume data still has no predictive power.

Proponents of the Random Walk theory contend that one can test daily, weekly, or monthly price changes and find that they are completely independent of past ones; if so, price movements are random. Other studies indicate that chart patterns have no predictive power. For example, a head and shoulders formation has ominous meanings to many chartists, but recent work shows that the market is just as likely to emerge from this pattern on the up side as the down. Of course, there are so many possible chart patterns that the evidence is not all in. The *Dow Jones −Irwin Guide to Common Stocks*, listed in the bibliography, describes some of the studies referred to above in more detail, and explains how they were made so that one can better judge their validity.

You will note that in this book we use charts to illustrate various matters that are being discussed. We find charts helpful in showing what has happened and where we are now. This is entirely different from using them to predict movements in the series under review.

WHAT CAUSES STOCK PRICE MOVEMENTS?

If past price movements neither cause nor predict future price movements, what does? There are a large number of influences that can be listed under three major headings: The general market, industry factors, and company-related information. Stocks have a strong tendency to move up or down with the market. They also tend to move with their industry classification or group. And, possibly most important, they move purely on company developments. The studies we have seen also show that different industry groups have different responses to the market's pull. For example, tobacco stocks, utilities, and retail stores do not move closely with the market, while railroads and metals track the market very closely.

The time period covered seems to dominate the results,

however. For example, in the brutal market collapse of 1974, the market was the driving force. Under more normal market conditions, the latter two, industry and company factors, seem to be more important. Our experience indicates that the company factors are more important in the long run, but that the other two may govern over shorter periods of time.

The important matters to analyze under each of these headings are as follows:

The Market.   What are the prospects for the economy? For example, which way are the leading indicators pointing? How will the financial factors, such as interest rates and the money supply, develop? What are the social and political trends? What is the outlook for the free enterprise system in the United States and the rest of the world?

The Industry.   What is likely to happen to the special factors affecting an industry's profitability? For example, interest rates are critical for the building industry, as are oil prices for the energy group.

The Company.   Is the company gaining or losing competitively in its industry? How fast are the earnings likely to grow? Are the finances strong? Does the company have special problems, such as labor troubles, or antitrust and other regulatory problems?

These matters are all interrelated, and are the factors that affect corporate earnings and stock prices.

THE EFFICIENT MARKET

Before we study the various factors that determine stock price movements, let us examine the question, "Can an investor do better than the market?" If he or she cannot, why bother with the substantial amount of work we outline in this book? The Efficient Market theory contends that stocks are efficiently priced to reflect all available market information because millions of investors, including at least 50 thousand professionals, having access to the same information, will quickly adjust the price to the facts, and stocks will sell for what they are worth. The market does anticipate earnings changes, dividends, and similar factors remarkably well. Also, when there is an earnings surprise, the move in the stock is quickly over, usually before all but the most nimble traders can take advantage of it. Many studies have examined how stocks react to dividend increases, stock splits, and other types of investment news, and show that the market is efficient, giving little opportunity to an investor to take advantage of such public information.

Even the more ardent advocates of the Efficient Market theory admit that some items of public information do have predictive value. For example, stocks sold heavily by insiders usually decline before the announcement, and continue to do so for some months afterward. Also, stocks bought by insiders tend to outperform the market. Various services monitor this information.

Another inefficiency worth noting is secondary stock offerings. These offerings usually occur after a stock has been strong, and, in most cases are followed by poor market perfomance. A secondary offering is one by an investor who has had a close relationship to the business, such as a venture capital firm that helped with the early financing.

Insider trading, whether in the market in modest amounts or in secondary blocks subject to registration requirements, have to be reported and are subject to legal restrictions. Insiders are not allowed to take advantage of material information. For example, if people knew that a tender offer was going to be made for a stock, they would be breaking the law if they bought the stock in advance of the announcement, no matter how they aquired that information. John Shad, the Chairman of the Securities and

Exchange Commission, recently said that "Every time there is a tender offer, almost without exception, if you look at the price of the stock two weeks before the offering and then on the day of the announcement, you'll see it has moved up in price. That suggests somebody knew something and that they took advantage."

Another inefficiency in the market results from the privileged position of the stock exchange members. They have access to information on sell orders overhanging the market and buy orders under the market. Their actions are reported, but not until two weeks after the event. Even so, it is worth monitoring their activities and this topic will be covered in a later chapter.

THE IMPORTANT MARKET INEFFICIENCY

In one fundamental respect, the market is extremely inefficient, and this is where the major investment opportunity lies. The ability of market participants to evaluate the prospects of a company and to reach a sensible conclusion about the stock's value is inconsistent, and at times irrational in the extreme. As night follows day, stocks go from outrageous overvaluation to absurd undervaluation.

Texas Instruments is a good example of the wide price swings that occur. In the poor market of 1970, the stock declined from 67 to 31—to less than half. The next year it rebounded strongly, and continued on up in 1972 and 1973, to a peak of 139. That was 108 points, or a gain of 348%. In the market collapse of 1974, it gave back most of the prior advance, declining to 59. In 1975 and 1976, the stock recovered irregularly to 130. In 1977 and early 1978, it dropped to 61, almost back to the previous low. The next advance culminated at 151 in the fall of 1980. Subsequently, it was cut in half to 70 in early 1982, and has recovered to over 100 since then. In the nearly 12 years covered, up to the 70 low in early 1982, the stock advanced

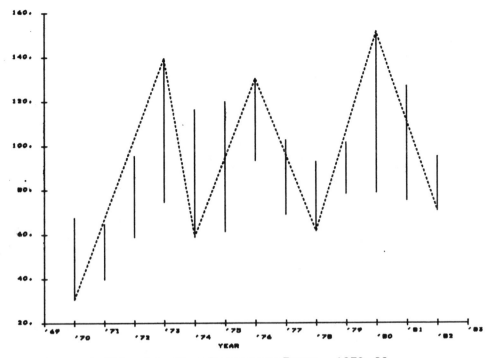

Figure 1.1   Texas Instruments Range — 1970–82

269 points and declined 266 points, in just those major moves, for a net gain of only three points. The chart above (Figure 1.1) shows the yearly price range, with the major price swings superimposed.

What was happening to the company's fundamentals during the time Texas Instruments stock was going through those gyrations? Earnings went from $1.36 per share in 1970 to $9.22 per share in 1980, declining only in 1975 and 1981. In Chapter 4, on estimating growth, we show data on Texas Instruments, our current earnings estimates, and our valuation.

Another example is Procter & Gamble. This is a very conservative stock, known as suitable for "widows and orphans" and regarded as not very volatile. However, as the

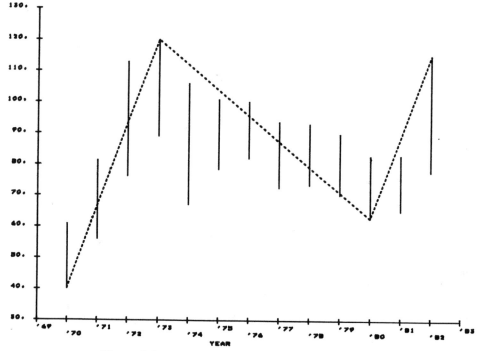

Figure 1.2   Procter & Gamble Range — 1970–82

chart in Figure 1.2 shows, there are good and bad times to
own the stock.

The stock was in a long decline, from a high of 120 in
early 1973, to a low of 63 in 1980. The 1980 low was even
below the 1974 low, in contrast to most stocks. From the
looks of this chart, one might conclude that something
had gone wrong with Procter & Gamble's earnings. Far
from it! Earnings grew from $2.60 per share in 1970, to
$9.39 per share in 1982. Both figures are for the fiscal
years ending in June. Earnings advanced every single
year!

Why did the stock lag the market until recently? The
reason is complex, but basically reflects the problems of
inflation and the fact that other kinds of businesses were

better able to pass on higher costs. With less inflation, the company's prospects look much brighter and the stock is responding accordingly. Procter & Gamble is discussed in more detail in Chapter 5, which discusses quality.

Is it possible for the average investor to know such things as when to own stocks like Procter & Gamble or Texas Instruments, when they should be bought, and when they should be sold? The readers of this book will have to judge for themselves. Obviously, we have been convinced for many years that a sensible approach to the valuation of securities, together with reasonable effort and good judgment, will yield consistent profits. As the old saying goes, "The proof of the pudding is in the eating."

We are not trading oriented. However, our worst mistakes over the years have been in failing to sell stocks that were clearly overpriced. Our time span is usually from one to three years. An examination of the above charts indicates that a two-year holding is fairly typical. This book does not offer tax advice, but it is usually best to plan on holding a profitable investment for the maximum 20% rate on long-term capital gains of over one year. Similarly, it frequently pays to sell investments that have gone wrong before a year passes, when you have a loss.

WHY USE A COMPUTER?

The methods described in this book evolved over a considerable number of years, and are based on work on financial analysis and portfolio management done by many people. As will be described in the next chapter, there are several ways of valuing stocks that give good results. When we began developing the forerunner of our present methods, our main tools were a columnar pad, a pencil with an eraser, and a slide rule. A personal computer is a tool of such greater power than those we had 40 years ago that it is like comparing a Fourth of July rocket to the space shuttle. We are using statistical methods that, before the computer, were impractical because of the time involved. New possibilities are opening up rapidly as less expensive hardware and better software become available. The only limits are found in the ingenuity of the investor and the computer programmer.

Our analytical objectives are not basically different from those we had before obtaining a personal computer. However, work can be done more accurately, in more detail, and one can cover many more stocks than previously. We are able to construct statistical series involving thousands of mathematical operations. These permit us to experiment with methods designed to show the probable direction of interest rates or stock prices. Several of the more promising of these are shown in subsequent chapters.

Presumably, the reader has either a good knowledge of how to use a computer, as well as some interest in investments, or else a good knowledge of investments and some interest in computers, and perhaps both. In the back of the book is a glossary of the analytical terms used, and also a bibliography of books that explain in greater detail some of the subjects we are only able to touch upon briefly.

As an example of what can be done with a computer, we have included the following chart of the stock market in log form (see Figure 1.3). The advantage of using logs is that it shows percentage changes on a comparable basis. Whether from 20 to 40, or from 80 to 160, the move is the same distance on the chart. The computer translated the monthly figures to logs in a matter of seconds. It will perform other mathematical functions with equal speed.

The chart also shows corporate profits, via the broken line, for comparison. We have included profit estimates through 1984. As is the case with all estimates used in this book, the figures come from reliable sources, but are subject to the limitations that exist in trying to foretell the future. A look at this chart, which covers more than 30 years of market history, shows how numerous the oppor-

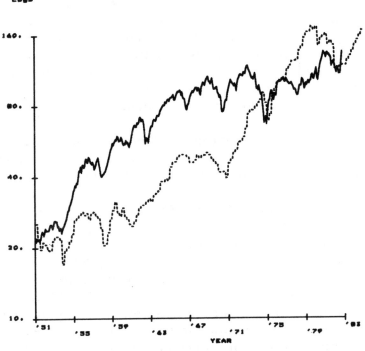

Figure 1.3   500 Stock Index — 1951–83
Corporate Profits — 1951–83

tunities have been to make 50% or more on stocks in the space of a year or two. Of course, there have been an equal number of times when you could lose a similar amount.

STOCKS WILL FLUCTUATE

Some years ago, I asked several investment friends what they thought about the following story. When J. P. Morgan, the elder, was at the peak of his power and influence in Wall Street, a brash young reporter asked him what the market would do. Mr. Morgan was quoted as replying, "It will fluctuate."

My question was what did Mr. Morgan mean? What was in his mind? The investors had a variety of ideas. One said it was just a brush-off to an impertinent question. Another said that if Mr. Morgan knew what the market was going to do, he would be foolish to share his knowledge with others. A third analyst thought that the response meant Morgan did not care to risk looking foolish in making such a uncertain prediction.

Another investor said that Mr. Morgan might have been thinking, "And as long as it continues to fluctuate, I will know how to profit from it." This last is the opinion that appeals to us.

The methods we and other professional investors use in trying to profit from fluctuations in stock prices differ in degree of complication. Ours is not the simplest, but it is designed to work on a small computer, and the information needed to make it work is readily available from several sources, as discussed in Chapter 3, "Sources of Data."

There is nothing abstruse or inherently difficult about our methods. As explained in the chapters that describe the computer programs, an elaborate computer system is not required.

2

Methods of Stock Selection Used by Professionals

THE CONCEPT OF VALUE

Oscar Wilde wrote, "A cynic is a man who knows the price of everything and the value of nothing." Whether investors are cynics or not, many know the price of stocks but have little idea of their value. If you ask them what a stock is worth, some give you a blank stare; they equate the current price with the value. Stocks rarely sell at the price they are worth. They fluctuate from overvaluation to undervaluation, and then back again. While a stopped clock is right twice a day, a stock seems to sell at its value twice every three years, more or less. Value means different things at different times. Analysts use such terms as breakup value, liquidating value, or appraised value.

It is considerably more difficult to determine the value of a share of stock than it is a pound of beef for a number of reasons. The beef is tangible; one can look at it. A pound is also a tangible measure, while a share is not quantified. It does not tell you how much of a business you own. American Telephone & Telegraph has 815,100,000 shares out-standing, so a share of stock represents an interest of 0.0000001227%. In a small company, with only a few million shares outstanding, a share of stock is still a very small interest. If an investor has 100 shares of a stock of a company that has five million outstanding, he has a 0.002% share in the company. Assume the company splits the stock two for one. The investor now has 200 shares of stock, but his or her share in the company remains the same. No wonder investors become confused.

If investors have a good idea about what a stock is worth, or what its value is, they will be able to take advantage of its price fluctuations. They will relate the price of the stock to the estimated value, and compare that with other stocks being considered for investment. Professional investors use a number of methods for estimating the value of a stock. Several of the more widely-used methods are described briefly in this chapter. Some of these methods work better on certain types of stocks than on others. Our approach is not original; a number of others use similar methods. However, we have developed a few variations or refinements that improve the results. The bibliography lists several books that describe in detail those methods developed by others in the profession. There is no single, widely-accepted way of valuing stocks. There are, however, certain elements common to most valuation methods.

EARNINGS ARE FUNDAMENTAL

In a broad sense, all widely-used methods of stock valuation are based on estimates of the future earning power of the company under review. In the case of an oil producer, the most commonly used method of valuing the stock is to estimate the amount of oil and gas reserves in the ground, then calculate a value based on those estimates. The calculation involves estimating the earnings that will result from producing the oil and gas, so this is not a basic exception. Similarly, if a company is going to be liquidated, at least a certain portion of the valuation will be based on what the assets can earn. If the assets can not earn anything, they may still have a residual value as a tax loss or for other reasons to some other business.

Few investors, professional or public, spend as much time as may be desired examining how the earnings of a company under review are calculated. A leading accountant applied accepted accounting principles to one company, and showed how he could obtain earnings ranging from $.80 per share to $1.79. The method used in inventory valuation and in calculating depreciation makes a material difference in the reported results. This is a very real problem, and one that has not been adequately addressed by financial analysts. Also, as will be discussed in subsequent chapters, certain industries have special accounting peculiarities. We are not referring to fraud. Fortunately, there is not much of that, even though a case hits the headlines every few years. In the example, the accountant used methods approved by both his profession and by regulatory authorities.

How do you handle this problem? You can get a partial answer by examining the tax rate and its reconciliation, which appears in the the annual reports. We show the significant accounting methods in the footnotes of our valuations, as is discussed in detail in Chapter 6.

Some analysts adjust reported earnings in their research reports for unusual accounting practices. However, this is less common than it should be. As explained in Chapter 5, the valuations take into account the effects of inflation on earnings, and other adjustments are made when appropriate. One should invest only in the stocks of companies that use clean and conservative accounting. If the accounting is promotional, it may be an indication that management is running the business in a risky fashion that will cause problems. When an examination of the accounting procedures indicates that it is materially less conservative than comparable companies, the stock should be dropped from consideration. There are more than 10,000 stocks listed in a recent *Standard & Poor's Stock Guide* (S & P's). While some are preferred stocks, there are at least 8,000 common stocks you can buy.

THE PRICE–EARNINGS RATIO

The price–earnings ratio, or P/E, is the price of a stock divided by the earnings for a particular year. Many reports show the P/Es for the most recent year for which the figures are actual, the current year as estimated, and the following year as projected. The P/Es shown in the stock tables use the last 12 months' earnings. Some services use an earnings figure made up of the last two quarters that have been reported, plus the next two quarters as estimated.

Most professional investors compare the P/Es of the stocks they are considering with historic P/Es, as well as with the present P/Es of other stocks or with market averages. International Business Machines (IBM) is selling at 60, or about 10.5× the latest 12 months' earnings, and about 9× estimates for 1982, ranging between $6.50 and $7.00 per share. IBM sold over 30 times its earnings, using the average of the annual high and low prices, back in the late 1960s and early 1970s, and occasionally over 40× earnings. Using $6.75 as the estimate for IBM's earnings for 1982 and $15 for the S & P Industrial average, you get the following comparison:

  IBM price 60 divided by $6.75 equals 8.9×
  S & P's price 122 divided by $15.00 equals 8.1×
  Or, 8.9 divided by 8.1 equals 110%.

Accordingly, an analyst might say, "IBM is selling at a 10% premium to the market, which appears reasonable, based on the company's above-average earnings prospects."

That statement does not say anything about the value of IBM. It merely offers the opinion that the price of IBM is reasonable. It is important to remember that the P/E is only a measure of price. By itself, it says nothing about whether a stock should sell at a market multiple, or else higher or lower. By the time this book is published, both the prices and the earnings figures may have changed. However, this and all the other examples were actual at the time of writing.

YIELDS

The investment manager usually takes the dividend into consideration, as well as the earnings and the P/E. The yield is calculated by dividing the dividend by the price. IBM is currently paying a quarterly dividend of $.86, or $3.44 per year. That gives a yield of 5.7%. Actually, the term *yield* is not appropriate to stocks; *return* would be better. *Yield* is a bond term, and takes into account any discount or premium in the price of the bond compared to the par value it will pay at maturity.

Many investment managers put a great deal of emphasis on a stock's dividend-paying ability because accounts such as pension funds and college endowment funds need current income to meet expenses. Similarly, retired individuals may be more concerned with the dividend return than young executives trying to build up their assets. Taxes are a primary consideration for many investors. Dividends may be taxed at a 50% rate, while a long-term capital gain is taxed at no more than 20%.

The safety of the dividend should be considered. An extremely high yield may mean the dividend is in jeopardy.

High grade bonds are usually better than stocks for current income. The suitability of various types of investments for different investors is discussed later.

THE DIVIDEND DISCOUNT MODEL

The first effort to assign a value to common stocks that received any general acceptance in the financial community was the Dividend Discount Model. The theory is that a stock is worth the sum of future dividends for a specific number of years, discounted at an assigned interest rate. *Discounted* means that a sum of money to be received a year later is worth less that the same sum received now, by the amount of interest that can be earned on it. For example, a discount rate the same as the yield on long-term government bonds would be about 12% at present. Accordingly, $100 dollars discounted for one year would be $89, and for 10 years would be $32. This is derived from discount tables, or a computer can make the calculations easily. Several of the texts listed in the bibliography have such tables in their appendices.

Early texts on this method stated that a stock was worth the discounted total of all future dividends, which is possible if the discount rate is higher than the growth rate. If, however, the growth rate is higher than the discount rate, the value would approach infinity.

A specific adaptation of this approach, used by a well-known Wall Street firm, estimates a growth rate for the earnings of the company under review over the next 10 years. It then assigns a pay-out ratio. For example, the company may pay out half its earnings on the average. This gives the expected dividends over the 10-year period, which are discounted and then added together. In this example, we assume a stock is earning $2 per share, and is paying out 50% in dividends. Using a growth rate of 8% per year and a discount rate of 12%, the value of the dividend in the tenth year is $.69. Why is this so? At 8%, a dollar will grow to $2.16 in 10 years. A dollar discounted 10 years in the future, at 12%, is worth $.32. Multiplying $2.16 by $.32 gives $.69. If we use a growth rate of 12% and a discount rate of 8%, the value is $1.44, more than double the first example.

This method adds a residual value, which is assumed to be equal to the estimated earnings at the end of the 10 years, multiplied by the reciprocal of the discount rate and then discounted. *Reciprocal* means dividing the discount rate into 100, so if the discount rate is 12%, the reciprocal would be 8.33.

The calculated value is divided by the price of the stock and the ratio is compared with similar figures for other stocks. One firm that uses this approach has developed a number of refinements. These include a quality rating, a growth persistency rating, an earnings variability rating, and an earnings trend factor.

This approach depends primarily on the validity of the growth rate used. A report published in September 1980, quite close to the top in the market, singled out Datapoint as the most attractive stock of some 275 reviewed. They assigned Datapoint a growth rate of 33%. Datapoint was 37 at the time, had a spectacular rise to a high of 67, then had an even more spectacular collapse to a recent price of 12. What went wrong? The company has suffered competitively, and earnings have been poor recently. We doubt that a 33% growth rate is still being used.

This same report listed Automatic Data Processing, selling at 24 at the time, as the most overpriced or least attractive stock reviewed. It is still 24. They assigned a growth rate of 11% to ADP. In 1979, earnings were $1.11 for the June fiscal year, and were $1.71 for 1982, a growth rate of 15.5%. ADP's earnings have been hurt less by the economic problems of 1981 and 1982.

Another version of this method, developed by one of the pioneers in Wall Street valuation methodology, is described in detail in *Investment Values in a Dynamic World*, listed in the bibliography. That system has some interesting aspects, but it has the same basic problem as the one described above. In our opinion, some of the more recently developed methods are easier to use and give better results.

HISTORIC TOTAL RETURN

Total return means the total amount of dividends and profits an investor receives in the course of one year. For example, one may buy a stock at 50 and receive a dividend of $2, or 4%, and sell it at the end of the year at 55 for a profit of $5, or 10%. The total return is 14%. In the terms used in the investment community, one does not have to sell the stock; one has the profit on paper.

The opposite table shows total returns on stocks and bonds back to 1926.

Note that bonds had a negative total return for the last four years in a row. However, bonds have had a positive total return in 42 of the 56 years, while stocks have had a positive return in only 37 years. Stocks, while more erratic, have had a better overall return of about 10%, as indicated in the first chapter. Obviously, when conditions are favorable, stocks provide handsome returns of 30% to 50% in one year. They also show large negative results on occasion. In the first 9 months of 1982, bonds fared much better. We now estimate that bonds gave the best total return on record, over 35%, for 1982. Stocks also provided a favorable return for the current year, but did not break any records.

ESTIMATED FUTURE TOTAL RETURN

There are a number of valuation methods that are based on the concept of future total returns. This concept is the one

	COMMON STOCKS	LONG-TERM CORPORATE BONDS
1926	11.6	7.4
1927	37.5	7.4
1928	43.6	2.8
1929	-8.4	3.3
1930	-24.9	8.0
1931	-43.3	-1.9
1932	-8.2	10.8
1933	54.0	10.4
1934	-1.4	13.8
1935	47.7	9.6
1936	34.0	6.7
1937	-35.0	2.8
1938	31.1	6.1
1939	-0.4	4.0
1940	-9.8	3.4
1941	-11.6	2.7
1942	20.3	2.6
1943	25.9	2.8
1944	19.8	4.7
1945	36.4	4.1
1946	-8.1	1.7
1947	5.7	-2.3
1948	5.5	4.1
1949	18.8	3.3
1950	31.7	2.1
1951	24.0	-2.7
1952	18.4	3.5
1953	-1.0	3.4
1954	52.6	5.4
1955	31.6	0.5
1956	6.6	-6.8
1957	-10.8	8.7
1958	43.4	-2.2
1959	12.0	-1.0
1960	0.5	9.1
1961	26.9	4.8
1962	-8.7	8.0
1963	22.8	2.2
1964	16.5	4.8
1965	12.5	-0.5
1966	-10.1	0.2
1967	24.0	-5.0
1968	11.0	2.6
1969	-8.5	-8.1
1970	4.0	18.4
1971	14.3	11.0
1972	19.0	7.3
1973	-14.7	1.1
1974	-26.5	-3.1
1975	37.2	14.6
1976	23.8	18.7
1977	-7.1	1.7
1978	6.4	-1.0
1979	18.5	-4.2
1980	32.4	-2.6
1981	-4.9	-1.0

we use in our method. The theory says that if earnings increase at a certain rate, and if the price earnings ratio remains constant, then the price of the stock will appreciate at the same rate as the earnings. That second "if" prevented our acceptance of this approach back in the 1960s, when this method was first proposed. In those years, the P/Es were extremely high—a P/E of 40 to 50 times earnings was common for the popular growth stocks of the day. These high P/Es continued until the sharp break in 1973–74. Since then, market P/Es have been generally under 10, as shown in the following chart (see Figure 2.1).

We use our total return method of valuation in compar-

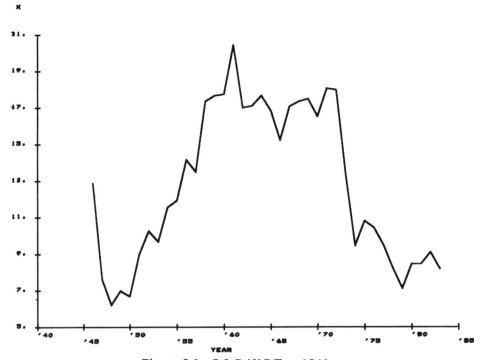

Figure 2.1   S & P AV P/E — 1941–

ing stocks to determine which are the most attractive values. The method is simple: Yield plus Growth equals Total Return; Total Return multiplied by a Quality Rating Factor equals Adjusted Total Return; Adjusted Total Return divided by the Price—Earnings ratio equals Relative Value. At the end of this chapter, we show a recent Valuation Report on IBM that we prepared for clients. The last line of the table shows the calculation. Chapter 4 explains in detail how we estimate the growth rate. Chapter 5 discusses the quality ratings. Later chapters detail the remaining factors that help you make sound investment decisions.

The most important aspect of this valuation method is that it deals in an orderly manner with the real world of investments. It is a simple way of showing the relationship between the benefits that can be expected from owning a stock (the total return) and how expensive it is to obtain those benefits (the price—earnings ratio). The method works. Obviously, if the benefits are large, you can afford to pay more for them. How well this or any other approach to valuation succeeds depends primarily on how accurate and reasonable the figures are that you put into the computer. The saying "Garbage in, Garbage out" certainly applies here.

RETURN ON INVESTMENT

Methods of valuation based on return on investment (ROI) are similar but not identical to the total return approach. Return on investment is earnings divided by a measure of the amount invested in the business. The investment is calculated by deducting current liabilities, such as amounts owed to suppliers or employees, from the assets. The assets consist of current assets such as cash, receivables from customers, and inventory, along with fixed assets including depreciated plant and equipment, and similar items.

Most of these methods deduct debt and preferred stock to obtain a figure usually referred to as common stockholder's equity, or book value. There are several variations we will not describe in detail. One method uses cash flow instead of earnings, and gross plant instead of depreciated plant. Cash flow is earnings plus noncash charges such as depreciation.

Return on investment is similar, but not identical, to total return. Assume a stock has a book value of $10 per share, and is also selling at $10 per share. In this example, earnings are assumed to be $1.50 per share, and dividends are $.50 per share, so the amount reinvested, frequently called the plowback, is $1.00 per share. The plowback can be expressed as a percent of book value and used as a measure of how fast the company can grow. This works out to 10% in this case, and is assumed to be the growth rate. In this example, the yield is 5%, $.50 divided by the price of $10, and the growth is 10%, so the total return is 15%. The ROI is also 15%, $1.50 earnings divided by the book value of $10.

If the stock is selling at a different price from the book value, the total return and the return on investment diverge. In the example above, if we assume that the stock is selling at 20 but all the other numbers remain the same, the total return drops to 12.5% (the dividend of $.50 divided by 20 equals 2.5%, plus the growth of 10%), while the return on investment remains the same at 15%. This is a peculiarity of the total return approach.

One system of valuation, used by a good research firm, expresses the P/E for the stock under review as a ratio to the P/E on the S & P's industrial index, as illustrated at the beginning of this chapter. They then take the return on equity (ROE) for the stock, and express that as a ratio to ROE on the S&P's. Next, the relative P/E is divided by the relative ROE. In this case, they are dividing it in the opposite direction, so the lower the result, the better the value. A report on IBM, published in the fall of 1981, showed the following figures. IBM was 60 3/8 at the time, and the S & P's was 151.91. The latest reported earnings were used in this calculation, rather than estimated future earnings. The relative P/E of 104, divided by the relative ROE of 145, was .72. The comment expressed was, "The relative value of IBM is extraordinarily depressed." While IBM is about the same, the market is 122, or about 20% lower, so that was a sound conclusion.

This is a simple method that works well a good part of the time. The deficiences are that it uses actual earnings rather than estimated future earnings, and that growth may be higher or lower than the portion of the earnings plowed back into the business. A company may grow at a faster rate than the plowback, or at a considerably slower rate. Some industries such as steel have reinvested a substantial share of the earnings, but have shown little or no growth. On the other hand, a few companies can grow at a faster rate than the plowback would support. An example of the latter is Digital Equipment, which has had an average return on equity of about 13% in recent years. It does not pay a dividend, so the plowback is also 13%. However, the growth rate has averaged 20%. This has been made possible by frequently raising new capital on advantageous terms.

Our valuation methods, and most others, are based on estimates of future earnings. Stocks sell on expectations, on hopes and fears, not on past realities. It would make investment simpler if this were not the case, as most of the problems in valuing stocks stem from the earnings estimates, but this is how the market works.

A LOOK AT THE RATIOS

There follows a series of charts showing some of these ratios going back to the immediate postwar period, 1946. As may be remembered, there was a postwar adjustment

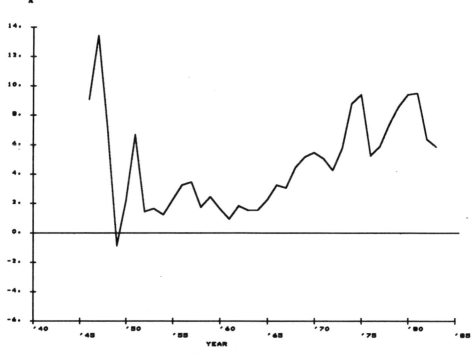

Figure 2.2   Change in Deflator — 1941—

lasting into the early 1950s. After that, as shown in the following charts, the country enjoyed a long period of prosperity, interrupted by several moderate recessions. By the late 1960s, inflation was beginning to be a problem. With troubles in the Middle East causing a 10-fold increase in oil prices in the 1970s and early 1980s, inflation has had a major impact on stock prices.

The first chart (Figure 2.2) shows changes in the deflator. This is a broad measure of inflation based on the Gross National Product.

The second chart (Figure 2.3) shows return on investment for the S & P's Industrial index. In this series, the investment is calculated as of the start of the year. Comparing the two charts shows business has not been able to

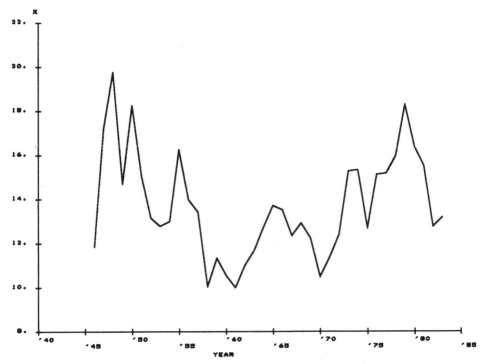

Figure 2.3   S & P's Return on Investment — 1941–

fully offset the effects of inflation. In the five years of 1960 to 1964, when inflation was at a 1.5% rate, the return on investment for the S & P's averaged 11.2%, a difference of 9.7%. In the five years of 1976 to 1980, when inflation was averaging 7.2%, the return on investment for the S & P's averaged 16.1, a difference of 8.9%. Thus, in spite of huge profits by the oil industry and a few other groups, business was unable to increase profits in line with inflation.

The next chart (Figure 2.4) shows average yields on the S & P's index. Dividends have not moved ahead as fast as earnings in recent years for reasons connected with inflation, which will be discussed later in the book. Yields are high because stock prices are depressed, as shown in the price earnings chart earlier in the chapter.

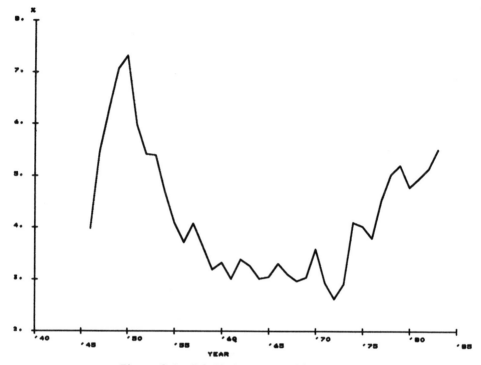

Figure 2.4   S & P's Average Yield — 1941–

The chart on the facing page (Figure 2.5) shows the plowback dividend by the book value, which, as you recall, is used as a measure of the growth rate.

The next chart (Figure 2.6) shows the total return, which is the sum of the data in the two previous charts.

The deflator figures are deducted from the total return figures to get an adjusted total return. Figure 2.7 shows how well this group of 400 industrial companies was able to cope with inflation.

The next chart (Figure 2.8) shows our adjusted relative value for the S & P's Industrial index. This is the adjusted total return divided by the price–earnings ratio. It is similar to the valuation method we use, except the growth rate

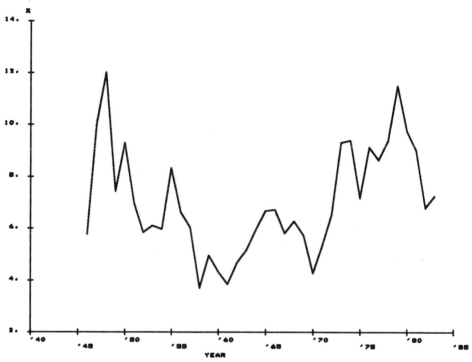

Figure 2.5   S & P's Plowback/Book — 1941–

is calculated differently and the inflation adjustment is not identical to the quality adjustment used.

The last chart (Figure 2.9) shows the market. This average rose from a low of 13 in the late 1940s to a high of 160 in 1980, more than 12-fold.

Estimates for the balance of 1982 and for 1983 are included in all except the market chart. They appear reasonable, but many uncertainties exist in the economy, although no more than is normally the case. All the estimates used in this book assume a moderate recovery in the economy, and an inflation rate well below 10%.

The market has been in a similar position, in many ways, to where it was in the late 1940s and the early 1950s.

Figure 2.6   S & P's Total Return — 1941–

In those days, people remembered vividly the long Depression of the 1930s and many expected the economy to slide back into one. There was much talk of a primary postwar depression similar to that which occurred in 1921. Price–earnings ratios were about the same then as they are now.

The consensus on Wall Street has been that when the economy emerges from the present recession, it will go back into a serious inflationary period. That opinion may be changing. Much depends on the good sense of the voters and our representatives in Congress. One of my former associates said recently, "I hope Congress is beginning to understand the basic law of economics, which is that there

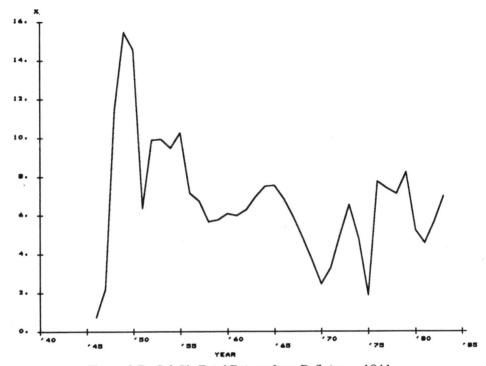

Figure 2.7   S & P's Total Return Less Deflator — 1941–

isn't any free lunch. If they give something to some people, they have to take it from someone else or from everyone through inflation." The recent strength in both the bond and stock market may be forecasting a noninflationary recovery.

USING THE VALUATIONS

This valuation work is used primarily as a screen in selecting stocks for further study. As will be explained, the computer has a filter routine that will select stocks by various attributes. For example, it will select stocks with

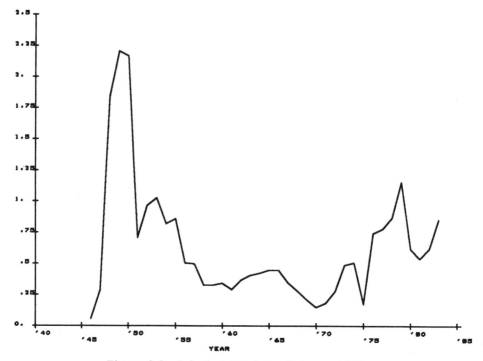

Figure 2.8   S & P's Adj Relative Value — 1941—

high growth rates, high quality ratings, high yields, low price to book value ratios and, most important, high valuations. The valuation takes into account all the foregoing factors except price to book value, but we look at each factor separately.

In Chapter 9, the 270 stocks currently being followed actively are shown. When a stock no longer meets certain criteria that we use in deciding which stocks are possibly attractive for investment, we retain the back data on a diskette so it can be updated quickly if some development restimulates our interest.

If a stock looks exceptionally attractive on our valuation work, we first recheck all the estimates. If they stand up and the stock fits in with the evidence on which groups are

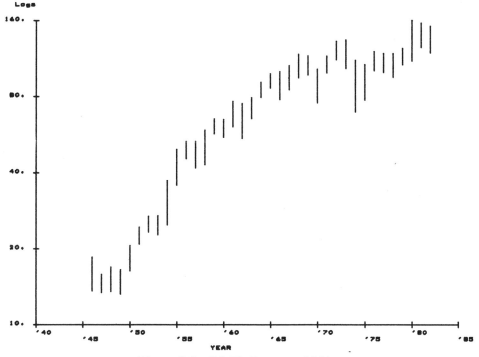

Figure 2.9   S & P's Range — 1941 –

likely to do well, and if the market as a whole seems favorable, we may begin to accumulate the stock in accounts. The usual procedure is to acquire an initial position, then add to the holding from time to time, based on what transpires.

Attempting to buy stocks that represent outstanding value means one is bucking the market. If the stock is depressed, it indicates that a considerable number of investors do not like it. Accordingly, a bullish opinion on the stock may be contrary to the market consensus. There is a theory of investing that goes by the name "Contrary Opinion," and a number of books have been written on the subject. However, our focus is value not contrariness.

The single most important thing to remember is that

other people may have information about the stock, the industry, or the market that we do not have. Therefore, it is sensible to move slowly and to keep rechecking the facts. The valuations are revised at least quarterly, and sometimes more frequently if there are new earnings figures or estimates. Stocks are repriced monthly, and some of current interest are priced weekly.

If it begins to appear that the earnings are not living up to the estimates, or if the estimates are being reduced by analysts who follow the stock, it may be a good idea to back away from that position. In our experience, the first downward revision of an earnings estimate is seldom the last.

On the other hand, if the stock's price is weak but the figures are working out as well as expected, or perhaps a little better, you should accumulate the stock slowly. It is too much to expect that you will be fortunate enough to start buying an out-of-favor stock at the exact bottom. When you succeed in catching the low, it is luck, not brains. Successful investing requires patience. As one of the deans of the analyst profession says, "We make more money with the seat of our pants than we do with our heads."

One very successful mutual fund manager, John Templeton, said recently, "The U. S. stock market today is the biggest bargain in history. We are at or near a low point in the market that will never be seen again in this decade." He also said, "We just buy bargain stocks wherever we find them. We buy them when others don't want them." On his record, his opinions deserve respect. These remarks were made before the market strength that began in mid-August 1982. Our previous charts tend to support those conclusions.

There follows a typical, brief IBM valuation report, of the type we prepare for clients, based on our computer valuations. We have been recommending IBM as an attractive value since the middle of 1981. While the stock has done better than the market, it remains one of the good values among the large capitalization blue chips we follow. Other stocks favored because of their sound investment attributes are used as examples in subsequent chapters, where the details of these methods and how they can be applied to the complex world of Wall Street are explained.

VALUATION REPORT

IBM   - INTERNATIONAL BUSINESS MACHINES - CBO - P - COMPUTER/DATA PROCESSING

YR MO	EARNINGS QT.	CUM.	% GROWTH	DIVIDENDS QT.	CUM.	BOOK	% RETAINED/ PRIOR YR	GROWTH YR CALCULATIONS		EARNS vs DEFL
										Base 73
81 3	1.25	6.18	19.1	0.86	0.00	0.00	0.0	4 YR $	13.40	86.6
81 6	1.37	6.24	16.6	0.86	0.00	0.00	0.0	5 YR $	15.10	100.0
81 9	1.18	5.91	3.3	0.86	0.00	0.00	0.0	4 YR %	17.58	105.4
81 12	1.83	5.63	-7.7	0.86	3.44	30.66	7.8	EST 1 %	15.50	102.9
								EST 2 %	14.00	116.9
82 3	1.30	5.68	-8.1	0.86	0.00	0.00	0.0	% RETAIN	11.34	126.7
82 6	1.68	5.99	-4.0	0.86	0.00	0.00	0.0	AVERAGE	14.60	137.1
82 9	1.58	6.39	8.1	0.86	0.00	0.00	0.0			122.2
82 12	2.19	6.75	19.9	0.86	3.44	34.40	10.8	QUALITY FACTOR mil		132.3
								CASH	1843.000	112.0
83 3	1.50	6.95	22.4	1.00	0.00	0.00	0.0	WORK	2902.000	129.1
83 6	1.80	7.07	18.0	1.00	0.00	0.00	0.0	DEBT	2704.000	142.7
83 9	1.75	7.24	13.3	1.00	0.00	0.00	0.0	CONV	0.000	Mkt Val
83 12	2.85	7.90	17.0	1.00	4.00	38.70	11.3	SHARES	594.260	35656

Av cost, Depr 11.1%, Plant 4 yrs, CD 57%, CC 98 %
QUAL: S&P 100 VL 100 CD 90 AV: 97 +0 +5 +0 = 102% P/B   1.55   +
VAL.: PRICE   60.00   YIELD   6.7+GR   15=   21*Q.R 1.02=21.63/PE   7.59= 2.85

EARNINGS - Estimates range from $6.50 to $7.00 for 1982 and from $1.00 to $1.50 higher in 1983. We are using $6.75 for this year and $7.90 next, but much depends on the strength of the dollar and what happens to world economies. The basic attraction, however, is that the huge investment in new products and services and new, efficient plant and equipment is beginning to pay off. In the four years 1979 through 1982 IBM will have spent about $26 billion or $45 per share on plant facilites and rental equipment. Even for IBM it is an extraordinary effort.

GROWTH - When the company is involved in a major plant and new product program margins suffer for a while but eventually recover. In the last year the normal problems of growth have been compounded by high interest rates and a strong dollar. The penalty from foreign exchange is estimated at about $1.00 per share in 1981. We project an acceleration in the earnings growth rate for several years ahead and estimate that $13 plus per share is a reasonable prospect for 1986.

QUALITY - The Government dropped the anti-trust suite admitting that they did not have a case. The cash flow figures should show a major improvement starting in 1982. This is a result of both internal efficiencies and tax benefits. Dividends were last raised in 1979 and an increase is likely soon. We think the payout will be about 50% in the future. While lower than the recent rate it should mean a $6.00 dividend by 1985.

VALUE - Although IBM stock has done about 20% better than the market recently it is still one of the better values of the blue chip stocks we follow. The near term acceleration of growth, the premier quality that has been enhanced further by the end of the anti-trust problem and the prospects for higher dividends make the stock a suitable investment for most accounts.

J C Jenks CFA

3

Sources of Data

STATISTICAL SERVICES

As discussed in Chapter 2, earnings are fundamental to any viable approach to stock selection. A source of accurate earnings figures and sensible earnings estimates is the first requirement. Our main statistical sources are *Value Line* and *Standard & Poor's.* Most of the larger libraries have both, as do many brokerage offices. Inexpensive trial subscriptions to *Value Line* are advertised in the financial press.

The Value Line Investment Survey covers 1700 stocks. The data is updated on a quarterly schedule. The reports come out weekly, with an index that contains recent earnings and dividend figures. *Value Line* offers other services, such as *Over-the-Counter Special Situations* and *Options and Convertible Securities.*

Standard & Poor's has a number of services. The most convenient are the small format stock report cards. These cover nearly every stock in which there is any significant interest. Again, they are updated regularly. S & P's has another very useful weekly service, called *Earnings Forecaster,* which contains earnings estimates on a large number of stocks made by a number of the leading investment firms. These are the services we use, but there are others that are helpful. For quality ratings and convenience, the compact *S & P's Stock Guide*, published monthly, is handy. Some brokers will give copies to good customers.

NEWSPAPERS AND PERIODICALS

The Wall Street Journal is, certainly, in a class by itself for financial and business news. Dow Jones also publishes *Barron's*, a weekly paper that contains voluminous financial data. Of the other weeklies, we think *Business Week*, published by McGraw-Hill, is especially good. *The Wall Street Transcript* is expensive, but full of analysts' reports. Of the big city newspapers, the *New York Times* has an excellent financial section, and there are a number of other papers that are good. For weekly international news, *The Economist*, now printed in the United States, is excellent and gives a European perspective on the American economy. There are many more financial magazines than we can read, some of which, not mentioned here, are also very good.

CORPORATE REPORTS

Most of the information used here originally comes from the annual and quarterly reports published by the companies in question. They also file reports with the SEC such as the annual 10 K, the quarterly 10 Q, and prospectuses in connection with public issues of securities. These are usually available from the companies but add little that is not in the stockholders' reports. If you become interested in a stock, write the company and ask to be put on the mailing list for quarterly and annual reports, and also ask for the most recent reports published. It pays to save these reports for at least a year or two, as it is quite likely that you will want to refer to them again.

BROKERAGE REPORTS

Many brokerage firms put out reports on stocks they follow or may be recommending to investors. We receive reports regularly from several firms. Also, friends send us studies on companies they think may be of interest. These studies give earnings estimates and frequently express opinions particularly useful in our work on such topics as growth rates. Brokerage reports alone rarely provide enough data to do a valuation. Their main uses are as checks on the earnings estimates and as sources of ideas about stocks we might wish to examine in greater detail.

Having managed a research department in Wall Street, I am well aware of the difficulty involved in analyzing a company's prospects and the attractiveness of a stock. The following is a brief explanation of what analysts do and how they do it, so that the reader can appreciate both the strengths and weaknesses in financial analysis. Brokers, investment bankers, mutual funds, bank and trust companies, insurance companies, investment counselors, and others have a number of investment analysts who specialize in a particular industry or a few related industries. Most of them are experienced, well-acquainted with the senior managements of the companies they follow, and very well-informed. They study the industry carefully, using data on supply and demand for the products or services; watch price trends; check with customers; and meet frequently with management. Their primary responsibility is to estimate earnings for the next quarter, the current year, and possibly several years ahead. Many use computers to make models of what a company's earnings should be under various economic or industry conditions. As in any other profession, analysts have different levels of experience and competence. Some have exceptional insight into what is happening and is likely to happen to both the industries and the companies they follow. Unfortunately, many and perhaps most analysts are overly optimistic a good deal of the time, and fail to recognize when things are going wrong and a stock should be sold. Negative reports on a company are rare, perhaps because analysts do not want to upset their friendly relations with senior management. Appendix B, Investment Analysis, discusses a recent development in investment analysis that has considerable promise.

Investment analysts are quite accurate on the earnings estimates when economic conditions are normal, but are less so when the economy is more volatile. It is in the best interest of a company's management to keep analysts well informed, but management rarely makes hard and fast predictions about earnings. However, management does try to guide an analyst's estimates. The financial press is full of such statements as, "Mr. Smith, President of XYZ Co., told analysts at a meeting in New York (or one of over 50 other cities where there are analysts' societies) that he believes analysts' estimates of $2.00 per share are in the ball park."

Unfortunately, analysts do not always see trouble coming. Some months ago, we became concerned about the fact that a stock we follow was not acting well in the market. We asked an analyst who had recommended the stock if there were competitive problems and if he had lowered his earnings estimates. He said no to both, and gave us a recent report he had written. Since then, reported earnings have fallen sharply, earnings estimates have been revised downward, and the dividend has been cut in half.

In this case, the analyst failed to recognize the impact of a new and aggressive competitor.

Problems can arise from events that are completely unpredictable. The poisoning of Johnson & Johnson's Tylenol capsules is an example. An earnings estimate for several years in the future is obviously more likely to go astray than a shorter estimate but, as we will discuss later, four- and five-year estimates can be quite accurate.

CHART SERVICES

There are several chart services that show how a stock is doing in the market, along with other data such as earnings. These are useful for taking a preliminary look at a stock before undertaking a more thorough appraisal. Standard & Poor's publishes the *Trendline* charts. *The Mansfield Stock Chart Service* is well organized and available at various schedules and prices. Many professionals use the *William O'Neill Charts*, which contain a good deal of information about who owns the stock and what brokers follow it, as well as quite complete company data. Trial subscriptions are available on many of these services, and are advertised in the financial papers such as *Barron's*.

FURTHER COMMENTS

Value Line is perhaps the best single service for most investors. It contains historical financial data, a description of the company, and details on how it is doing, with estimates of future earnings. Their system for selecting stocks is short-term oriented, relying primarily on the trend of earnings and whether they are better or worse than expected. While *Value Line* has a good record of stock selection over all, we do not rely, to any major degree, on their recommendations. In spite of its name, the service pays scant attention to relative value. Most of the figures are accurate, and when errors do creep in, they are corrected promptly. The estimates of future earnings are generally reasonable. However, in our experience, they are not among the first to detect a change in the earnings trend. *Value Line* usually includes capital gains and similar nonrecurring profits in the quarterly and annual earnings figures. We do not.

All the numbers necessary to do a valuation are available in *Value Line*, except the S & P's quality rating and the figures needed to update the deflator when one moves the data a year ahead. As mentioned earlier, the former is available in the *S & P's Stock Guide*, and the latter, along with a great many other statistical series, in *Business Conditions Digest*, a government publication.

INDUSTRY DATA

There are a number of services and publications designed to provide detailed information on a particular industry. For example, the *Best Insurance Reports* covers the insurance industry with separate volumes on *Property and Casualty*, and *Life and Health*.

In the trade magazine field, there are far too many publications to even mention. McGraw-Hill publishes one for every industry of any consequence. There are dozens of magazines on computing, and perhaps more. While trade publications are full of information, much of it is of little interest to investors. The problem is time. Most of us are not able to read more than two daily papers, two weekly magazines, a few monthly publications, the statistical services, and occasional reports from brokers. We find it is best to do less reading, but to do it more thoroughly, and to make notes on matters that concern our investment interests.

OTHER INFORMATION

While we have discussed only printed sources of information, it is an excellent idea to be able to call someone for information when there are unexpected developments. Investors able to do so should attend annual stockholder meetings of companies in which they are interested, introduce themselves to the management, and ask for the names of individuals they might call when they have questions. Also, a full-service broker is usually worth the modest additional commission because the account executive can check with the firm's research department when questions arise.

We look at a great many earnings estimates and note them on our computer printouts. When there is a wide dichotomy in the estimates, we seek other experts and try to form our own opinion. However, we are no longer making our own estimates on as many stocks as when I was a full-time analyst. On becoming a portfolio manager, I had to rely on others for the figures. The average investor should not rely on his or her own earnings estimates. In the next chapter a useful way to project future earnings is described. It can be helpful in checking other estimates.

SCHLUMBERGER VALUATION

The following valuation on Schlumberger shows what the numbers are and where they are explained in more detail in later chapters.

Note that the valuation on Schlumberger is high. The stock is down from a previous peak of 87 in 1980. We believe that the company will be regarded in the future as a high-technology business, with favorable prospects that are not entirely dependent on oil-well drilling activity. Accordingly, the stock is one of the more attractive blue chips in our work, and is worth consideration by investors. In subsequent chapters, we will use other stocks that appear to have investment merit as examples.

B

```
Schlmb- SCHLUMBERGER LTD - CBO - OILFIELD SERVICES/EQUIP IND
10-29-1982   A                         E              C              D
        EARNINGS       %    DIVIDENDS       % RETAINED/   GROWTH       EARNS
YR MO   QT.  CUM. GROWTH   QT.   CUM.  BOOK PRIOR YR  CALCULATIONS    vs DEFL
                                                                     Base  75
81  3   0.94  3.51  39.2  0.17  0.00  0.00  0.0   4 YR $    9.00      41.7
81  6   1.03  3.72  33.6  0.17  0.00  0.00  0.0   5 YR $   10.25      51.8
81  9   1.16  4.00  31.4  0.20  0.00  0.00  0.0   4 YR %   19.66      75.0
81 12   1.24  4.37  35.1  0.20  0.73 14.60 32.4   EST 1 %  18.00     100.0
                                                  EST 2 %  16.00     124.0
82  3   1.21  4.64  32.2  0.20  0.00  0.00  0.0 E % RETAIN 21.44     161.1
82  6   1.21  4.82  29.7  0.20  0.00  0.00  0.0   AVERAGE  18.77     189.4
82  9   1.12  4.78  19.4  0.24  0.00  0.00  0.0              F       228.8
82 12   1.21· 4.75   8.7  0.24  0.88 18.47 26.5   QUALITY FACTOR mil 294.5
                                                  CASH    1726.700   364.9
83  3   1.15  4.69   1.1  0.24  0.00  0.00  0.0   WORK    1729.300   370.1
83  6   1.20  4.68  -2.9  0.24  0.00  0.00  0.0   DEBT     284.700   365.9
83  9   1.25  4.81   0.6  0.28  0.00  0.00  0.0   CONV       0.000  Mkt Val
83 12   1.40  5.00   5.3  0.28  1.04 22.45 21.4   SHARES   293.500   10713  J
        Av cost, Depr 11.6%, Plant 5 yrs, CD 90, CC 85, Res 4.0%   K      I    H
QUAL: S&P 100 VL 100 CD  88 AV:  96  +5  +5  +0 = 106%  P/B  1.63         -
VAL.: PRICE  36.50   YIELD  3.1+GR   19=  22*Q.R 1.06=23.12/PE   7.30=  3.17
                       G
```

A- Earnings are primary, not fully diluted, for most stocks. Significant non reoccuring items are eliminated. Growth is based on the cumulative figures.

B- The exchange on which options trade if any.

C- The four year estimate for earnings is for 1986 at present. The four year growth rate is from 1982 to 1986. If there is an estimate after 5yr the growth calculation is from 1983 to 1987. See chapter 4.

D- This series currently starts with 1972. See chapter 4.

E- This is the earnings retained for the year as a percent of the prior years book value.

F- Figures are in millions. Debt includes unfunded pension liabilities and preferred stock if any. See chapter 5.

G- These are the S&P and Value Line ratings expressed numerically as explained in chapter 5. CD stands for constant dollar earnings which are expressed as a percent of reported earnings. We add 5 if working capital exceeds debt and 5 more if cash exceeds debt. We subtract 5 if there are convertible securites. See chapter 5. These refinements give a premium to the super strong companies such as Schlumberger.

H- This is the relative value. If the valuation has a plus over it the 12 months estimated earnings growth is more than 10% ahead of the estimated long term growth rate. If a minus it is more than 10% below the growth rate.

I- Price divided by book value. Especially useful for bank stocks and similar businesses.

J- Market value of common stock in millions.

K- The foot notes show the principal method of inventory valuation, depreciation as a % of gross plant, the average age of the plant and other data. See chapter 5.

4

Estimating Growth

When analysts use the term *growth*, they are usually referring to the percentage growth in earnings per share, adjusted for stock splits and stock dividends. The period covered may range from one year to the next, but more often covers a span of four or five years. For these purposes, we use four years from the current year or four years from next year. At present, we are using the latter because 1982 was a depressed year, and growth rates calculated from it would be unreasonably high.

GROWTH FROM PRICE INCREASES

Recent years of high inflation have given a false idea of how fast the earnings of some businesses are growing. With inflation waning, as it has since early in 1981, growth rates are also slowing sharply. In Wall Street terms, we are in a period of *disinflation,* meaning a slowing in the rate of inflation, but not deflation. However, the latter has occurred in many industries that benefited the most from inflation, such as metals and petroleum.

Several years ago, many analysts were projecting continuing price increases at a 10% rate or higher for petroleum products. The major oil companies have shown little growth in physical output. Domestic reserves have been drawn down, and foreign reserves have been expropriated in many cases. Recently, the physical volume of petroleum products has been declining. However, the 1980 Iran-Iraq conflict resulted in a substantial amount of capacity being removed from production, as well as sharply higher prices. More recently, Saudi Arabia has cut its production in half in an effort to stabilize prices. This has been reasonably successful until now, but there is increasing pressure on the oil-price structure.

How does one project growth rates for an industry such as oil? Obviously, the past 10 years of tight supplies and rising prices are not good guides. It may turn out that the years 1981 and 1982 were important turning points, so projecting the past into the future would be unrealistic.

Furthermore, the oil industry, as with other extractive industries, has an accounting problem that has not been properly addressed by either accountants or analysts. The question is, how should the earnings from production of crude oil and gas be calculated? Many oil and gas fields last for years if properly managed and maintained. Some of the oil being produced now was found during a time when costs were much lower. That oil is subject to special taxes, the so-called Windfall Profits Tax, but even so it may be of lower cost than oil now being found in such remote areas as the Beaufort Sea or off the coast of Newfoundland. Some analysts contend that the industry should adopt replacement cost accounting. This means that oil production would be expensed at a figure equivalent to the present cost of finding reserves. There are objections to this from the industry, and there are some obvious difficulties in doing it. If a company is not able to find enough new oil to replace the reserves it has used up, how would this accounting problem be handled? This is the case with a number of firms, and thus it seems unlikely that replacement cost accounting will be adopted. However, if petroleum prices remain flat for a few years, the effect on earnings of the rising cost of finding new reserves will be somewhat the same.

One well-known consulting firm that specializes in appraising oil companies said, in a report written in 1980, that "The production of Texaco's oil and gas reserves will provide a relatively steady flow of operating profits at an annual rate of about $3.1 billion through 1985. This forecast reflects a progressive decline in production, offset by rising oil prices." While this opinion appears overly optimistic at present, the important question concerns what Texaco will do with this cash flow. Can they reinvest these funds in a way that will produce a rising stream of earnings in the future? We doubt that the oil industry will show an average rate of growth in earnings over the next few years. However, there are exceptions, especially in the case of companies that are primarily searching for natural gas, which is still undervalued in relation to oil.

A good check on growth rates is to look at the estimated return on investment compared with past returns on investment. For example, Exxon had an average return on investment of 12.5% prior to the OPEC-induced price increases. Accordingly, a recent report, estimating a growth rate based on future earnings amounting to 19% on investment, seems too optimistic.

Growth based on gains in physical volume is more likely to persist than growth based on price increases, so note which of the two is occurring.

CYCLICAL GROWTH

The next problem to be considered is how the fluctuations in the business cycle affect estimates of growth. There are a number of excellent and rapidly growing businesses that are quite cyclical. An example we will use is Texas Instruments, an innovative leader in integrated circuits, with strong operations in military electronics, oil-field seismic systems and other products.

TEXAS INSTRUMENTS VALUATION

```
TexIns- TEXAS INSTRUMENTS INC - CBO - ELECTRONICS INDUSTRY
11-07-1982
         EARNINGS     %    DIVIDENDS         % RETAINED/   GROWTH            EARNS
YR MO    QT.  CUM. GROWTH  QT.   CUM.  BOOK  PRIOR YR  CALCULATIONS        vs DEFL
                                                                         Base  73
81  3   1.47 8.49    4.8  0.50  0.00  0.00   0.0    4 YR $   19.00         62.6
81  6   0.44 6.53  -23.6  0.50  0.00  0.00   0.0    5 YR $   21.50        100.0
81  9   1.15 5.38  -39.8  0.50  0.00  0.00   0.0    4 YR %   22.65         97.4
81 12   1.56 4.62  -49.9  0.50  2.00 53.44   5.2    EST 1 %  18.50         61.4
                                                    EST 2 %  16.00         91.6
82  3   1.17 4.32  -49.1  0.50  0.00  0.00   0.0    % RETAIN 12.94        104.0
82  6   1.56 5.44  -16.7  0.50  0.00  0.00   0.0    AVERAGE  17.52        116.6
82  9   1.57 5.86    8.9  0.50  0.00  0.00   0.0                          132.0
82 12   1.80 6.10   32.0  0.50  2.00 57.95   7.7    QUALITY FACTOR mil    147.1
                                                    CASH     286.200       67.6
83  3   1.90 6.83   58.1  0.50  0.00  0.00   0.0    WORK     538.200       86.3
83  6   2.20 7.47   37.3  0.50  0.00  0.00   0.0    DEBT     211.900      126.3
83  9   2.55 8.45   44.2  0.50  0.00  0.00   0.0    CONV       0.000    Mkt Val
83 12   2.85 9.50   55.7  0.50  2.00 65.75  12.9    SHARES    23.629      2835
       Various, Depr 17.1%, Plant 2.5yrs, CD 32.3, CC 67.3%
QUAL: S&P 90 VL 100 CD 67 AV: 86  +5  +5  +0 =  96% P/B  1.83        +
VAL.: PRICE 120.00    YIELD 1.7+GR  18=  19*Q.R 0.96=18.36/PE 12.63= 1.45
```

The figures are actual through the third quarter of 1982. Earnings have been hurt by write-offs, foreign exchange charges, and the weak economy. It now appears that there will be a vigorous improvement in 1983, and continuing into 1984. Preliminary earnings estimates for 1983 vary at around $10 a share. While our confidence in these estimates is not unbounded, we are reasonably certain that the company has a bright future and we estimate that the next cyclical peak in earnings will be on the order of $20 per share.

Using Texas Instruments as an example, the growth calculations are as follows. The four year estimate is $19.00 per share for 1986. We derived this figure from various sources. *Value Line* is using an estimate of $20.00 for 1985 to 1987, so our estimate is compatible. The five year estimate is $21.50. A routine for estimating these figures is described later in this chapter. The four year growth estimate in the third line is calculated from 1983 to 1987. It is high because 1983 earnings estimates are lower than if it was a normal year. *Value Line* is using an estimated future growth rate of 18.5%. Other estimates average around 16%. The % RETAIN means the amount of earnings retained after payment of dividends expressed as a percent of book value. The calculation is based on the prior year's book figure. This is the plowback figure explained in Chapter 2. While the four year % figure may be high, the % RETAIN is low; accordingly, the average of these four figures seems reasonable and goes into the calculation of value on the last line of the table.

As discussed in the first chapter, Texas Instruments has had a growth rate of 21% in earnings and 18% in cash flow between 1970 and 1980. While that was a difficult ten years in many respects, it was also an inflationary ten years. Did Texas Instruments benefit from the inflation? It appears that they did not, except in their small seismic activities. The integrated circuit business is one of the few that have sharply reduced prices in recent years, especially recently. However, the business is cyclical, and it is important to attempt to calculate growth rates from a good year to a similar year.

HOW RELIABLE ARE THE GROWTH ESTIMATES?

How realistic are our estimates of future earnings and rates of growth? We have been struggling with the problems of looking into the near future for many years. We have before us the *Value Line* estimates made in the fall of 1976 for the average of 1979 to 1981, which equates with an estimate for 1980. On Texas Instruments, they were using $7.40. The actual was $9.22 for 1980, but a $7.40 average for the three years was quite close. We examined 15 other big blue-chip stocks. The estimates were high on four, low on 11. They were badly high on General Motors, for understandable reasons, and very low on Exxon and Schlumberger because of the energy boom. They were quite close on the rest. We have reviewed various projections, our own and others, with similar results. If the estimates are done carefully, and if the economic assumptions are reasonable, the figures are usually reliable.

GROWTH CALCULATIONS—THE ESTIMATE ROUTINE

The last column, "EARNS vs DEFL," calculates an index of the annual earnings, back to 1972 to the present, which are divided by an index of inflation, the Gross National Product (GNP) deflator. This is another way of looking at growth, and shows whether the company was helped or hurt by inflation. These figures do not enter into the valuation calculations.

There is a program in the package that calculates past growth rates using the Log of Least Squares method. This is called LOGTREND. It will also project past trends into the future. This gives an estimated growth rate of 15.9% for Texas Instruments, and earnings for 1986 of $17.63 per share, based on 1970 through 1981 figures. In using the routine, if the last year is subnormal, start with a poor year, as was 1970 for Texas Instruments.

A method on which we place more reliance is our Estimate Routine. This is intended for companies like Texas Instruments that reinvest huge amounts of money in new plant facilities and equipment. There is a relationship between the amount of money spent on plant and equipment and future sales and earnings. While it varies from year to year, it has some predictive value.

The first column is capital expenditures per share as reported, and as estimated for several years ahead. Management officials usually state what they expect to spend at least one year ahead, and frequently have five-year capital

TexIns

YEAR	CAP EXP/ SHARE	SALES/ SHARE	INC IN SALES/ SHARE	SALES/ INC PRIOR YR CAP	PM % E	EARNINGS/ SHARE
77	8.73	89.70	17.12	2.87	5.70	5.11
78	13.44	110.67	20.97	2.40	5.56	6.15
79	18.71	141.25	30.58	2.28	5.37	7.58
80	23.32	175.22	33.97	1.82	5.26	9.22
81	14.48	178.37	3.15	0.14	2.59	4.62
82	15.25	192.85	14.48	1.00	3.20	6.17
83	18.00	217.25	24.40	1.60	4.50	9.78
84	20.00	253.25	36.00	2.00	5.00	12.66
85	22.00	298.25	45.00	2.25	5.50	16.40
86	24.00	347.75	49.50	2.25	5.50	19.13

budgets that they are willing to discuss. The second column of data, sales per share, are entered up to the latest figure available. The subsequent years are estimated as follows. The computer calculates the increase in sales per share and divides that by the prior year's capital expenditures. These figures are shown in column four. From inspection, or perhaps by using an average, we then enter what we think this ratio might be several years into the future. On that basis, the computer then calculates future sales. Meanwhile, we enter past earnings per share, and from inspection of the profit margins, we enter figures that seem logical for the future. The computer then calculates estimated earnings for the period under review, usually four years ahead but perhaps longer. This approach has applicability for certain types of companies, but not for all. We do not rely on it heavily, but it is an example of the type of extrapolation that is easy with a computer. The estimates derived this way are revealing when compared to other estimates or actual results. They can act as warnings of changes in trends for an industry or a company.

Another way to check growth rates is to deflate the sales using some measure of inflation such as the GNP deflator, which we use in the Earnings versus Deflator routine described above. This result is then divided by an index of industrial production, to take out cyclical influences. This gives a reasonable approximation of historical internal growth. Those figures can then be projected into the future, based on one's estimates of future inflation and the level of business activity. By using estimates of profit margins, the earnings can be calculated. We will not illustrate this procedure because we are still working on it. To be really useful, this will have to be done on an individual industry basis. That is, different industries have different inflation rates and different degrees of correlation with industrial production. A good deal of effort is being put into procedures such as this, which are referred to as "model making," and this approach has great promise for the future. However, from the point of view of this book, it is a side issue because, as discussed earlier, we are not recommending that investors rely on their own earnings estimates. Some other useful approaches to solving the problem of trying to see into the near future of a company or an industry can be run on a small computer. Certain correlation techiques will be discussed briefly in Chapter 10.

COMMENTS

Cyclical companies do not lend themselves very well to our work. To get a fair appraisal of the value of a stock, we base it on a normal year. At times, we are tempted to conclude that there isn't any such thing for some businesses. We do not follow many cyclicals, although we do occasionally look at stocks like General Motors. In any case, it is much harder to calculate a growth rate for a steel stock than it is for a drug stock. For that matter, in recent years, it would be hard to prove that the steels have had any growth. Certainly, after adjusting for inflation, most of them have not. With very few exceptions, we do not attempt to follow stocks whose earnings have not at least kept up with inflation over the last five to 10 years. Basically, we are not interested in problem stocks or turn-around situations. Some investors do well with this type of investment, but it impresses us as swimming against the current. There is an old expression on Wall Street that "Turn-arounds take seven years." What this probably means is that they take seven years longer than expected.

Our fundamental approach is to buy growth and make sure we are actually getting it without paying too much for it. It is instructive to take a look back at the prices reached by some stocks in the late 1960s and early 1970s. Polaroid sold at 19 recently. What do you think the high was? It was 149. Xerox was 36; the high was 172. Burroughs was 36; it has sold as high as 126.

Growth rates do not remain constant for long periods of time. Many investors who do not use computer routines calculate growth rates from point to point, using compound interest tables. That is, they arbitrarily select a base year, then arbitrarily select another year and compare the two earnings figures, and then look up the growth rate in the compound interest tables. If, for example, both Company A and Company B earned $1 per share last year, and both are expected to earn $1.59 in four years, according to the compound interest tables, the growth rate is 12.4%. However, let us assume that company A is going to have accelerating growth rates of 5% the first year, 10% the second, 15% the third, and 20% the fourth. On the other hand, Company B's growth is decelerating at rates of 20% the first year, 15% the second, 10% the third, and 5% the fourth. In both cases, the earnings go from $1 to the $1.59 figure, but Company A will obviously sell at a much higher P/E at the end of the period than Company B.

We recently received a report on computer-related stocks from one of the large, well-regarded firms in Wall Street, showing expected future growth rates for some of the faster growing companies. They projected 25% for Data General, while we were using 16%. Others follow, with our estimates in parentheses. Datapoint 30% (21%), Prime Computer 40% (30%), Wang 37% (26%), and Tandem 47% (35%). At this time, it appears that both their and our estimates are high in several cases.

In checking the records of various research organizations, we have found most of them err on the optimistic side. A look at the compound interest tables will make it apparent why growth rates of much above 15% are very difficult to sustain. At 15% per year, $1 of earnings turns into $4 in 10 years and $16 in 20 years. At 20%, it turns into $6 and $38. At 30%, it turns into $14 and $190, at 40% it becomes $29 and $837, and at 50% it becomes $58 and $3,325.

For readers who are mathematically inclined, the book *Quantitative Techniques for Financial Analysis* listed in the bibliography, gives detailed information on some of the matters discussed in the chapter, as well as interesting suggestions on other methods of analysis that can be run on a personal computer.

One final note of caution: most management officers have an optimistic view of how fast their companies can or should grow, so it pays to check out such estimates to see if they are actually being achieved.

5

Quantifying Quality

After experimenting for several years with our stock selection approach of total return divided by the price—earnings ratio, it became clear that the method works better if quality is expressed in numerical terms and then factored into the equation. As the reader will have noted by now, the total return number is multiplied by a quality factor that usually, but not always, reduces that figure before it is divided by the P/E to give the final valuation. As with our growth calculations, we could not find one single way of expressing quality that worked well with most stocks, so several figures are averaged.

QUALITY RATINGS

Quality ratings for stocks and bonds are expressed in letters rather than numbers. After examining the S & P's ratings found in the *Stock Guide,* and the *Value Line* rating called *Company's Financial Strength* found in a box on the lower right, and after a good deal of experiment and testing, we finally settled on the following: S & P's, A+ 100%, A 90%, A– 80%, B+ 70%, B 60%, B– 50%, C 40% and for Value Line, A++ 100%, A+ 92.5%, A 85%, B++ 77.5%, B+ 70%, B 62.5%, C++ 55%, C+ 47.5%, C 40%. Standard & Poor's also has a D rating, which means the company is in reorganization. The *Stock Guide* explains, on page 7, how S & P's determines its quality ratings. The consistency of growth is a very important factor. If a blue-chip stock with a high rating has several disappointing quarters, the rating is frequently reduced. *Value Line* has a somewhat different method, as explained on page 57 in their booklet *Value Line Methods of Evaluating Common Stocks*. Both are sound approaches. Every month, S & P's lists ranking changes on page 2 of the *Stock Guide*. Occassionally, both services give a higher rating than appears justified, simply because a company is big and has been in business for a long time. While a ranking may be moved down one notch when it does not make sense compared to similar stocks, we rarely use a higher rating than the services. Frequently, stocks of small and relatively young companies are not rated by S & P's. They also do not rank bank stocks. In those cases, we make comparisons and assign a rating that seems appropriate. If a stock is not in *Value Line*, the same procedure is used.

BALANCE SHEET FACTORS

After some experience, it appeared that there were other factors that were not adequately reflected in the results. Note the exceptional cash and working capital strength of Schlumberger shown in Chapter 3, for example. The Procter & Gamble valuation below will be used to illustrate the following discussion.

P & G is being split two for one in February 1983. These figures are not adjusted for the split.

```
ProctG- THE PROCTER & GAMBLE CO - ASE - HOUSEHOLD PRODUCTS IND
11-07-1982
        EARNINGS      %      DIVIDENDS          % RETAINED/    GROWTH           EARNS
YR MO   QT.   CUM.  GROWTH  QT.   CUM.   BOOK  PRIOR YR  CALCULATIONS         vs DEFL
                                                                             Base   73
81  3  2.09  6.91  -10.3  0.95  0.00   0.00   0.0    4 YR $    14.40          97.2
81  6  1.74  7.18   -7.7  0.95  3.80  46.68   7.8    5 YR $    15.85         100.0
81  9  2.70  8.44   21.1  0.95  0.00   0.00   0.0    4 YR %     9.56          95.4
81 12  2.31  8.84   24.3  1.05  0.00   0.00   0.0    EST 1 %   11.50          91.5
                                                     EST 2 %   11.50         104.4
82  3  2.39  9.14   32.3  1.05  0.00   0.00   0.0    % RETAIN  11.80         113.5
82  6  1.99  9.39   30.8  1.05  4.10  50.35  11.3    AVERAGE   11.09         117.0
82  9  2.99  9.68   14.7  1.05  0.00   0.00   0.0                            121.4
82 12  2.60  9.97   12.8  1.05  0.00   0.00   0.0    QUALITY FACTOR mil      123.8
                                                     CASH           578.000  104.8
83  3  2.65 10.23   11.9  1.20  0.00   0.00   0.0    WORK          1201.000  132.6
83  6  2.20 10.44   11.2  1.20  4.50  56.20  11.8    DEBT           846.000  145.8
83  9  3.30 10.75   11.1  1.20  0.00   0.00   0.0    CONV             0.000 Mkt Val
83 12  2.85 11.00   10.3  1.20  0.00   0.00   0.0    SHARES          82.893     9284
          June, Lifo, Depr 4.7%, Plant 6 yrs, CD 65%, CC 79%
QUAL: S&P 100 VL 100 CD  79 AV: 93 +0  +5  +0 =    98% P/B   1.99
VAL.: PRICE  112.00   YIELD  4.3+GR   11=   15*Q.R 0.98=15.07/PE  10.18=  1.48
```

PROCTER & GAMBLE VALUATION

Procter & Gamble has a very high quality rating. Both S & P's and *Value Line* give it their highest ratings. This is because both earnings and dividends go up every year like clockwork. Cash dividends have been paid every year since 1891. However, as shown in the deflator figures, the company has had to struggle to stay ahead of inflation. Note the Quality Factor figures below the Growth figures. The first is cash in millions of dollars, the second is working capital, the third is debt, which includes pension fund liabilities and preferred stock, if any. The next figure shows covertible securities, if any, and the last figure is the number of shares of common stock outstanding.

Pensions are fully funded. There is a nominal amount of preferred stock outstanding. Cash is substantial but, because of a recent acquisition, it is lower than normal. If cash had exceeded debt, the computer would have added 5%. Since working capital is larger than debt, it does add 5%. See the next to last line in the valuation. If there are convertible securities, which is not the case here, 5% is subtracted unless they are nominal in amounts. These refinements are arbitrary, and result in the highest quality rating 110%. However, it helps to distinguish between the super strong, like Procter & Gamble and Schlumberger, and stocks considered merely strong.

While we most often use figures for pension liabilities as reported by the company, if the liability is substantial, it may pay to examine how it is calculated. A low interest rate assumption is conservative. For example, IBM uses 5.5%, while General Motors uses 10%.

We do not favor convertible bonds. A company is better advised to use straight debt or, if debt is not prudent, sell more common stock. We buy converts on occasion, but not on the original issue. If they are selling well below par and give a fairly good return, they have a utility for certain accounts. Our view may be influenced by the outlook for the economy and by interest rates. As of this writing (fall of 1982), certain convertible securities seem fairly attractive.

When analyzing financial stocks, such as banks and insurance companies, there are complications. In these cases, cash does not mean the same thing, and it is useless to try to calculate a working capital figure. Accordingly, there is nothing with which to compare the long-term debt. After some experimenting, we arbitrarily decided to use 1% of total assets as a figure for cash, and 2% of total assets for working capital. We freely admit that it is difficult to justify those percentages. Why not 2% and 4%, for example? As long as it is kept fairly conservative, it does not seem to matter much which figure we use, as long as it stays the same for all the companies being analyzed. The purpose is to express in numerical terms matters that are somewhat subjective. As long as the results make sense, it does not pay to fuss more than necessary with the details. Keep the objective in mind. A company with a strong balance sheet is less likely to get into difficulty than one heavily burdened with debt.

THE INFLATION FACTOR

The effect of inflation on earnings is expressed as a factor after CD, meaning Constant Dollars. This term refers to a method of restating earnings to show the effect of inflation. Some annual reports also show a method called Current Cost. Accordingly, we are experimenting with a new procedure described below. Both figures are shown in the footnotes when available. *Value Line* has been showing a figure for Constant Dollar earnings for some years. This figure is divided by the figure for reported earnings, in order to arrive at the factor we have been using. The result is averaged with the two quality ratings, as discussed earlier. The other adjustments are then added.

For two main reasons, earnings as reported are usually overstated because of the effects of inflation. This is the case first because inventory profits result from rising prices, and second because depreciation accruals, which are based on historic cost, are not adequate to replace worn-out or obsolete facilities. Many of the larger companies have gone over to the Last In–First Out (LIFO) method of inventory accounting, which takes care of that problem quite well if physical volumes of inventories remain fairly constant.

With inflation diminishing, and because most companies have gone over to LIFO, this quality adjustment factor may be less important in the future than it was in the past. A few industries have remained on the First In–First Out (FIFO) method or the Average Cost method because costs were dropping fast enough to offset inflation. Integrated circuits are a good example. Texas Instruments uses Average Cost for most inventories and LIFO for some.

Our new procedure is another rather arbitrary method that cannot be defended on any basis, except that it seems to improve the results. When the Constant Dollar and Current Cost figures are materially different, we use the higher of the two if the company is on LIFO or if it has little or no inventory. If inventories are on FIFO, we use the lower figure. If inventories are carried at Average Cost, we average the two figures. If there are no figures available, put in a figure that is the average of the S & P's and *Value Line* quality ratings. These are all subject to the minimums explained below. When several methods of inventory accounting are used, they are shown as "Various" in the footnotes, and we use our judgment as to which figure should be used, based on our knowledge of the company and its industry.

Depreciation is a complicated matter. The 1981 tax law permitted a faster write-off of plant and equipment, but the 1982 law rescinded some of those benefits. The basic problem is that most manfacturing businesses find that the depreciation allowed for tax purposes is too low to replace worn-out or obsolete facilities. Accordingly, they are paying more taxes than they should. Also, the ability to pay dividends is diminished and payouts are lower than in the 1960s.

The government publishes figures showing the effect of inflation on earnings. There is a major difference, as shown in the chart on the next page (Figure 5.1).

Note that the inflation-adjusted earnings have been holding up better than reported earnings recently. As discussed later in the book, this is one of the indicators we use in determining the probable direction of the stock market.

Many companies show almost no earnings on an inflation-adjusted basis. Affected the worst are basic industries such as steel. Also, the electric utility industry has this problem, as do others. For this reason, we do not follow either steel companies or electric utilities, and also because they show little growth. There are a few stocks in the computer that show very low inflation-adjusted earn-

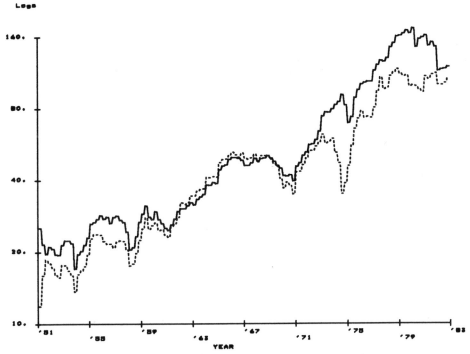

Figure 5.1   Corporate Profits —1951—
Profits Adjusted — 1951—

ings, such as tire and rubber companies and some basic chemical concerns. To avoid too severe an effect on the quality ratings, we use the following rule of thumb. We do not use a CD rating below 60% if the firm is on LIFO accounting, we do not go below 50% if they are on the Average Cost or the Retail method, and we do not rate below 40% if they are on FIFO or any other accounting method.

The footnotes on the Valuations show the fiscal year if it is not the calendar year, the method of inventory accounting, depreciation as a percent of gross plant, average age of the plant, figures for constant dollar and current cost earnings expressed as a percent of reported earnings when available, and occasionally other information peculiar to any particular company.

Any reader interested in looking at details of current cost or constant dollar accounting will find it explained in the annual reports of most large companies. We also list a standard text on accounting in the bibliography, which will supply such an explanation of this type of accounting.

OTHER EFFECTS OF INFLATION

Another matter is worth mentioning on the subject of the effect of inflation on earnings. Inflation is floating away debt so that it may be paid off eventually in depreciated money. Many annual reports show the theoretical effect this has on adjusted earnings. This is not factored into our work because it gives results that do not make sense in many cases. For example, it might result in a higher quality rating for a company with heavy debt, compared to a similar company with little or no debt. It is true that inflation is floating the debt away, but in the meantime, the company may be seriously burdened by the high interest charges or the need to refinance the debt when it comes due.

We are not entirely satisfied with these methods for averaging the effect of inflation on earnings into our quality ratings. Also, for certain types of companies, the figures may not be available or may mean very little. The financial service companies, such as banks and insurance companies, pose a problem here as well. They do not have inventories, and depreciation on buildings and equipment is a very minor item compared to most manufacturing companies. The problem is the effect on their loans and investments of the high interest rates that go with inflation. Banks and insurance companies carry their bonds and mortgages at cost or amortized values. Obviously, if

they have some 7% long-term bonds or mortgages acquired some years ago, for example, those investments are not
worth what they cost. The AT&T 7% bonds of 2001 were
selling at 68 as this book was written. They sold under 50
earlier in 1982.

Another problem with insurance companies will not be
discussed in detail. They are required to keep their books
in a particular way for reporting to the state insurance
commissioners who regulate the industry. Those figures
are very conservative. For example, all out-of-pocket costs
such as sales commissions are expensed as incurred. The
earnings figures prepared by the accountants for reports
to investors try to match expenses against income. Accordingly, sales commissions are capitalized and then amortized over a period of years, based on various consider-
ations. There are other material differences as well. Analysts are not entirely satisfied with the accounting methods used in corporate reports to stockholders. While the so-
called convention reports to the commissioners are overly
conservative, the reports to stockholders have proven too
liberal in some cases. Accordingly, it is advisable to keep
the quality ratings on insurance stocks on the conservative side. This is a specialized field of investment, and our
methods should be supplemented with additional information from qualified insurance industry analysts.

Another factor of concern to the investor in insurance
stocks is the revision in the tax law passed in 1982. Previously, much of the investment income received by the life
insurance companies was sheltered from taxes. This has
been changed. In considering insurance stocks, it is advisable to look at tax rates and to secure estimates on what
effect the new law will have on earnings for each company
under review.

It has been mentioned that dividend payouts are lower
than they were before inflation became virulent. One reason for this is inadequate depreciation; the other is taxes.
Corporate tax rates in the United States are the highest in

the world except for those in Sweden. In addition, the dividend recipient is also taxed. This is double taxation, which is obviously unfair and discriminatory, and should be changed.

For this and other reasons, many investors do not want dividend income. They prefer the smaller growth stocks that plow the earnings back into the business. For that reason, and for others connected with market factors, many of the smaller growth stocks are selling on the same basis or higher than the better quality stocks. In other words, the market is not paying as much attention to quality right now as it has in the past. This does not make us believe that our quality ratings are wrong. It is a market phenomenon that we have seen before.

There is an old rule on Wall Street that in the early stages of a new bull market, when everybody is bearish, it's best to buy the speculative stocks, but as the bull market ages, it's time to get into quality. When quality does not seem to be costing much of a premium, more rather than less attention should be paid to it. The last chapters of this book discuss the factors that go into making successful stock investments. However, we wish to mention now that, while our single valuation figure is intended to take into account everything of consequence, it is advisable to look at the components as well.

The next three chapters explain the computer programs in some detail. They are reasonably easy to run. There is a diskette available with this book containing all the programs, as well as valuation data on 30 stocks. The stocks have been selected for their long-term investment attractiveness. They also represent a variety of different types of investments, ranging from the big blue-chips to a few, small, high-technology growth stocks.

6

The Software Package

The following three chapters cover the programs that assist us in making stock selections. For the most part this section is presented as a manual for the use of these programs. Some familiarity with the IBM Personal Computer software will be required if reconfiguration is chosen, but neither a knowledge of the IBM DOS or BASIC will be needed to run the programs, in that they comprise a complete package that takes control as soon as the computer is turned on. In other words, it is a turnkey system.

Getting the programs operational is an entirely different matter that depends on whether the reader decides to start from the available diskette or from the source listings. The diskette provides the programs, system files, and a starting set of stock files. This master diskette does not contain the IBM Personal Computer operating system, however, and is write protected. No attempt should be made to use the master diskette as a working diskette. Working diskettes must be set up by copying files to blank diskettes, as will be explained shortly.

Those who would type the programs into the computer should consider that, all told, there are thousands of lines of code, and tens of thousands of characters to be typed correctly. It is not by any stretch of the imagination as easy to type as simple text. Typing mistakes that lead to faulty program operation may be very time consuming to correct. It can be done, but this method is not recommended. The program listings are intended primarily as documentation.

The programs provided are: AUTOEXEC.BAT, START-UP.BAS, MANAGER.BAS, STOKINDX.BAS, STOCK-PGM.BAS, ESTIMATE.BAS, LOGTREND.BAS, SCAT-TER.BAS, and SETUP.BAS. The programs must all reside on the same diskette, and should be used in the default drive (in a multi-drive system); however, the A-drive is not mandatory. AUTOEXEC.BAT and SETUP.BAS are auxilliary programs. STARTUP.BAS and MANAGER.BAS serve to handle the overhead of a complex software package but do not provide any stock selection features in themselves.

The data files used are grouped into two types: system data files and stock files. The system data files are: CURDATE.SYD, LETTERS.SYD, GRUPGRPH.SYD, DRIVES.SYD, SYMBOLS.SYD, PRICES.SYD, and DEFLA-TOR.SYD. The stock files include an index, STOCK.INX, related to a collection of stock data files with the extension .DAT. Also, earnings estimate files with an .EST suffix and corresponding index named ESTIMATE.INX are included.

In a multi-drive system, only the system data files and STOCK.INX must reside on the same diskette as the programs. ESTIMATE.INX and the *.EST files should be on their own diskette, free of any other files. The stock data files should reside on as many diskettes as are required to store them. The stock data diskettes are not limited in storage capacity (each data file requires only 2048 bytes), but rather are limited in the number of files that may be stored on them; 64 for single-sided, and 112 for double-sided drives using IBM Release 1.0 or 1.1 software. Consideration for a hard disk drive will be covered later.

Under a single drive floppy system the capabilities of this package are limited, but for a personal portfolio may well be thoroughly adequate, even with having just a single-sided drive. The stock selection package is designed to plateau with two floppy drives.

SETTING UP WORKING DISKETTES

A program diskette should first be set up as follows. (We will assume a two drive system is being used.)

Place an IBM system diskette in drive-A and format a blank diskette mounted in drive-B using the command:

```
A>FORMAT B:/S
```

Then copy BASIC to this diskette with:

```
A>COPY BASIC.COM B:
```

Now replace the IBM system diskette in drive-A with the stock selection master diskette.

Transfer the batch file using:

```
A>COPY AUTOEXEC.BAT B:
```

The programs are copied using:

```
A>COPY *.BAS B:
```

The system data files are then transferred:

```
A>COPY *.SYD B:
```

And also the stock index:

```
A>COPY STOCK.INX B:
```

Data diskettes should now be set up by remounting the IBM system diskette in drive-A and formatting two blank diskettes in drive-B using the commands:

A>FORMAT B:

And an affirmative to the prompt:

Format another (Y/N)? Y

Remount the stock selection diskette in drive-A and transfer the stock data files using:

A>COPY *.DAT B:

Then remount the remaining formatted diskette in drive-B and copy the estimate files with:

A>COPY ESTIMATE.INX B:
A>COPY *.EST B:

All that is left to do is label these diskettes "Stock Selection Programs," "Stock Data," and "Stock Estimates," respectively.

HARD DISK CONSIDERATIONS

If you have an IBM Personal Computer with a hard disk drive and are using IBM Release 2.0 software, then the method to use is to define a directory path from the root directory of the hard disk to a subdirectory, that might be called STOCKS, using the MKDIR command. Then use the CHDIR command to make the STOCKS subdirectory the default level. All files may be stored together since there is no limit on the number of files that can exist in a subdirectory. Use a global copy to transfer all files from the stock selection master diskette to the hard disk with:

COPY A:*.*

When the stock selection programs are to be run on the hard disk a CHDIR statement must designate the STOCK level subdirectory before the first program (START-UP.BAS) is run, and/or the drive defaults in the programs should be changed to reflect the proper directory path.

PROGRAM LISTINGS CONSIDERATIONS

Should you have no intention of typing the programs in then you may wish to skip this subsection.

If you are contemplating typing the programs in from the listings in Appendix-A then first we suggest that you read the whole book, including reading the program listings to decide for yourself if the potential rewards are worth the effort involved. Then refer back to this section.

The main reason for typing the programs in is where you have a computer, other than an IBM Personal Computer, using a version of Microsoft BASIC which is compatible with PC BASIC. It should be possible under these circumstances to use the programs with another computer. However, modifications to various routines will be required to reflect different BASIC features and keyboard screen and disk I/O conventions.

Type in the programs and save them on one diskette, but do not attempt to run any of them before all have been entered. Then make a backup copy of this diskette. Now go through the program listings and change all program code that obviously will not work with your computer to code that uses your computer's capabilities and which duplicates the intended function. When this is done to your satisfaction, make a backup copy of this diskette and label it "Converted."

You are now ready to test the programs. Should you receive a syntax or other error message, correct the offending code immediately and rerun the program. After all program modes are tried and all errors corrected the package should be fully operational.

First, run the SETUP.BAS program to create the system data files and STOCK.INX, and also to designate default drives for program and data files. Then, run the START-UP.BAS program to test the rest of the stock selection package. All programs should be started by chaining through the path of STARTUP.BAS to MANAGER.BAS to the application program and back to MANAGER.BAS. After correcting an error, restart the package by running STARTUP.BAS. The exception to this rule is LOG-TREND.BAS which can be run as a stand-alone program.

We hope and trust that this method will be rewarding. Special consideration should be given to an awareness that subtle typing errors may result in program code which does not lead to syntax or other error messages. Such errors usually come about because a variable name has been misspelled or a literal, such as a number, has been typed improperly. The section of code that is being executed when the error occurs can often be identified from the remarks in the listings. Then a careful line by line comparison with the source listings should identify the error.

STOCK GROUPING

For organizational reasons, and because of some firmware limitations on the number of files that can be stored together on a floppy diskette, stock data files are grouped.

Every stock must have a group number assigned to it, and all stocks of any particular group must reside on the same diskette. Where the groups are small, several groups of stocks may reside on one diskette.

For our purposes we have found it convenient to group stocks into 21 categories, which we store on six double-sided diskettes. But our conventions need not be followed. For the small portfolio, it is actually preferable that they not be used. A small portfolio can be considered to reside on a single diskette. In this case, stocks should be left undifferentiated by giving them all the same group number (Group 1).

The stock groupings we use are the following: (1) Aerospace, (2) Building, (3) Basic Chemicals, (4) Specialty Chemicals, (5) Basic Industry (including consumer durables), (6) Consumer Softgoods, (7) Paper and Wood Products, (8) Drug and Medical, (9) Energy Services, (10) Oils, (11) Food, (12) Machinery, (13) Metals and Mining, (14) Miscellaneous, (15) Retail, (16) Financial Services, (17) Other Services, (18) Technology (except computers), (19) Computers and Computer Services, (20) Transportation, (21) Utilities and Communication Equipment.

Groups 14 and 17 are catch-alls for companies that are hard to classify. Additionally, a Group 22 could be set up for dormant stocks; that is, companies that currently are not being followed actively, but where there is an expectation that future developments might rekindle interest. This would be for the purpose of making space available on an active diskette. Group 0 is reserved for internal use.

It is possible to assign up to 255 groups; however, group numbering must be sequential, and having 255 groups would be both unwieldy and impractical. The fewer the number of groups you choose to have, the better.

Grouping, therefore, can serve two purposes: to locate stocks on a diskette and to categorize by industry. The former is necessary. The latter is optional.

THE PROGRAMS

Here we will give a general overview of the programs and their related data files.

AUTOEXEC.BAT

The batch file in its simplest form serves the dual purpose of configuring BASIC for the application and starting a BASIC program. For the stock programs this is very simple; the command BASIC STARTUP is all that is required. No more than three files will be open concurrently, no memory need be set aside for any purpose outside of BASIC, the file buffers are adequate at 128 bytes, and no input communications buffer is currently used. Should you supply your own batch file or otherwise choose to enter the stock selection software package with RUN, you should enter at STARTUP.BAS.

STARTUP.BAS

The STARTUP program is the first program called after BASIC is loaded. Its purpose is to do housecleaning chores before the stock programs take control of the computer's operation. These tasks include setting the screen to text mode, setting the CAPS LOCK state to uppercase letters, determining on which drive the stock software disk is mounted; getting the date and start-up time of the previous interaction with the stock programs from the file CURDATE.DAT and updating as appropriate, and then chaining to the manager program.

MANAGER.BAS

The manager is the root for a hierarchically organized collection of programs which comprise a variety of stock selection tools. The manager reads the file, DRIVES.SYD, that tells the system where to look for stock data files. Then it presents a menu of programs and calls the selected application. In turn, when you are done with an application, control returns to the manager for another selection.

Currently, there are five application programs in the package. They are STOKINDX.BAS, STOKPGM.BAS, SCATTER.BAS, ESTIMATE.BAS, and LOGTREND.BAS. The benefits of a manager program are that application programs can easily be added to the package, and that it allows wide capabilities that would be unmanageable in a single BASIC program. Organizing associated routines in stand-alone packages conserves memory. Because of this, 64 Kbytes is both the minimum memory required and the maximum memory useful to the stock selection package. An IBM PC needs only a full complement of memory chips on the system board.

STOKINDX.BAS

The STOKINDX program serves the purpose of maintaining an index to the stock data files and, most importantly, collects information from the stock files for the purpose of stock comparison, thus leading to informed stock selection. Stock selection is not an automated process. The programs will not say, "BUY (SELL) 'XYZ' COMPANY OR YOU'LL BE SORRY," but it does provide information that is very useful in choosing stocks to buy or sell.

There are four broad categories of capabilities provided in STOKINDX. First, it gives the user access to the index through reading, searching, and selecting. Second, it provides routines to maintain the index. Third, it includes an alphabetic pointer to stocks and exchanges. Fourth, it offers a capability for repricing stocks in a variety of modes.

The data file STOCK.INX is the index itself. The index resides wholly on the system disk, and almost all operations with it involve disk activity. The limitation is that the inherent disk access delay is a noticeable factor that becomes more and more apparent for some routines as the size of the index is enlarged. The overriding benefits are that changes made immediately become permanent, and a large index may be maintained unhampered by RAM limitations. Both a hard disk drive and use of a disk simulator in RAM improve performance. The latter technique allows a potential hazard for lost data, though. We have tried it using a batch file that copies STOCK.INX to the simulated drive before executing BASIC STARTUP, and then copies the file back to diskette when the stock selection package is exited. However, minor power interruptions are common enough (such as from lightning) and so, from our experiences, we do not recommend that a disk simulator be used without an uninterruptible power supply and an especially conscientious operator.

Stocks are organized in the index in the following ways. Foremost, they are ordered by the exchange on which they are traded. NYSE stocks come first, AMEX stocks next, and OTC stocks follow. Only stocks on these three exchanges are supported, but the program structure does not rule out the inclusion of other exchanges. Within an exchange the stocks are arranged pseudo-alphabetically. What does this mean? Simply, the first letter of all entries in the index must be in alphabetic order. This is a requirement that the operator must maintain because the index program has no sorting capability.

A stock is entered into the index using a code name of six letters or less. The first character should be a capital letter, but those following may be any combination of capitals and lowercase letters that is most comprehensible. We use an ampersand occasionally.

For an index entry name, we use the identifer used in the *Wall Street Journal's* stock tables, or a close approximation of it. Some obscure abbreviations are expanded for easier identification. Also, we adhere to the convention of following the same entry order as appears in the *Wall Street Journal* tables. This leads to an odd state of affairs, since the printed tables are predominantly ordered alpha-betically by company name but are not necessarily in alphabetic order by code name. As such, the index cannot be sorted, and so entries are position dependent. Search-ing is sequential from the beginning of the index and insertions, deletions, and moves entail mass repositioning of entries. The exchange identifiers are also index entries, so stock numbering will be discontinuous across exchange boundaries.

Although recognized as an antiquated structure, for a reasonable portfolio it is workable. We have followed as many as 560 stocks using this method and, quite frankly, this is way too many to follow. Currently, we try to limit ourselves to 300 active stocks. We regularly add and delete stocks from our active list, but keep the inactive stocks' data in reserve.

We cannot advise about how many stocks the reader should follow. This would depend on whether you are an institutional or individual investor. For maintaining the data base, the availability of a large office staff contrasts greatly with a single person who has only a few hours over the weekend to spare. Start small and enlarge until an obvious point of diminishing returns is apparent, then back off a bit for maximum efficiency. One must realize early that not every stock can or should be followed.

Another file accessed by STOKINDX is LETTERS.SYD. This consists of three tables (for the three exchanges) of stock code names, paired with index locations showing the first stock for each letter of the alphabet. For small port-folios, this information is of no particular value, but as the size of the index grows, it becomes more and more useful. Its general purpose is to tell the operator where to begin looking for a stock in the index. This helps especially for the move and insert routines, because they require enter-ing an index location for the destination of the activity. The actual choice of when to update LETTERS.SYD is left to the discretion of the user. For the computer to modify LETTERS.SYD every time a change is made to the index would entail a time penalty that is not justified for the average portfolio, so dynamic updating has not been implemented.

The two files SYMBOLS.SYD and PRICES.SYD are provided to allow repricing stocks by modem and a remote data base. A program to access a remote data base is not provided, but a simple method of reading and writing to these files to accomplish remote repricing is described in the next chapter for those with this capability.

Another file that is written to, but never read from, by STOKINDX is GRUPGRPH.SYD. This consists of a collection of up to 52 entries from STOCK.INX which are assembled for input to the program SCATTER.BAS, described below.

SCATTER.BAS

SCATTER.BAS is a program for plotting scatter diagrams on the screen. STOKINDX.BAS makes available to SCATTER.BAS data that is most helpful for stock selection, using the file GRUPGRPH.SYD for graphic presentation as a comparison of any two stock parameters. For example, 52 technology companies could be assembled, and then each company plotted on the screen, based on its unique values of growth and quality. This provides both a comparison of a particular company's growth with its quality, and a comparison of the growth/quality of one company with that of the others in the set. This can be a powerful tool for identifying strong, weak, and average performing stocks, and also serves as a check on the validity of the data entered.

STOCKPGM.BAS

This program serves the purpose of maintaining the data on each stock, and of doing the calculations required to arrive at a numeric representation of a company's relative value. It also does the work of updating the calculated figures to reflect price fluctuations, and storing the results in STOCK.INX for later comparative purposes.

STOCKPGM.BAS is the sole access to the stock data files as suffixed by .DAT. They are created, modified, and displayed in convenient ways.

The program also accesses a system data file called DEFLATOR.SYD, which stores historical information on the rate of inflation. Some companies are benefited and others harmed by inflation, but none are immune to its influence.

ESTIMATE.BAS

The program ESTIMATE.BAS has the sole purpose of projecting earnings per share based on historical and estimated data, and is useful because of the assured proclivity of stocks to sell at prices based on the prospects for future earnings. It is a wholly self-contained program that maintains its own index, ESTIMATE.INX, and data files with the .EST suffix. The generic suffix .DAT is not used, in order to distinguish estimate files from the stock files of the same name. The program is unusual in that it works in two modes. During the setup mode, it expects entry of specific historical data and derives other figures. In the update mode it expects entry of estimates of the derived figures (such as profit margin) and then calculates back to the projected sales and earnings per share.

LOGTREND.BAS

LOGTREND.BAS is a logarithmic regression analysis program used to project company growth. The equivalence of the slope of a semi-log chart and a growth rate is utilized by the computer just as it would be by visual inspection. The program uses no files but rather expects immediate data, particularly historical earnings. It then calculates the equation of best fit and projects the figures by years. You may then either enter a time and the program will provide the expected value, or you can enter a value and the program provides the time when that value is expected to be reached.

SETUP.BAS

This program is used to create system files when they do not already exist. These are the files: STOCK.INX, GRUPGRPH.SYD, LETTERS.SYD, DEFLATOR.SYD, CUR-DATE.SYD, SYMBOLS.SYD, PRICES.SYD, and DRIVES.SYD. The first three files are formatted as they should appear. DEFLATOR.SYD is loaded with the deflator constants up to 1983 (projected). The user is also given the opportunity to designate the drives to be used for programs and data files. The program need not be used if you are starting from the available diskette (and will be using drive-B for stock data) because the files are already provided and B is the default data drive. The program may be used at any time, however, (such as to change the drives) without harm, as existing files will be recognized and remain unaltered.

USER INTERACTION WITH THE PROGRAMS

In order to make the programs usable, we have adhered to a set of conventions that will make the programs predictable.

All input is through the keyboard. The output is predominantly visual on the screen; hardcopy output from a printer will never be generated unless specifically requested. Limited use of the internal speaker is employed to announce the completion of the group revaluation routine, which is moderately time consuming for large groups.

The programs are menu driven in order to make them comprehensible. This means that a prompt will be presented whenever an informed choice is to be made. The prompt will indicate the range of choices and the proper method for selecting whatever operation is desired. However, the programs do not contain a help feature, so the reader should make it a point to consider the remarks that follow and refer to this book as a guide. The user must understand the fundamentals of stock selection as covered in the theory sections of this book to be able to use these programs effectively.

All selections are made by typing a character or pressing a function key. Except for the function key menus, a question mark will be presented when a choice is to be made. The proper characters to type will also be presented in parentheses, and the user should type the indicated characters exactly as they appear. Lower case will be accepted for choices. Single key input is fast, but it does not allow corrections. However, the programs are highly forgiving, and one can escape from an unwanted selection by using the ENTER or Esc key. A routine will reject invalid selections, with the exception that pressing the ENTER key alone has a default meaning at every level of the program.

The ENTER key by itself is used for the following purposes. Where none of the indicated selections are wanted, then prompting may return to a higher level. The program may bypass the current menu and display additional selections. The program may initiate a default action. A message may be displayed as the result of some activity or error, and the program will wait for the ENTER key to be pressed before proceeding.

The ENTER key is a general means of getting out of trouble, but it should not be used in a few particular cases. When actual data is requested a prompt will be presented followed by either a colon or an equals sign. The data is to be typed followed by the ENTER key. If an error in typing has occurred, then corrections may be made using the

IBM editing conventions before pressing ENTER. A colon indicates that the requested data is optional, and so the ENTER key by itself may be used to bypass having to enter data at the point. The equals sign, however, means that the program requires entry of the requested data in order to operate properly. It is a very good idea to comply with this as if it were a demand. The IBM PC will, however, enter zero into a numeric variable on receipt of ENTER alone.

The programs resist crashing well. The sometimes extremely usable and at other times frustrating proclivity of the IBM PC to buffer keystrokes requires that no more than the required amount of typing be done. But when the operator knows exactly what key strokes to use to get into a wanted routine it is a time-saver to type them all at once before the prompts are presented.

A routine will recover from inadvertently leaving the drive door open on the data disk drive, and will also recover when the wrong data diskette is in the drive. However, the diskette containing the programs and system files should always remain in its drive, and the door to this drive should never be open while the programs are in operation.

Routines are not generally receptive to requests to terminate while in the middle of an operation, but two that are are REPRICING and GROUP REVALUATION. The formal method of exiting a particular mode is through Esc. As mentioned, the ENTER key also serves this function in less important cases.

When system data files are to be written to disk, the activity usually takes place immediately. When data files are to be permanently modified, the programs need authorization to do so. This is accomplished by means of the (W)RITE to disk selection. A conscious effort should be made to remember that files must be written to disk, but it will be difficult to inadvertently lose data because a specific request is required to escape without writing to the file. This convention is to prevent the loss of back data in the event that there is any difficulty entering new data.

It is a good idea to write new data to a file before any attempt is made to list it to a printer. The programs test for printer availability, but do not monitor data transfer and will not recover from a communications breakdown.

The programs are generally most usable by an operator who is interested in the results. Although, certainly, data can be entered by clerical staff, there is a weakness in the organization of the program package. This is that the user must, in most instances, know the stock code names and their groups to be able to access the data. For the investor who chooses the stocks and regularly reads the *Wall Street Journal* stock tables, this is no problem because this information is ingrained. For others, it requires memorization. In this case, it may be beneficial to have a printed listing of stock names, code names, and groups at the computer for reference when necessary. Although STOCK.INX can be printed out, this listing does not provide a correlation between code name and company name, and no provision for this is provided in the programs.

CONFIGURATION CONSIDERATIONS

The programs will work without modification in an IBM Personal Computer with 64 Kbytes of semiconductor R/W memory, two floppy disk-drives (preferably double-sided), and a Monochrome/Printer Interface Adapter, or the Color/ Graphics Interface Adapter and a separate Parallel Printer Adapter. By adding redirection of LPT1: to COMx: in the batch file, or by designating a COMx: output device in the output routines, an Asynchronous Communications Adapter can by used to communicate with a serial printer. This section will cover the modifications needed for other hardware, and will also cover some operating options.

The program package will not work with less then 64 Kbytes of memory. Any memory above the first 64 K will be of no additional benefit except for extensions such as a disk simulator, resident modem driver, etc.

If single-sided drives are used, then the stock data files are limited, under IBM Release 1.0 or 1.1 software, to 64 stocks per diskette, and the stock estimate files limited to 63, plus the file ESTIMATE.INX.

Several estimate diskettes may be set up, but each diskette must have its own ESTIMATE.INX in order to reference the files on it. The estimate index is limited to 100 entries on double-sided drives. For single-sided drives, the constant L1 at the beginning of ESTIMATE.BAS should be changed to 63 or less. Optionally, an extension different from .EST may be used by changing the constant EXT$. Since the operation of ESTIMATE.BAS is independent of the other programs, except that it returns to MANAGER.BAS when exited, a separate diskette may be used for estimate files on a single drive system. One should remember to change diskettes before returning to the manager, however.

For all programs, selection of an output file is used to direct specified data to either the screen or to the printer. This method benefits programming and allows an easy change of output device. The output select routines are located at the end of each program. File #3 is used for output, and only the device reference need be changed to adapt to the user's requirements.

STOKINDX.BAS references file only on the system disk. The index itself (STOCK.INX) is a variable-length, random access file limited to a maximum of 999 entries. Each record is designed to hold one string and seven single precision numeric values. The string size is set at 15 characters by constant W2 to hold a stock code name, a five character ticker symbol, and 4 bytes to hold group and class numbers, a star stock flag, and a relative performance token. Constant W1 sets a total record size of 50 bytes. Constant NL sets the length of the code name. These constants can be changed to reflect savings in disk space or the availability of additional capabilities. The code name could be set to eight characters to equal the DOS restrictions on name length, or additional numeric calculations from STOCKPGM.BAS could be stored in STOCK.INX. As it now stands a field size of 44 bytes would be adequate to store the data, and it might be chosen. If changes to these constants are contemplated, they should be made in the programs STOKINDX.BAS, STOCK-PGM.BAS, SCATTER.BAS, and SETUP.BAS, but based on the nature of the changes in some cases, internal program modifications would also be required. Only imperative reasons would justify changes to these field and record size constants.

For proper operation, STOKINDX.BAS requires a limit on the maximum valid group number. The constant LGRP should be changed to the chosen value, if our convention of a maximum of 21 groups will not be used. The limit is 255. The same constant LGRP in STOCKPGM.BAS should also be changed to the chosen limit.

The constant DD$ in STOCKPGM.BAS determines the default stock data file drive, and is equated to "B:." For a single-drive system, either change it by running SET-UP.BAS, or else change the default specification in STOCKPGM.BAS. There is a significant limitation on the number of stocks that can be followed in a single floppy system. This is because of storage limitations on floppy disk and restrictions in the number of files. In this case the DOS, BASIC, programs, system data files, stock index, and data files must all reside on a single diskette. The maximum number of stock data files then equals the number of files available on the disk less the number already stored (usually 18), or else it equals the floor of the available space on the diskette divided by 2098 bytes; whichever is smaller.

We expect that many IBM PC's will be purchased with Advanced BASIC and the Color/Graphics Interface Adapter to allow use of the many graphics features the computer offers. Business, however, may choose the Monochrome Adapter instead. The string edit routine in STOCK-PGM.BAS uses the LOCATE statement to change the size of the cursor for insertion purposes. The standard cursor (a blinking underline at line seven) is changed to a block cursor from lines four to seven, and then back to the underline on line seven again. This will be unacceptable with the 7×9 character of the B/W Interface. Therefore enable the optional constants CSR1, CSR2, and INSS at the beginning of the program to reflect the display adapter being used.

7

Using The Programs

This chapter covers the details of how the programs are used.

GETTING STARTED (AUTOEXEC.BAT & STARTUP.BAS)

If you have not yet done so, follow the instructions in Chapter 6 for setting up working diskettes. Now make backup copies, to alleviate any concern over side effects arising during this stage of familiarization.

Place the program diskette in drive-A, put the stock data diskette in drive-B, and use a Ctrl-Alt-Del sequence to re-boot the computer. The batch processing command, >A BASIC STARTUP, will appear, BASIC will be invoked, and the program STARTUP.BAS will begin with the message:

STARTUP Program

System drive A:

Upper-case set

Input date, or (P) if Previous, ENTER if Current date is correct...

Previous date was   dd-dd-dddd

Current date is ?   cc-cc-cccc

New   date   < _

The date dd-dd-dddd is the last date stored in the file CURDATE.SYD. The date cc-cc-cccc is the date known to the system. The current date should be entered in IBM format, or either of the displayed dates chosen. When entering a date, a single integer will be accepted as a new day for the current month.

Then the message:

Input time, or press ENTER if Current time is correct...

Previous time was   tt:tt:tt

Current time is ?   ss:ss:ss

New   time   > _

Similarly enter the correct time. The program then stores the date and start-up time in the file CURDATE.SYD. It is optional to enter the time, but the date will be printed on various listings, so it is good practice to keep the date current. The advantage of storing the date in a file is that it need not be reentered if the computer is shut off and restarted in the same day. Similarly, if the computer has been left on after other programs have been run, restarting the stock package will allow bypassing the New time prompt with ENTER, in which case the clock reading will be entered into the file.

The first message means that the program MANAG-ER.BAS has been found on drive-A. Six locations are checked in the following order: A:, B:, C:, D:, E:, and F:. These correspond to the IBM floppy and hard disk drive designators.

THE MANAGER (MANAGER.BAS)

Five programs use the function keys for routine selection:
they are MANAGER.BAS, STOKINDX.BAS, STOCK-
PGM.BAS, SCATTER.BAS, and ESTIMATE.BAS. Each
will display a diagram of the function keys at the center of
the screen, and will identify the routine corresponding to
each key. The diagram will only be available to the applica-
tions programs if these programs are chained to form
MANAGER.BAS, because the manager uses the COMMON
statement to pass an array containing the diagram data to
the other programs. A block activity indicator will appear
below the diagram whenever a key is pressed.

The manager prompt is:

STOCK VALUATION Programs   Esc Exit to DOS

                        MANAGER

STOCK INDEX
Program   F1   F2 STOCK FILES Program
SCATTER DIAGRAM
Program   F3   F4 STOCK ESTIMATES
                                  Program

LOG TREND Program F5

Esc here executes a SYSTEM command to return computer control to the operating system. The function keys
cause the selected program to be chained.

THE STOCK INDEX PROGRAM (STOKINDX.BAS)

It is best now to become familiar with the STOCK INDEX
program because it is the heart of the system. An index

entry must be placed in STOCK.INX before a new stock data file can be set up.

On entry STOKINDX.BAS will prompt with the function key diagram as follows:

STOCK INDEX Program   Esc Exit to MANAGER

Overwrite index	(shift) F1		
Insert stock	F1	F2	Read index
Delete stock	(shift) F3		
Move stock	F3	F4	List by group
Create alphabetic list	(shift) F5	F6 (shift)	List by class decade
List first stock alphabetic	F5	F6	List by class
Reprice * stocks	(shift) F7	F8 (shift)	Search for ticker symbol
Reprice by decade	F7	F8	Search for code name
Read modem prices	(shift) F9		
Store symbols (modem pricing)	F9	F10	Select by criteria

We will now describe each routine.

READ

On key F2, the screen will be cleared and the following prompt presented:

Read from stock number: _

As explained in the previous chapter, the index entries are position dependent. As such, they are most easily referenced by location, but may also be referenced by code name. To start with the first entry, enter 1 with ENTER, and you will be given the following prompt:

Options
(G) Store for SCATTER graph
(A) Averages
(P) Printout
Esc Escape from routine
? _

G indicates that up to 52 sequential stock entries should be extracted from the index and stored in the file GRUPGRPH.SYD for later display as a scatter diagram.

A will have the program calculate an average for all parameters starting with the stock at the selected location and continuing to the last entry in the index.

P will redirect output to the printer.

Pressing ENTER by itself gives an uncomplicated listing on the screen. The listing will be preceded by a heading:

Sym Name Class Group Price Val. Growth Yield P/B Qual. Mkt V.

Then, up to 20 entries from the index will be displayed. # is the location of the entry in the index. Sym is the ticker symbol, as used to access data over the QUOTRON system. Name is the code name for the company. Class is the economic classification, as covered elsewhere in the book. Group refers indirectly to a diskette on which the company data is stored, and refers directly to an industry group. Price is for the most recent price entry that was (or is to be) used for valuation calculations. Val is the comparative valuation figure for the stock: it may be followed by a space, + or _ as explained earlier. Growth is explained on the chapter on growth. Yield is the actual or estimated percentage return of dividends. P/B is the ratio of price to book value, Qual. is the quality rating, and Mkt V is the market value in millions of dollars. Optionally, an entry under Name may be followed by an asterisk, indicating that the stock is a star stock, designating a stock of special interest.

At the end of the listing of 20 entries will be the prompt, Continue, or not Esc?. ENTER will continue displaying entries from the index at the top of the screen, and Esc will exit from the READ routine.

LIST BY GROUP

Select F4 and answer the prompt, Group <0-21>:.

Twenty-one is the maximum valid group number, but, as mentioned earlier, this may be changed by the user. An options prompt similar to that for READ will be displayed, except that the middle option will be:

(A) Add prices to these stocks

This is the best method for repricing stocks by group. The manual repricing routines allow entry of a numeric value, use of the destructive backspace key for corrections, ENTER by itself if the price is unchanged, and Esc to exit the routine (after confirmation of this intention).

A Group listing will be identical to a READ listing, except that the average of the parameters will be displayed at the end of the listing, along with the date.

The prompt that follows, Press any key to continue, is preparatory to clearing the screen for selection of another routine.

LIST BY CLASS

This routine is identical in operation to LIST BY GROUP except that it lists by subclass. The prompt is Classification <0-255>:.

LIST BY CLASS DECADE

This routine gives the prompt, Classification decade <0-6>:.

There are only six major economic classes that we employ. These are signified by the tens place in the class number. A maximum of 24 class decades is possible. The zero class decade (with 0 to 9 subclasses) is reserved for unclassified stocks.

SEARCH FOR STOCK BY CODE NAME

Answer the prompt, stock code name:, with the exact code name for the entry sought, and, if the entry is in the index, it will be displayed in READ format. Then a prompt:

Change (S)ymbol, Star Stock (Y/N), (C)lass, (G)roup, (P)rice? _

will allow revision of the indicated parameters. When no more changes are needed, bypass this prompt with an ENTER and you will be asked, Esc Escape update?. This is to exit without writing the changes to the index.

SEARCH FOR STOCK BY TICKER SYMBOL

This routine is identical in operation to SEARCH BY CODE NAME. Note that ticker symbols must not use lower-case letters.

SELECT BY CRITERIA

This routine, called using function key F10, is a very useful aid to stock selection. It does a multi-way selection of the index entries, extracting only those with parameters better than predefined minimums; less than a maximum for Price/Book Value, and within a range for Market Value.
The prompt is:

Select by criteria

Input limits for multi-way selection from STOCK.INX

Valuation limit: _
Growth limit: _
Yield limit: _
Total Return limit: _
Price/Book limit: _
Quality limit: _
Enter market value limits in $ millions
Low limit: _
High limit: _

The criteria refer to the corresponding fields of the index entry, except for Total Return (Growth plus Yield).
The limits are lower bounds, except for Price/Book and market High. Parameters not important to the purpose at hand should be disabled by entering zero (a large value for Price/Book, because a low value is the favorable condition). If Price/Book is zero, then the routine will be exited before

starting. A value of zero for High market value will be interpreted as unlimited.

Then the options are presented as:

Options
(G) Store for SCATTER graph
(P) Printout
Esc Escape routine
? _

The most effective way to use this routine is to start with
moderate criteria, observe the listing that results and then
rerun more stringently. In this way, stocks are weeded out
until only the most interesting ones remain. The routine
may also be used to select stocks in one category by disab-
ling all other parameters. In any case, a stock must still be
judged by its blend of characteristics, both quantitative
and qualitative.

MAKING CHANGES TO THE INDEX

An individual entry in STOCK.INX is modified in five ways:
(1) by an initial setup using Overwrite or Insert, (2) as
mentioned, through the SEARCH routines, (3) through
the various repricing methods, (4) as a result of a group
valuation carried out by STOCKPGM.BAS, (5) by the Delete
and Move routines. Only Move has no internal influence on
an entry. The others affect various fields within an entry.
    A minimal stock entry must exist in the index before one
may do anything with stock data. This is done through
Overwrite or Insert. Overwrite replaces the data at a
selected location in the index with a new entry. Insert, as it
implies, inserts a new entry at a specified location. Move is
similar to Insert except that an existing entry is inserted at
a new location and deleted at its old location. Delete irre-

vocably erases an entry from the index, but it does nothing to the data file itself.

The index is not confined to storing just stock entries, but also stores market separators and an end-of-index marker.

Whereas a stock entry must begin with a capital letter, the other entries are based on special characters. An entry with # as the first character will be interpreted as the separator between the NYSE stocks and the beginning of AMEX stocks. Similarly, = separates AMEX stocks from OTC stocks. An asterisk (*) is the end-of-index marker. An entry beginning with any of these symbols will not be displayed in stock entry format, but, rather, will invoke a special prompt or action.

Because of the requirement for a special end-of-file marker, one should not attempt to write to an index location outside of the index. An Overwrite to the location following the last entry will destroy the end-of-file marker with notable repercussions. Writing a * entry within the index will truncate the index at that point. Overwriting at a location containing a market separator will eliminate the market distinction, which is fine only if AMEX or OTC stocks are not being followed.

Overwrite

The first prompt is, Overwrite at stock location:. The location for a new entry should be determined before entering this routine, but ENTER alone will exit without difficulty. The current entry at the chosen location will be displayed with the prompt, <location#> Stock code, or (END) to exit routine=.

Typing END (end) is the only way to exit this routine. A stock code name of up to six letters should be entered. The routine will then prompt in turn for:

Ticker symbol :
Classification:

Group number =
Star stock (Y)?
Price :

All are optional except Group number. If the group is not yet known, then zero is a satisfactory response, but it will have to be changed later when you decide which diskette will be used to store the file data and which group it will be affiliated with for doing group revaluations.

Then the prompt, (C) Clear data fields, Esc Escape update?, will give three options: (1) if C then it sets the fields for Val through Mkt V to zero and does the write; (2) if Esc then the routine will allow reentry of the data for the same location or the option to end; (3) if ENTER alone, then the write will take place, but the Val to Mkt V fields will retain the values they had for the previous entry at that location.

After a successful write, the next index location will be addressed and the process will repeat until you type END (end).

Insert

The INSERT routine is substantially the same as WRITE, except that the only option at the end is Esc Escape update?. Otherwise, all index entries from the chosen location will be pushed up one position, the data fields at the selected location will automatically be set to zero, and the routine will return to the outer level prompt after the one insert is completed.

Delete

DELETE gives the prompt, Delete stock code name:, and will then remove an entry from the index if it exists exactly as named. ENTER alone at this prompt exits. The actual data file itself is not affected by deletion from the index, but can be eliminated as an option in the STOCK FILES program.

Move

The prompt here is:

Move stock code name:

Followed by:

Insert prior to entry #:

Pressing ENTER at either prompt cancels the operation.

If the stock to be moved is found below the location for insert, then the entry will appear at the location immediately preceding the one designated. If the stock is found after the location for insert, then it will appear at the location. In both cases the new entry will appear before the entry at the designated location.

THE ALPHABETIC LIST

The routines List first stock alphabetic and Create alphabetic list together allow easier access to the index, especially for a large index.

The Create routine has no modes. It searches through STOCK.INX to locate the first stock that appears for each letter of the alphabet for each of the three exchanges, stores this information in the file LETTERS.SYD, and then returns to the outer menu. No escape option is offered because there is no real hazard.

The List alphabetic routine reads the LETTERS.SYD file if the alphabetic list is not currently in memory, and displays exchange name, location number, and corresponding stock code name. It is useful as a coarse locator prior to READ and other routines.

REPRICE

The REPRICE routines allow three additional methods for pricing stocks.

The Reprice * stocks routine allows repricing of only those stocks designated of special interest. It is a fast means of repricing, but even though it can be exited before completion, it cannot be restarted in the middle of the index. The message, Enter (E) at end of line to indicate error, allow changes, means that corrections can be made immediately after a price is entered. Then two messages are presented, Esc to escape routine, and Price ENTER if same. The first star stock is found and presented as:

    <location> <name> * <price>:

Either the new price should be entered, ENTER if the price is unchanged, or else Esc. Esc leads to the prompt, Esc Escape routine?. Otherwise, the percentage change in price is shown followed by (E)?. An E response will present the line again for entry of the correction, and the following ENTER causes the routine to search for the next star stock.

If general repricing is desired, use the Reprice by decade routine. The first messages and prompt are:

Manual pricing by decade
During routine, Esc to escape group of ten.

Enter prices from stock number: _

The starting location should be entered; however, it will likely be modified by the program because actual repricing will begin on a decade boundary plus one (i.e., 21, 31). Entry is similar to star stock repricing, except that Esc instead of a price or ENTER by itself will cause an immediate jump to a correction routine, then continuation with the next decade of stocks. Another difference is that corrections are only possible (after ENTER has entered the price) at the end of a group of 10 stocks. The prompt, Any price errors (Y), Esc Exit?, allows corrections, exit, or continuation with the next 10 stocks. If Y then the prompt, Which # <1 to 10>:, refers to the local position in the list. After all corrections are made, ENTER will proceed to the next stock decade.

The advantage of this method of repricing is that it can be terminated at any time and then restarted at the appropriate decade boundary. This is the method used to accomplish a complete manual repricing of the index.

We have tried to make repricing as painless as possible, even though some tedium is inherent in manual methods. Even with a numeric keypad, looking up prices in the paper and then typing them in is slow and antiquated.

The best method for repricing is automatic, and can be done over the phone lines using the Dow Jones News/ Retrieval Service. This has not been implemented fully, but a method for automatic repricing is provided by using the Store symbols and Read modem prices routines. The user will have to provide an interface to the remote data base with the following capability. Your program should read the file SYMBOLS.SYD to extract a stock ticker symbol. The symbol is then presented to the remote data base, along with the query for a price; the price is received and written to the file PRICES.SYD followed by a terminating character (comma, carriage return). If a price is not available, your routine must enter zero into PRICES.SYD. This process is repeated until the end-of-file marker for SYMBOLS.SYD is found, and an end-of-file marker is appended to PRICES.SYD. Definition of the proper protocols and modem hardware will, of course, be necessary. Dow Jones Reporter is the name of a software package for the IBM PC to access this service.

The interface for remote pricing at the stock programs end is to first use the Store symbols routine to transfer the ticker symbols from STOCK.INX to SYMBOLS.SYD, run the remote data base program, and, using the Read modem prices routine, transfer prices from PRICES.SYD to STOCK.INX. No changes to the order of stocks in

STOCK.INX are to be made between running the Store symbols and Read modem prices routines. If such is done, then Read modem prices will exit on the first mismatch of STOCK.INX and SYMBOLS.SYD ticker symbols.

STOCK DATA FILES (STOCKPGM.BAS)

After placing an entry in STOCK.INX, we return to the manager and chain to STOCKPGM.BAS to set up a stock data file. You should put the proper group diskette for the new entry in the data drive at this time.

The outer level of prompts using the function key diagram is:

STOCK FILE program   Esc Exit to MANAGER

    Stock display   F1   F2 Set up new file
    Do group valuations   F3   F4 Change deflator
                                        constants
    List data disk files   F5

SETTING UP A NEW DATA FILE

Now press key F2 for the New file routine and it will ask for Stock code for new file:. Enter the code name and the routine will search to make sure there is an entry for it in the index. If there is no index entry then the routine will exit. Otherwise, it will search the data drive to determine if the stock file already exists. If so, a message to this effect will be presented, and the user will be able to exit or continue as if it were a new file.

The NEW FILE routine is a means for entering data in a systematic way. The first prompt for data is:

    Stock heading (input company name, group, etc)...
    <code name> -_

The code name is automatically placed at the front of the heading. The heading should contain the full company name, group name and number, and any other useful information that fits on the line.

Next comes First year for data=. The data file will store four years of quarterly data. The first year should be two years prior to the current year and the last year is next year's projections. The first year data, however, is not diplayed when a data file is called up, but is entered in the Set up mode to maintain continuity in the figures that are calculated. The prompt should be answered with the appropriate year, in the format of either two or four digits.

Then the prompt, First quarter end month (2,3,4)=, should be answered based on the month (February, March, April) that ends a company quarter. Corporations choose a variety of fiscal years, and this complicates the storage, calculation, and presentation of the data. Most will be calendar years with a March quarter. If the fiscal year ends on some odd week, we ignore this when answering the next prompt, Quarter in which fiscal year ends (1-4)=. So, for example, a January 3rd end will still be placed in the fourth quarter.

The routine will now prompt for quarterly data by displaying year (as two digits), month (1-12), and Quarterly earnings=. The four quarterly earnings are entered in turn, and a similar prompt will be displayed first for dividends, then for book value for the year-end quarter. Then a prompt, Any errors in (E)arnings, (D)ividends, (B)ook?, allows corrections by type. (Any error in dividends, for example, will require reentry of all four dividend figures, but not others). ENTER alone leads to the next prompt, (Esc) Exit from quarterly data input?. By selecting Esc, one is not required to enter additional yearly data but may jump directly to the entry of growth data.

We recommend that at least all back quarterly data be entered using the NEW FILE routine. The first year must be entered by this method, but the other data may be entered somewhat more flexibly in the display/modify mode, so it is simply a matter of preference whether to escape here or not.

Entering the growth figures now begins with, 4 yr $ Earnings estimate=. This for the estimate four years hence. Then, 5 yr $ earnings estimate:. Following this is the prompt, Est 1 % Growth estimate=, and after this an Est 2... prompt. These are for entry of growth rate estimates derived from various sources.

Then the program prompts for balance sheet figures with:

    Enter values in millions
    Cash =
    Working capital =
    Debt =
    Convertibles outstanding =
    Shares =

The figures must be entered in millions to make later calculations correct and to allow proper formatting for display. The first four are dollar values.

Again, a prompt will be presented allowing the ability to correct errors; however, errors must still be corrected by reentering the data in groups, so it may well be better to postpone corrections until the display phase.

Then comes the valuation and footnotes section requiring the following:

    S&P Quality rating=
    V.L Quality rating=
    C.D (Constant dollar) rating=
    <code name>- Price=

    Footnotes (67 Characters max.):

    Any errors in (V)aluation or (F)ootnotes?

Then a routine is called to enter data necessary for deflator calculations. This routine is explained a few paragraphs down under the heading of THE DEFLATOR ROUTINE.

After this we are at the end for entry of initial stock data.

The new stock data will then be displayed on the screen, followed at the last line by the prompt, Esc Escape update of file <code name>?. As data entry should have gone without a hitch, press ENTER. Pressing Esc will prevent the data from being written to the file, and the data will be lost.

The program now returns to the outer level of prompts.

Various calculations will have been done before display, and all will be correct, as long as correct figures have been entered.

We will now describe displaying a stock file, using the F1 (Stock display) selection, to explain the methods for modifying existing data.

DISPLAYING STOCK DATA

STOCK DISPLAY prompts for Stock code:, and after the code name is entered, the program will either get the file from disk or give a message why the file cannot be retrieved. In this routine only, typing all capitals for the code name will retrieve the file.

The display is identical to the display presented after a new file is set up. An inability to complete deflator calculations on an out of date file will be brought to your attention, since deflator calculations are done every time a file is called for display.

The bottom line prompt is now:

(N)umeric, (H)eading, (F)ootnotes, (S)plit, (Y)ear update, (D)eflator?

All the data except for the hidden first year can be modified using these selections. We will explain the DEFLATOR routine first because this same routine is used by the Set up new file routine just described.

The Deflator Routine

The first prompt is:

New base year for deflator calculations: _

This should be entered as either a two- or four-digit value, not more than 11 years prior to the current year.

The corporate earnings can then be entered, changed, or left the same. The instructions are:

You may change back earnings or bypass an entry with ENTER alone.

On the next line is the prompt, <year>, <current value> Earnings:. This will be repeated for twelve years and stock data will redisplay.

Earnings may be changed, or else only the base year can be changed to put the deflator figures on a new footing. This can be done as often as you like for experimentation with the base year. As covered in another chapter, the choice of a base year should be made carefully to reflect business conditions that were representative of the company.

Actually, the last figure entered will not be used if the last year of quarterly data has any valid cumulative earnings figure. The next to last figure entered will not be used if the next to last year contains an earnings figure corresponding to the year-end quarter.

Year Update

YEAR UPDATE automatically scrolls the figures to make space for another year of data. A description here is hardly warranted. Trying it out will show where it has moved the yearly figures up and supplied zeroes at places for new data.

The only prompt is Esc Escape Year Update routine?. The year update cannot be undone after this, but no permanent change will be made to the data until a write to disk is authorized.

Adjusting for Stock Splits

SPLIT automatically adjusts for stock splits or stock dividends. The prompt is, New shares added as a percentage of stock outstanding=. If a company has done a three-for-two stock split, then 50% more shares have been issued, so 50 should be entered. A 4% stock dividend requires entry of 4, etc. A split can be negated by repeating with the converse value. Minus 33.3% undoes a three-for-two split. There will be round-off errors, however, so undoing a split is not recommended; instead the file should be recalled from disk. Pressing ENTER is the same as 0% added stock; there will be no change.

Heading and Footnotes

These routines are screen oriented; the data will be changed in place. Left and right cursor keys, Ins and Del are active, and Esc exits from the text correction routine. If you change the company code name in the heading, you should be aware of two effects: the dash must remain the seventh character of the heading for the file to save properly, and the data will later be saved under a file of the new code name. A new code name should be overwritten or inserted into the index at the earliest opportunity.

Changing Numerics

This routine is a flexible method for screen editing of the numeric data. Its function is to map positions on the screen to the corresponding array variables. Most of the cursor control functions have been implemented including left, right, up, down, Tab for a five space jump right, Shift Tab for five space jump left, Home, End for end of current screen line, ENTER for a new line, and the delete arrow deletes as it would under system controlled editing.

The routine will only allow data to be changed in specific places including year (which will renumber all the years), month (similarly changes all the months), quarterly earnings, quarterly dividends, book, 4 yr $, 5 yr $, Est 1%, Est 2 %, Cash, Work, Debt, Conv, Shares, S&P, VL, CD, and Price. All other figures are calculated.

The routine gives the message *Num pad for cursor control, top row digits for data.* Although many are used to and prefer a numeric pad for data entry, the dual function of the pad for cursor control poses a dilemma. Since cursor control is necessary, we suggest that you not use the Num Lock key to shift between cursor control and the numeric pad but rather use the top row digits and period (not decimal point) for data entry, and dedicate the pad for cursor movement. Manually shifting the pad mode eventually leads to confusion as to which state it is in, entry of erroneous data, and the aggravation of cursor displacement just when you are in place to enter data.

To use this routine, simply place the cursor where the data is to go and begin typing the number. If the cursor is not within a field valid for changes then nothing will happen; otherwise the characters will be displayed as typed. Digits, minus sign or hyphen, and period (for the decimal point) are accepted. Then, pressing any cursor control key or ENTER will cause the cursor to return to the start of the entry, and another press of the key will cause the expected cursor action. The return of the cursor to the beginning of an entry quickens the input of columnar data. Press Esc to exit the NUMERIC routine. Recalculation will be done and the data will be redisplayed.

When none of the data modification routines is wanted, press ENTER and the following prompt appears: (W)rite to disk, (P)rintout, Esc Exit?. If changes have been made that are to be saved, answer with W. Esc returns to the outer level of prompts without writing. P directs a listing in screen format to the printer. ENTER by itself redisplays the data and the data modification prompt.

THE DEFLATOR CONSTANTS

The F4 choice allows changing the values in the DEFLATOR.SYD file. These constants, representing the yearly inflation figures, are used to calculate the deflator values for every stock. Recalculation is done every time a stock data file is displayed, so the most recent constants are always reflected in the results.

If a stock data file is not valid to the same or previous year of the last deflator constant, the deflator calculations cannot be completed. This usually means that a file has been rescued from the doldrums and needs year updating to make it current.

Changing the deflator constants is similar to changing the back earnings also used in deflator calculations. The prompt is, (Y)ear update all constants, (W)rite to disk, Esc Exit?. This prompt is displayed at the top of the screen after all the constants have been displayed line by line. The last figure is the year corresponding to the preceding deflator constant, and serves to coordinate the series with earnings data.

The ENTER key to this prompt allows the constants to be changed one by one, or left the same (as desired). Y pushes all the constants up one year (duplicating the last value), and increments the index year. W writes the modified data to DEFLATOR.SYD. Esc returns to the outer level of prompts.

GROUP VALUATIONS

The F3 selection is used to update stock files and STOCK.INX to reflect changes in stock prices. The index file, STOCK.INX, is opened and a stock entry for the chosen group is located, the price is extracted, the file is called from the data drive, calculations are done, select data is written back to the index, and the data file is written back to disk; this is done automatically, and in three modes.

The first prompt is, Do valuations on group numbers:. Since a group number refers to a data diskette, the group numbers should be entered and the proper diskette now inserted into the data drive.

The next selection is, Valuations on whole group (G), star stocks (*), single stock (S)?. G does a valuation on every stock found in the index belonging to the selected groups. * does the same except that the stock must also have the star flag assigned to it. S prompts for Stock name:, searches the index until the code name is found, and the program does an update valuation on this stock alone. It then asks if it should continue with the group valuations. Given an affirmative, it will behave as G mode from there on.

At the end of a group valuation the computer will BEEP and present the message Group <group #> has been done.

As stock valuations are completed, a line of information similar to stock index format will be displayed on the screen so that the operator can follow its progress.

LISTING DATA FILES

It is a useful feature to be able to execute BASIC commands from within a program. This capability is provided in IBM PC BASIC. The F5 selection will do the equivalent of a FILES <data drive>:*.DAT. By this means, you can review the files on the diskette to determine if a file is on the diskette or to refresh your memory of the stock code name that must be used to call up a file. Files are stored under uppercase only, so the name displayed may not indicate the code name used in the index; however, a file can be called for display using all capitals.

You can delete a file as an option to this routine. The prompt is:

Option to delete a stock data file. Input code name, or ENTER when done.
Delete stock: _

Only the name should be entered, not the extension .DAT. We delete a stock only when trading is permanently suspended (due to merger, bankruptcy, etc.), or after reassignment to another group and diskette.

This completes an explanation of how to use STOCKPGM.BAS.

SCATTER DIAGRAMS (SCATTER.BAS)

The purpose of the scatter diagram program is explained elsewhere, and only its operation will be covered here. The program begins with the display:

SCATTER DIAGRAM program

Loading data...

If data has never been written to GRUPGRPH.SYD, the message will be presented:

No data. Initialize GRUPGRPH.SYD from STOCK INDEX program

This to remind the user to store data using one of the STOCK INDEX program options. SCATTER.BAS will be exited.

Otherwise, the function key diagram will be presented as:

SCATTER DIAGRAM Program   Esc Exit to MANAGER

    Review data   F1   F2 Select parameters

The F1 selection will display the data in an expanded format similar to a listing from STOCK INDEX. A capital or lower-case letter will also be assigned to each stock.

The F2 selection will display a list of parameters, as follows:

Select the parameters to plot on the Y and X axes...

(1) Price

(2) Value

(3) Growth

(4) Yield

(5) Price/Book

(6) Quality

(7) Market Value

(8) Total Return

(9) Price/Earnings

Y-parameter= _

To display a scatter diagram, enter the number of the parameter to be plotted along the Y-axis. The parameters are the same as the corresponding columns of a stock index entry, except that Total Return and Price/Earnings are derived from the others. Then answer X-parameter=, and the program creates the scatter diagram.

The 25th line describes the parameters as:

<Y-parameter> (y-axis) VS <X-parameter> (x-axis) Esc to exit

The 24th line shows the limits as X-low, Y-range, X-high.

The top line shows Average, the average of Y-axis values and the average of X-axis values followed by Letter:. The intervening lines of the screen contain the scatter diagram, in which each data point is assigned an uppercase or lowercase letter. Lines are drawn for the averages of the set, except that price and market value are not averaged.

Answering the prompt with any letter will cause the corresponding data point to be identified to the right with the company name and value of Y- and X-parameters; the cursor will move to that location of the screen where the point is plotted. The letter displayed may not be the same as that selected if several companies are plotted to the same point; in this case the letter of the last point plotted will prevail. After a short delay, the cursor will move back to the prompt to repeat the process.

Entering Esc will exit from the point-identify mode, and the program will return to the outer level prompt for selection of another scatter diagram.

When the parameters are both positively correlated, such that an increase in value is preferable, then stocks in the upper right quadrant will be of greater interest than stocks elsewhere on the screen. Of course, price/book and price/earnings have negative significance. Plotting Price against any parameter is basically meaningless.

STOCK ESTIMATES (ESTIMATE.BAS)

Entered from the manager with the F4 selection, this program will give the following message:

ESTIMATE.INX found of drive <default drive>:

If you have started the program without first mounting an estimate data disk, then an alternate prompt is presented:

Mount Estimate data disk on drive <default drive>: _

If the file is still not found then the message and prompt is:

Estimate data disk not on line
Drive for estimate data (A,B,C,D,E,F,)=

and the program will wait for a valid drive designator. Then the prompt:

(E)stimate or (B)lank diskette to drive <drive id>?

allows running the program with a new data drive, or setting up a new estimate data diskette.
    Loading a formatted, empty diskette and entering B will lead to the prompt:

(C)reate estimate data disk on drive <drive id>?

C will authorize the program to create the file ESTI-MATE.INX formatted with empty entries. For ENTER alone, the program will allow an exit to the manager.
    Answer the first question with E and the program loops back to make sure a diskette with the ESTIMATE.INX file has indeed been loaded on the data drive. Then it displays the function key diagram:

STOCK ESTIMATES program   Esc Exit to MANAGER

    Display index   F1   F2 Set up new file
    Read file   F3

The F1 selection causes display of a 100 entry index numbered as 20 rows of five entries each, with the prompt,

(R)ead or (D)elete?, at the bottom. Typing ENTER will cause a return to the outer menu. Either R or D leads to the prompt, File name or #:. Typing either a code name or the position in the index of a file will lead to the selected action. An invalid name or position will lead to a message. D clears the entry with spaces and KILLS the file. It is quick and ruthless, so the only protection from inadvertently losing a file is to not input a valid file name or number.

R gets and displays the selected file. The outer menu Read file (F3 selection) does the same.

The F2 selection prompts for New file name:. A six-character name indentical to a STOCK.INX entry should be used. File already exists is displayed if this is the case, and if not, First year=, instead. The first year selected should allow at least six years of back data to be entered to ensure proper operation of the program. A blank file will be written to the data drive, and the file is displayed in columnar format:

<file name>

| Year Cap Exp/ | Sales/ | Inc in Sales/ | Inc Sales/ | PM% Earnings/ |
| Share | Share | Share | prior yr Cap E | Share |

<data>

(N)umeric, (Y)ear update, (S)tock split, (P)rintout?

The choices here work substantially the same as in STOCKPGM.BAS, and there is little point in explaining them except to mention some differences in the Numeric prompts.

After setting up a new file, the display will be flagged for setup mode. Selecting N will cause carats ($\wedge$) to be placed below columns and the message:

Setup mode- Enter back data in columns 2, 3 and 7 of rows 1 to 6

We then enter the historical data for capital expenditures per share, sales per share and earnings per share. This should not be interrupted before it is done because the setup prompt will never be presented again for the current file, and calculations will seem quite odd if six years of data have not been entered.

On exiting the numeric entry routine, calculations are made and the data is redisplayed. Now select the N choice again and the prompt will be:

Update mode- Enter new data or correct back data in columns 2, 5, and 6

Upon exiting the numeric routine this time, new calculations will be done and the empty columns filled with the results.

Pressing ENTER instead of one of the four selections will allow a write, exit, or repeat of the previous prompt.

GROWTH PROJECTIONS (LOGTREND.BAS)

LOGTREND.BAS is called from the manager with the F5 selection and begins with the heading and prompt:

LOGARITHMIC LINEAR REGRESSION Program
To calculate the growth rate of yearly data

First year: _

Enter the year as a four-digit value, or bypass with ENTER if it is of no concern that the data be so tagged. The prompt will then be:

<year> or 1:

Sequentially enter the data followed by ENTER until the data is exhausted, then press ENTER only. The results of the regression analysis will be presented as:

Number of points: <number of data points entered>
LN(Y)= <linear equation of X>
Zero year: <first year minus 1>
Growth: <percentage rate>
Degree of fit: <fraction from 0 to 1>

Then press ENTER and tabular data will be presented in the order: year, original data, and projection. Starting with the first year that does not have entered data, the projected value will be followed with Esc Exit?. Answer with ENTER and the next year's projection will be displayed, up to a maximum of 50 years. Esc gives the prompt:

Find value for any time? Enter time: _

Enter a year, either within or outside of the span displayed, and with a fractional part if desired (e.g. 1984.416), and the projection will be shown as F(<year>)=<value>. Then the inverse prompt will be displayed, Find time for any value? Enter value:, and the result will be, <value>=F(<time>). Pressing ENTER alone will bypass the prompt, and ENTER as the response to both queries will exit from this mode, leading to the heading, and the new menu:

(R) Review data
(N) New series
Esc Exit to MANAGER
? _

R returns to display the equation data. N returns to the first year prompt.

After the year prompt, pressing ENTER in place of the requested first data value will offer the opportunity to return to the manager.

It is interesting to experiment with growth projections, but you should recognize that the results may be of questionable significance because corporate conditions may change radically at any time, thus deviating abruptly, and perhaps permanently, from the expected rate. For some companies, however, there seems to be a real underlying growth trend, and it is useful to know if the company is currently above or below this value.

CHAPTER REMARKS

We sympathize with the reader who has likely found this chapter either tedious or confusing, or both. If the remark holds true that a picture is worth a thousand words, then practice must be worth ten-thousand words. The redemption is that actually working with the programs will be considerably easier then reading about them.

You should go through all the routines, modes, and selections to see the effects of every choice. The overall structure of the software package should then become transparent and this chapter's tedium nullified. A subsequent review of this chapter will place it in a different perspective, in that it can be viewed as a reference rather than as a text.

We do not doubt that some perplexity must remain, especially if you have covered this chapter without running the programs and following them dynamically as you read.

The next chapter gives an overview of the programs with the intention of showing how the programs are used to our benefit.

8

Software Overview

Now that you are becoming familiar with how the software is used, you may question what, exactly, to do with it.

This chapter is not meant to substitute for reading the other chapters in this book, because understanding growth, quality, and the other fundamentals of stock valuation is a necessary prerequisite. The programs can provide meaningful results only if accurate data is first supplied. Since stock valuation is a predictive matter, a certain amount of the data supplied to the programs must also be estimates. This data must be fundamentally sensible for these methods to work.

Viewing the program package from the manager shows five program selections associated with the first five function keys. This order also correlates to the general usefulness of each program.

If you are starting with an empty data base, then your first priority is to build up a data base of your own. Even if you are starting with the data base supplied with the diskette, you will most likely be interested in other stocks and will want to know their relative value as soon as possible. The following description will show how to set up a new stock file.

SETTING UP A NEW FILE

First, select F1, the STOCK INDEX program, from the manager.

Then select F2 to read the index, and do a simple read, from stock number one, by ignoring the options. The purpose of this is to determine where in the index the new entry is to be placed. If the data base is empty, then all you will see are market separators; so you will later select location 1 for your first stock if this stock is on the NYSE, location 2 if the stock is AMEX, or location 3 if the stock is OTC. If the data base has stock entries, you will continue to display the index until you find the exchange separator and then the alphabetic location in which you want the stock. If you follow our convention, you will place the stock in the same relative position as it appears in the *Wall Street Journal* stock tables. Make a mental note of the location number, with an awareness that the new stock entry to be inserted will appear before the stock currently there.

Now return to the outer (function key) menu and select F1, Insert stock. Answer the first prompt with the location, and then input the code name chosen for the new stock. This should be identical, or at least similar, to the code name in the *Wall Street Journal* tables. Next input data for the five prompts that follow if this information is available. It is all optional, except that a group number must be designated for the new stock because this number determines which diskette will contain data for the stock. Use our conventions, your own conventions, or group 1 if no particular grouping conventions will be used (thus indicating data diskette one).

Write the data to the index, and your new stock is now in place in the index.

Next you will want to set up a data file on the new stock. Exit to the manager and select F2, The STOCK FILES program. Place the diskette you wish to use to store data on the stock in the data drive and select F2, Set up new file. Then, enter the code name previously used for the index entry. The routine will check the index to make sure an entry of this name does indeed exist, and then you proceed to enter initial data for the new stock.

The heading will show the code name and a dash. Now enter the complete company name, and group with which it is affiliated if typing by industry is important to you. Then enter the first year for historical quarterly data. This should be two years prior to the current year. You might choose three years prior, but then the data would not be as useful as data containing longer estimates.

It is assumed that you have acquired a source of data on the stock in question, and will enter the data in the orderly manner requested. Quarterly data is straightforward because it only includes earnings, dividends, and book value.

You should then enter one or more earnings and growth estimates and the company balance sheet figures. The LOGTREND and ESTIMATE programs will later allow a check on the growth and earnings estimates.

Then enter the quality ratings, recently quoted stock price and footnotes.

Now enter a base year for inflation calculations. The base year must be within 11 years prior to the current year. Then the routine prompts for the yearly company earnings in turn.

The stock will be displayed, and you press ENTER at the prompt to write the new data to disk. The data for the new file is in place and the STOCK FILE program can be exited.

If you now wish to check the growth rate estimates, you should call up the LOGTREND program and enter back earnings, beginning as far back as you think relevant, and observe the results. If the growth rate resulting from this data is different from the growth projections, you should seek a reason for the difference. If the LOGTREND projection seems more reasonable, go back to the STOCK FILES program, call up the stock using the Stock display selection, and use the numeric routine to change these figures.

If you wish to check the earnings projections, call up the ESTIMATE program. The ESTIMATE program will search for the drive containing ESTIMATE.INX. If no such file is found, follow the program instructions for setting up an estimate files diskette. Otherwise, at the outer menu select F2, the new file routine. Enter the stock code name and the first year for the data; the first year should allow six years of historical data. An empty estimate data display will be presented, and you should choose the N selection to enter numeric data. Then, enter the data for capital expenditures per share, sales per share, and earnings per share. After this, exit the numeric routine and select the numeric routine again. You will now be in update mode and should enter projected capital expenditures per share, a reasonable figure for the expected increase in sales divided by the prior year's capital expenditures, and expected profit margins. Exit again and the display will now show an expectation of earnings per share several years hence.

If the earnings per share estimate four years from now is significantly different from the earnings estimate entered when setting up the data file, you should either search out a reason for the discrepancy or input new projections for the update mode estimate data. When the results finally seem reasonable, then, if there is good reason to do so, you should return to the STOCK FILES program and amend the projected earnings for the stock. Year updating the estimate file will allow projections farther out; but, of course, the more remote, the less reliable they will be.

KEEPING THE DATA CURRENT

For data to be meaningful, it must be kept up-to-date. This entails a variety of user actions that will be covered in the order of increasing frequency.

The task that occurs least often is a yearly update of the data. The year update selections in the ESTIMATE and STOCK FILES programs, referring to estimate and stock data files respectively, are used to make room for another year of figures. This is to be done on each file when data becomes available and there is no place to store it. This must be meaningful data, since there is no point in year-updating a file just to extend projections into the highly speculative future. The estimate files should extend no more then five years (four is better), and the stock data files should have from a few quarters less to a few quarters more than a one-year projection. When it is decided to do so, select Year update and then immediately use the display and modify mode to enter new data.

Also, once a year it will be necessary to update the deflator constants file. This is easily done in the STOCK FILES program using the Y option of the Change deflator constants routine, and then inputting the new value for the GNP deflator at the end of the list.

The stock data files will require an update of quarterly data when the figures become available. If you are using *Value Line* as a data source, this effort will be spread out over the 13 weekly issues of each volume. Otherwise, it will all seem to pile up at once because most companies are on calendar years.

Whenever a reputable source comes out with new projections on a stock and they are significant, it is a good idea to update the estimates in the stock data file before the next group valuation is done.

The factor that most influences a valuation is price, and since prices fluctuate daily during the work week, repricing is the action most often required. It usually makes no sense to reprice every day, since the price fluctuations over any particular day, and even over several days, tend to be minor. If the market is especially active and you expect to be trading on the information provided, you would want to reprice the data base before making investment decisions.

Otherwise, repricing once a week, or as infrequently as once or twice a month may be adequate. Institutional investors will chose to reprice more often, and private investors will probably prefer a less imperative schedule.

Repricing is done to the stock index entries, and may be done by any of six methods. As an option, prices may be entered manually when listing by group, class, or class decade. Manual repricing can be selected on all stocks of special interest, or on the whole index or a sequential subsection of it. The sixth method is remote repricing over the phone lines using a modem. This is the preferred method for a large data base and for institutional investors.

After a complete or selective repricing of the index is done, the stock files should be updated to reflect the influence of the current price. You then select Do group valuations in the STOCK FILES program, and have the routine revalue the stocks for all groups, or only those groups that have had prices changed in the index.

The data is now up-to-date in both the files and the index.

EXTRACTING USEFUL INFORMATION FROM THE DATA BASE

With all the data maintenance tasks done, the main purpose of the software package is to extract the information from the data base that is meaningful to stock trading. This is accomplished by using the three methods of viewing, selection, and comparison. The place to start for this is the STOCK INDEX program.

We recommend that you regularly select the Averages option of the Read routine and start at stock location one. This routine will then present averages over the whole stock data base for the parameters valuation, growth rate, dividend yield, price to book value ratio, and quality rating. The point being that you will then know by inspection if a stock is better or worse than average, relative to these five parameters. Also, the list by group and by class routines present averages for the group or class, with similar partitioning into better or worse categories.

The Select routine allows you to set favorable limits on eight stock parameters and to select only those stocks that are equal to or better than the limits. This also allows you to partition stocks into lists such as high value, high growth, high yield, low price to book ratio, or high quality, and into either large, medium, or small companies, or any combination of attributes.

You can make comparisons by mentally measuring the figures of one stock against those of another. This is more easily done by selecting the Store for SCATTER graph option in the routines Read, List by group, List by class, List by class decade, and Select by criteria. After this option has loaded the data on up to 52 selected stocks into the GRUPGRPH file, the SCATTER DIAGRAM program can be called from the manager and a scatter diagram created on any pair of nine stock parameters. You then see data points corresponding to each stock displayed on the screen at favorable or unfavorable positions that we humans translate through our ability to evaluate patterns. Pattern recognition is a task that people do well, but computers do poorly or with great difficulty. The scatter diagram will show exceptional or unusual stocks at both the limits of the screen and in particular quadrants relative to the averages, and may also show individual clusters of stocks that tend to have similar characteristics. As you no doubt sense, this can be a powerful tool for discovering interesting stocks.

SOFTWARE REMARKS

It is important for the reader to understand that this software is not to be viewed as a video game having much action but little substance. The programs are not algorithms that run to completion and then are finished.

Instead, the programs provide a minimum of bells and whistles, but have a maximum of what we consider useful tools that can make the process of stock selection more reliable and systematic, and thus easier. The programs will not do our thinking for us, but help to clarify our thinking about stock investments. Soon you will determine for yourself how best to use this software package. We hope this chapter points out a direction in which to head.

9

Economic Groups

Up to this point, the focus of this book has been on how to calculate a valuation on a stock that is meaningful compared to other stocks or to a market index. These valuations can be used in comparing stocks with dissimilar economic characteristics. However, it is a little like saying, "here are some apples that are good values and here are some oranges that are good values." The question is, "At a particular season of the year, are apples or oranges the better value?" With stocks, of course, where we stand in the economic cycle and the outlook for inflation, interest rates, and similar factors determine which are likely to be the best values.

CLASSIFYING STOCKS BY ECONOMIC CHARACTERISTICS

As recent events demonstrate, the business cycle is still with us. Also, as we have seen in recent years, changes in the inflation and interest rates have had a major impact on stock prices. The more successful professional investors try to tailor their stock portfolios to anticipated changes in the economy. Many have an economist filling a senior position in the organization, or else they retain the services of outside economic consultants. The services we use, such as *Value Line* and *Standard & Poor's,* publish their own economic forcasts, and their earnings estimates and investment advice are based on this work. We also receive reports on economic matters from brokers and other sources.

After examining various methods of grouping stocks into useful classifications, it became apparent that most of them used far too many groups for our purposes. The problem is to keep any system of classification simple enough so that it can be effectively applied to the average investor's holdings. *Standard & Poor's* uses 61 major stock classifications, and a number of these are divided into subclasses. For example, Building Materials has four subclasses and Machinery has six. *Value Line* has 94 industry groups. For purposes of storing data on the diskettes, we use the *Value Line* classification, but with a few exceptions.

As pointed out earlier, we do not attempt to follow stocks in all industry groups. Most of the stocks we do follow can be classified into one of five major groups and a minor one, as explained below. However, a few stocks do not fit into any classification because they are diversified into several industries that have different responses to shifts in the economy. These are put into a zero or miscellaneous classification. The groups ending in zero, 10, 20, and so on are also miscellaneous classifications in that the stocks do not fit into the subgroups below. We have constructed indexes of these groups that are shown later in this chapter. These indexes are updated weekly.

In selecting the stocks for the group indexes, the largest capitalization stock in four of the important subclasses is used. However, in the chemical group, Dow Chemical was substituted for duPont because of the Conoco merger. Because prices change, and accordingly the market capitalization, the stocks may no longer be the largest in every case. For example, Johnson & Johnson's capitalization has, at times, exceeded Merck's in the drug and health-care field.

0) MISCELLANEOUS—Not elsewhere classified.

10) BASIC—Companies that produce products or services sold to other businesses or durable goods sold to the consumer, generally cyclical.

11) Machinery and heavy equipment: Caterpillar Tractor.

12) Basic chemicals, plastics and fibers: Dow Chemical.

13) Electrical equipment and appliances: General Electric.

14) Autos. trucks and parts: General Motors.

15) Aerospace

16) Business services except advertizing media.

17) Transportation

18) Specialty chemicals

19) Sales of such products

20) CONSUMER—Companies that produce consumable or low-priced products that are usually advertized and are not very cyclical

21) Soft drinks: Coca Cola

22) Drugs, hospital, and health care products: Merck

23) Tobacco and brewing: Philip Morris

24) Household and personal products: Procter & Gamble

25) Containers and packaging

26) Food

27) Consumer goods sales

28) Entertainment, advertizing media, and services

29) Hospitals

30) TECHNOLOGY—Companies producing components and equipment with a high technology content, sold primarily to other businesses. They are usually capital goods and range in cyclicality

31) Electronic instruments: Hewlett Packard

32) Computers and office equipment: IBM

33) Oil industry technical services: Schlumberger

34) Integrated circuits and components: Texas Instruments

35) Computing services

36) Military electronics

37) Technology sales

38) Crime prevention devices and services

39) Communication devices

40) ENERGY—Oil, gas, coal, uraninum, and products and services for producing them, also means of transportation. They are moderately cyclical and price sensitive

41) Integrated oils: Exxon

42) Oilfield equipment and supplies: Halliburton

43) Nonintegrated oil and gas producing: Superior Oil

44) Natural gas transportation and production: Tenneco

45) Coal and uranium mining

46) Transportation of coal and oil

50) INTEREST SENSITIVE—Companies that deal in money and credit or are especially sensitive to the availability and cost of credit

51) Financial services with the public: American Express

52) Insurance: American International Group

53) Regulated utilities: AT&T

54) Banking: BankAmerica

55) Building and building supplies

56) Consumer credit
57) REITs
58) Insurance agencies
59) Savings and loan
60) INFLATION BENEFICIARIES—Products that are perceived to rise in price more than the inflation rate and benefit from a weak dollar
61) Gold, silver and gem mining
62) Nonferrous and strategic metals
63) Land holding concerns

The following chart (Figure 9.1) shows the Basic group, together with an index of earnings (the dotted line). The earnings are actual through the third quarter of 1982 and are estimated thereafter. The figures are adjusted for

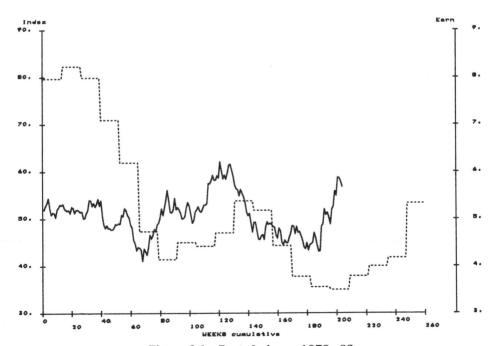

Figure 9.1   Basic Index — 1979–82

splits. If a company reports a loss, we use zero in calculating the earnings index.

From the earnings projections, it is apparent that a modest recovery is expected in the economy, starting in early 1983 and gaining momentum as the year progresses. The uncertainties are numerous, however, and the estimates depend on Congressional actions on Social Security, the budget, taxes, unemployment, and similar matters.

Other factors that will affect earnings of some basic industry companies are the strength of the dollar and how the financial problems of countries such as Mexico are handled. We do not expect that basic industry will return to normal profitability until 1984 or 1985. These basic industry companies are benefiting from lower inflation and

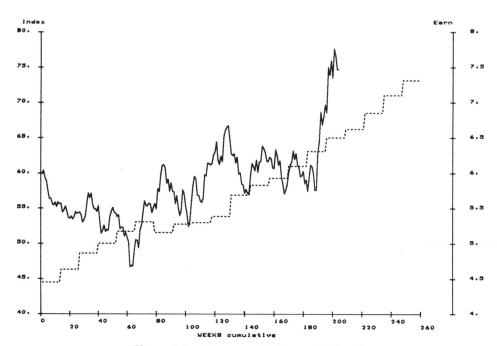

Figure 9.2   Consumer Index — 1979–82

declining interest rates, but less so than many other businesses.

At the end of this chapter, there is a list of all the stocks we are currently following in each group. We also include certain stocks that do not fit well into any of these groups.

The next chart (Figure 9.2) show the consumer group, together with earnings and estimates.

Consumer stocks are considerably less sensitive to the business cycle than those in the basic group. Many of them, food processors for example, are benefiting from lower raw material costs, particularly agricultural commodities. When consumer prices are stronger than producer prices, this group benefits compared to the basic industry group. High interest rates and a strong dollar have affected this group also, but perhaps not as seriously as some of the others. Many large international consumer concerns have developed considerable expertise in handling currency fluctuations. Consumer stocks have been doing well recently, but because they lagged behind other groups in the inflationary years they are not overpriced based on our valuations.

The third chart (Figure 9.3) shows the technology group, together with earnings and estimates.

This group is in a very favorable position assuming the economy recovers reasonably well. However, like the basic group, foreign competition resulting from the strong dollar is a problem for some businesses. Long term, the risk/reward ratio in the technology group appears excellent. Stocks in this group become overpriced on occasion and, based on the valuations, some already are. We follow a number of the smaller technology companies. In 1980 and 1981, many of these stocks had extraordinary advances. Some of the new issues, particularly, attracted a great deal of speculative buying. When the "hot" new issues rise to large premiums, it is an infallible sign of too much speculation; this is a warning to tread cautiously in the market. We follow a disproportionately large number of technology

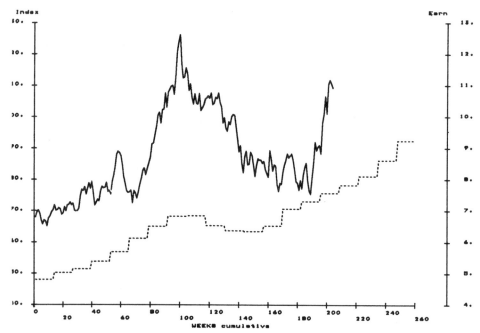

Figure 9.3   Technology Index — 1979–82

stocks, some being rather small and speculative. Later in this chapter, we discuss some of the problems involved in investing in emerging growth stocks.

The fourth chart (Figure 9.4) shows the energy group, together with earnings and estimates.

We are not very confident in these earnings estimates. It appears that OPEC may be in trouble. If they cannot restrict production more effectively, crude oil prices will continue to be weak. On the other hand, companies with a good potential for finding additional gas have excellent prospects unless, of course, Congress changes the current law providing for gradual decontrol of gas prices. Since the price of gas should eventually reach the energy equivalent of oil, which is more than double the average of 1982

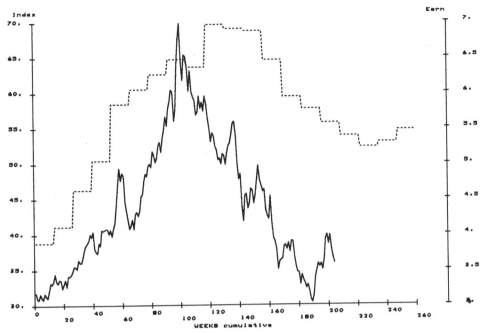

Figure 9.4   Energy Index — 1979–82

prices, the longer prospects seem favorable. The commodity oil service companies have also been hurt by current trends in the industry. They had a huge boom and, in many cases, overexpanded. However, from this level, it may not pay to be too bearish on the energy group because it has had a large correction.

The fifth chart (Figure 9.5) shows the interest sensitive group, with earnings and estimates.

Some of the stocks in this group, such as the banks, are more sensitive to short-term rates while others such as the building industry are more sensitive to long-term rates. The following chart (Figure 9.6) shows the yields on long-term Government bonds (the solid line), and on 91-day Treasury bills.

Predicting interest rates has been nearly as hard as trying to predict the stock market. Leading authorities on Wall Street were saying, early in 1982, that short-term rates would decline but long rates would not, and that as the economy began to grow again, both short- and long-term rates would rise to new highs. In August of 1982, these experts reversed their positions and touched off a huge advance in both stocks and bonds.

While there are very large demands for credit from the government to finance the huge projected deficits, overall credit demands from business and consumers are moderate. The building industry is operating at a low level, and the consumer seems to be in a mood to defer certain expenditures in favor of savings. With interest rates higher by a considerable margin than the inflation rate, the consumer is less likely to invest in tangibles and more likely to invest

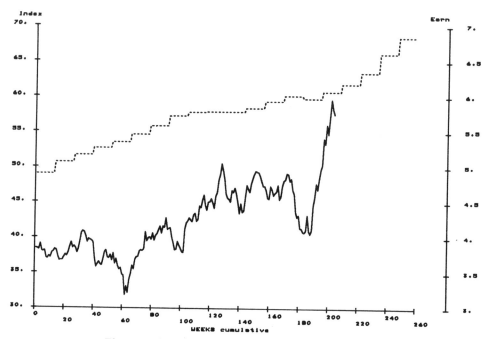

Figure 9.5   Interest Sensitive Index — 1979–82

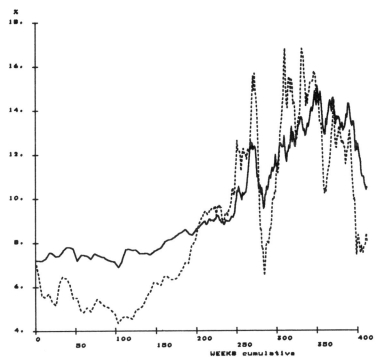

Figure 9.6   Government Yields — 1975–82

in financial instruments such as bonds and stocks. We discuss some of these matters in greater detail in Chapter 10.

The final group is one we call inflation beneficiaries. We neither keep a chart on this group nor follow many stocks of this type. If we become convinced that all efforts to control inflation are going to fail, and that there will be more inflation, not less, these are the stocks to own. Gold and other tangibles will also do well. However, we are reasonably optimistic because, for the first time in many years, there is an awareness in government that the nation has limited resources and that we must cut government spending and taxes, reduce regulation and government interference with business, get people off various forms of relief and back to work, stop monetizing the government's debt and inflating the money supply, and encourage savings and investment.

Will the economy emerge from the recession without having inflation flare up? The last chapter discusses how one can factor macroeconomic information into the investment decision-making process.

THE SUMMARY VALUATIONS

The stock lists at the end of this chapter show summary valuations on actively followed stocks. There are at least an equal number of others, for which we have data in the computer, that can be updated easily. The stocks are arranged by the market on which they trade, with the stocks on the New York Stock Exchange first, followed by those on the American Stock Exchange, and then the Over the Counter stocks. This simplifies entering prices.

We suggest that you run your own valuations on stocks that interest you, and then compare your results with ours. The growth rates and quality ratings will probably be reasonably similar. These stocks are priced as of November 30, 1982.

Because of space limitations, the summary valuations do not show the earnings estimates we are using. However, it is easy enough to calculate the earnings from the figures by running the equation backwards. Add the Yield and the Growth to get the Total Return. Multiply that by the Quali-Factor and divide by the valuation. This gives the P/E. Divide the price by the P/E and you have the estimated earnings for 1983 used in the valuation. There will be small rounding errors. Note that the valuations are based on the estimate of earnings for the year ended December, 1983. Since some companies have fiscal years that are different, the year could end November of 1983 or January of 1984.

EMERGING GROWTH STOCKS

The reader will note that there are a large number of stocks in these tables that have small market capitalizations and many are traded over the counter or on the American Exchange. The investment characteristics of a small concern that has been in business for only a few years are very different from those of the large, established business. While our valuation methods work quite well on small growth stocks most of the time, there are still some problems. Note the growth rates. Some are so high that, as pointed out earlier, we know they are not sustainable for more than a few years.

There are a few special rules to follow when investing in junior growth stocks. Do not invest in just one: buy several on the theory that if one works out handsomely, it will pay for disappointments in the rest. Consider the company's competitive position very carefully, as discussed in Appendix B. A small concern may appear to have a very strong product and market position, only to be supplanted by another company in a very short time. Consider placing stop-loss orders at about 15% under the market in order to cut your losses when something goes wrong, as it does frequently with this kind of stock. We discuss this and other trading stategies in Chapter 12.

Some investors may decide to use mutual funds that specialize in this kind of investment. The Surveyor Fund, of which I am a director, emphasizes high technology investments with a large share of assets in emerging growth stocks. This is one of the Eberstadt group of funds. Another larger fund of this type is the T Rowe Price New Horizons Fund. It normally has about 100 different stocks, which implies considerable diversification; but since they are all highly volatile stocks, the fund is not for widows and orphans or the faint-hearted.

Why bother with these kinds of speculative stocks? The answer is very simple. You hope to strike it rich. Even a small investment in extremely successful companies, such as Digital Equipment or Computervision, when the stocks first came public has turned into a fortune. My former associates at Eberstadt, before I was with the firm, invested about $1 million in Haloid in the Chemical Fund. Haloid became Xerox, and the holding was eventually sold for a profit of about $100 million.

Some of the smaller capitalization growth stocks listed here will fail, or merely limp along on the edge of failure. Some will sell out to larger concerns, frequently on a basis favorable to the stockholders. A few will grow and prosper. Investors who can accept the risk, and who are not primarily concerned with current income, should consider having part of their funds in this type of investment.

#	SYM	NAME		CLASS	GROUP	PRICE	VAL.	GROWTH	YIELD	P/B	QUAL.	MKT V.
32	CBT	CabotC		0	4	20.50	1.71+	9.04	4.88	0.90	85	652
34	CSL	Carlis		0	5	31.75	1.36-	13.18	3.15	1.83	82	294
51	DSN	DenMfs	*	0	6	23.50	1.64+	9.87	6.81	1.08	79	219
58		DJInd		0	14	103.93	1.17+	.7.32	5.77	0.99	81	260
123	MMM	MMM	*	0	3	74.13	1.09+	8.89	4.59	2.11	93	8707
131	PPG	PPG		0	2	50.25	1.44+	9.24	5.09	0.97	80	1731
154		S&PInd	*	0	14	154.65	1.25+	9.18	5.30	1.08	80	804
183	TYL	Tyler		0	2	19.50	1.22+	15.72	3.49	1.13	70	183
192		ValueL		0	14	35.00	1.16+	9.42	4.69	1.17	80	960
AMEX												
OTC												
217	CRIV	ChrlsR		0	8	36.00	1.05+	14.84	1.44	2.24	86	96
227	DYTC	Dynatc	*	0	8	23.63	1.11-	22.52	0.00	3.47	80	110
12-04-1982												
11		AV.		0	0	0.00	1.29	11.75	4.11	1.54	81	0
								15.86				

#	SYM	NAME		CLASS	GROUP	PRICE	VAL.	GROWTH	YIELD	P/B	QUAL.	MKT V.
11	AME	Ametek		10	12	35.75	1.69+	13.37	4.71	1.83	91	324
55	DOV	Dover	*	10	12	29.38	2.83-	15.60	3.73	1.52	106	805
70	FMC	FMC		10	12	29.50	1.78-	9.52	5.74	0.72	71	1016
96	ITW	ITW		10	12	37.75	1.30	11.43	3.18	1.35	93	464
128	NRT	Norton		10	12	32.00	1.35+	8.83	6.87	0.96	78	543
AMEX												
OTC												
222	CPER	ConslP		10	7	32.75	1.48-	8.00	6.11	1.00	93	355
12-04-1982												
6		AV.		0	0	0.00	1.74	11.13	5.06	1.23	89	0
								16.18				

#	SYM	NAME		CLASS	GROUP	PRICE	VAL.	GROWTH	YIELD	P/B	QUAL.	MKT V.
29	BY	BucyEr		11	12	14.88	1.47+	11.82	5.82	0.72	74	309
35	CAT	CatrpT	*	11	12	39.25	1.42+	11.80	6.84	0.88	80	3475
40	CMZ	CinMil		11	12	29.25	0.67-	25.59	3.00	1.53	86	546
182	TKR	Timkn	*	11	5	48.75	1.56+	9.65	4.92	0.65	94	547
AMEX												
OTC												
231	GULD	GouldP	*	11	12	18.88	1.59+	13.48	4.24	2.21	92	299
247	NBSC	NBrunS		11	12	17.50	0.80+	19.28	0.00	2.21	65	39
12-04-1982												
6		AV.		0	0	0.00	1.25	15.27	4.14	1.36	82	0
								19.40				

#	SYM	NAME		CLASS	GROUP	PRICE	VAL.	GROWTH	YIELD	P/B	QUAL.	MKT V.
56	DOW	DowCh	*	12	3	26.25	1.59+	14.46	6.86	0.98	78	4977
59	DD	duPont	*	12	3	37.63	1.62+	10.72	6.91	0.80	69	8871
151	ROH	RohmH		12	3	74.00	1.15+	11.14	4.05	1.12	80	956
AMEX												
OTC												
12-04-1982												
3		AV.		0	0	0.00	1.45	12.11	5.94	0.97	75	0
									18.05			

#	SYM	NAME		CLASS	GROUP	PRICE	VAL.	GROWTH	YIELD	P/B	QUAL.	MKT V.
26	BDK	BlackD		13	12	17.38	1.00+	8.98	5.29	1.03	80	605
42	CSP	CombEn		13	12	33.75	3.43-	12.91	6.87	0.99	96	961
66	EMR	EmrsEl		13	18	58.75	1.34	13.14	3.74	2.25	93	4030
80	GE	GenEl	*	13	18	92.50	1.45-	12.09	3.89	1.85	95	20945
85	GSX	GenSig	*	13	18	42.75	1.61-	12.94	3.93	1.32	91	1185
AMEX												
OTC												
214	AMAT	AppldM	*	13	12	21.88	0.00	0.00	0.00	0.00	0	0
12-04-1982												
5		AV.		0	0	0.00	1.77	12.01	4.74	1.49	91	0
									16.76			

#	SYM	NAME		CLASS	GROUP	PRICE	VAL.	GROWTH	YIELD	P/B	QUAL.	MKT V.
63	ECH	Echlin	*	14	5	19.25	1.01+	12.71	3.12	1.63	68	393
82	GM	GMot	*	14	5	59.88	0.94+	8.63	4.01	0.96	68	18180
AMEX												
OTC												
12-04-1982												
2		AV.		0	0	0.00	0.98	10.67	3.56	1.29	68	0
									14.23			

#	SYM	NAME		CLASS	GROUP	PRICE	VAL.	GROWTH	YIELD	P/B	QUAL.	MKT V.
27	BA	Boeing	*	15	1	32.63	1.28+	10.35	4.29	1.06	92	3150
36	CEA	CessAr		15	1	23.25	1.08+	18.78	1.72	1.20	87	447
71	FEN	Fairch		15	1	15.88	1.60-	12.10	5.04	0.81	70	208
150	ROK	Rockwl		15	1	41.38	1.67+	10.19	4.35	1.35	90	3144
188	UTX	UnTech		15	1	55.25	1.65+	10.43	4.71	0.99	80	2978
AMEX												
210	TFX	Telflx		15	1	28.63	1.16+	18.74	1.40	2.98	76	133
OTC												
239	KAMNA	Kaman		15	1	27.38	1.29	11.75	2.63	1.09	83	93
263	WYMN	WymanG		15	1	25.25	1.43-	14.08	3.17	1.54	85	483
12-04-1982												
8		AV.		0	0	0.00	1.40	13.30	3.41	1.38	83	0
									16.71			

#	SYM	NAME		CLASS	GROUP	PRICE	VAL.	GROWTH	YIELD	P/B	QUAL.	MKT V.
60	DNB	DunBr	*	16	17	98.00	1.19+	14.77	3.06	4.71	110	2753
130	PHH	PHH	*	16	17	35.38	1.03+	15.20	2.37	2.95	82	541
133	PKR	ParkPn	*	16	5	14.50	1.11+	15.70	3.59	1.57	85	245
AMEX												
OTC												
219	CCLR	ComClH	*	16	17	52.75	1.65-	18.08	3.41	4.57	98	475
225	DATC	DataCd	*	16	17	12.13	1.08+	13.34	1.98	1.47	85	74
234	IMSI	IMSInt	*	16	17	21.88	0.88+	13.69	1.10	2.10	81	205
248	NEILB	Nielsn	*	16	17	63.25	1.34	15.86	2.15	2.71	99	710
12-04-1982												
7		AV.		0	0	0.00	1.18	15.23	2.52	2.87	91	0
									17.76			

#	SYM	NAME		CLASS	GROUP	PRICE	VAL.	GROWTH	YIELD	P/B	QUAL.	MKT V.
5	ABF	AirbFt		17	20	16.00	1.11+	15.66	5.00	1.58	61	75
45	CNF	CnsFrt	*	17	20	47.50	1.64+	13.80	3.62	1.16	89	638
67	EAF	EmeryA		17	20	17.00	0.53+	9.62	2.94	3.01	65	267
72	FDX	FedExp	*	17	20	73.13	0.89+	16.34	0.00	3.39	76	1518
79	GEL	Gelco		17	20	26.13	1.48+	16.45	4.59	1.19	57	309
105	LTC	Leasw	*	17	20	35.00	1.42+	13.64	4.57	1.37	67	417
197	XTR	XTRA		17	20	19.88	1.22+	15.90	3.22	0.79	51	124
AMEX												
OTC												
233	HARG	HarpGr	*	17	20	25.00	1.55-	18.38	1.28	1.89	85	101
254	ROAD	RoadSv	*	17	20	56.75	1.47+	14.58	2.82	2.20	103	1125
12-04-1982												
9		AV.		0	0	0.00	1.26	14.93	3.12	1.84	73	0
									18.05			

#	SYM	NAME	CLASS	GROUP	PRICE	VAL.	GROWTH	YIELD	P/B	QUAL.	MKT V.
4	APD	AirPro	18	4	36.50	1.48+	11.65	2.47	1.05	78	1043
25	BIG	BisThr	18	4	22.38	1.69+	13.08	3.58	1.34	82	950
112	LZ	Lubrzl *	18	3	18.63	1.05+	7.19	5.80	1.46	97	730
125	MTI	Morton *	18	4	52.63	1.41+	14.51	3.04	1.40	77	881
143	RAYC	Raychm *	18	4	70.00	0.81+	14.94	0.69	2.20	83	654
AMEX											
206	GLK	GrtLk *	18	4	37.50	1.16+	16.93	1.71	2.03	86	271
209	PLL	PallCp *	18	4	44.88	0.97+	19.30	1.16	4.67	85	605
OTC											
216	BETZ	BetzL	18	4	40.00	0.92+	13.03	2.50	3.77	99	633
242	MILI	Millpr *	18	4	27.50	0.98+	16.74	1.45	1.86	85	368
250	PLIT	Petrlt	18	4	29.63	1.75+	14.67	3.71	2.12	97	351
252	QCHM	QuakrC	18	4	21.00	1.58+	14.45	3.05	1.17	92	73
259	SIAL	SigmaA *	18	4	38.50	0.70+	13.11	1.14	2.98	83	332
12-04-1982											
12		AV.	0	0	0.00	1.21	14.13	2.52	2.17	87	0
								16.66			

#	SYM	NAME	CLASS	GROUP	PRICE	VAL.	GROWTH	YIELD	P/B	QUAL.	MKT V.
86	GPC	GenuPt *	19	5	44.00	1.10-	12.21	3.18	2.39	101	1565
163	SNA	SnapOn *	19	12	26.00	2.12+	14.82	4.57	1.64	92	442
AMEX											
OTC											
240	LAWS	Lawson	19	5	28.00	1.28+	15.72	1.29	2.05	93	140
12-04-1982											
3		AV.	0	0	0.00	1.50	14.25	3.01	2.03	95	0
								17.26			

#	SYM	NAME	CLASS	GROUP	PRICE	VAL.	GROWTH	YIELD	P/B	QUAL.	MKT V.
18	AVY	Avery	20	6	37.00	1.17+	11.81	2.70	1.48	81	333
50	DLX	DeLuxe *	20	17	35.75	1.32-	12.72	3.36	2.77	98	824
62	EK	EstKod *	20	18	94.25	1.67+	11.93	4.03	1.84	106	15316
97	ITC	InsrTc *	20	11	11.88	1.31+	13.09	5.05	0.66	65	23
99	IFF	IntFl	20	6	24.50	1.10+	10.08	4.41	2.49	92	895
107	LNX	Lenox	20	6	45.00	1.52+	10.90	4.44	1.35	90	202
122	MB	MiltBr	20	5	28.00	0.98+	7.93	4.57	1.04	77	207
AMEX											
201	BFD.B	BrnFB *	20	11	36.38	2.07	14.64	2.75	1.98	100	916
OTC											
251	PHYB	PionHB	20	11	25.63	1.47-	16.48	3.12	2.13	83	818
12-04-1982											
9		AV.	0	0	0.00	1.40	12.18	3.83	1.75	88	0
								16.00			

#	SYM	NAME	CLASS	GROUP	PRICE	VAL.	GROWTH	YIELD	P/B	QUAL.	MKT V.
41	KO	CocaCl *	21	11	49.50	1.39-	10.11	5.25	2.25	105	6716
53	DOC	DrPep	21	11	13.38	1.28+	11.40	6.58	1.76	76	271
135	PEP	Pepsi *	21	11	41.00	1.40	11.72	4.20	1.83	85	3813
AMEX											
OTC											
12-04-1982											
3		AV.	0	0	0.00	1.36	11.07	5.34	1.95	88	0
								16.42			

#	SYM	NAME	CLASS	GROUP	PRICE	VAL.	GROWTH	YIELD	P/B	QUAL.	MKT V.
1	ABT	AbotLb *	22	8	38.25	1.04	14.50	2.51	3.04	86	4674
9	AHS	AmHosp *	22	8	44.25	0.86+	11.91	2.08	2.46	96	3140
23	BAX	BaxtTr *	22	8	49.88	0.78	14.56	1.04	2.65	82	3538
75	FGN	FlowGn *	22	8	13.50	0.71+	13.20	0.00	1.14	65	111
101	JNJ	JohnJn *	22	8	46.50	1.31+	14.88	2.49	2.63	103	8698
108	LLY	LillyE *	22	8	59.75	1.70	11.21	4.69	1.95	106	4539
120	MDT	Medtrn *	22	8	50.00	1.17	15.07	1.44	2.70	91	784
121	MRK	Merck *	22	8	82.75	1.38+	12.96	3.63	2.48	104	6122
138	PFE	Pfizer *	22	8	73.25	1.00+	13.91	2.73	2.65	87	5550
155	SGP	SchrPl	22	8	41.00	1.19+	8.18	4.29	1.46	100	2182
162	SKB	SmkB *	22	8	64.88	1.98-	15.33	4.32	2.66	105	5361
174	SYN	Syntex	22	8	52.75	1.51	15.31	2.65	2.64	93	1829
190	UPJ	UpJohn	22	8	44.75	1.36+	9.32	5.36	1.24	87	1351
AMEX											
OTC											
218	COBE	CobeLb *	22	8	34.75	0.80+	12.46	0.00	1.21	68	73
230	FOPHY	Fortia *	22	8	46.38	0.70+	21.86	0.52	5.87	85	893
238	ITEM	Intrmd *	22	8	18.25	1.60+	17.41	0.00	1.53	76	189
12-04-1982											
16		AV.	0	0	0.00	1.19	13.88	2.36	2.39	90	0
								16.24			

#	SYM	NAME		CLASS	GROUP	PRICE	VAL.	GROWTH	YIELD	P/B	QUAL.	MKT V.
13	BUD	Anheus		23	11	68.00	1.10-	13.38	2.35	1.89	76	3282
89	GHB	HeilmB	*	23	11	37.50	1.50	14.51	2.35	2.14	86	496
139	MO	PhilMr	*	23	11	62.25	1.72	13.14	4.18	1.77	84	7808
147	RJR	ReynIn		23	11	49.25	2.38-	10.04	6.50	1.03	89	5145

AMEX
OTC
12-04-1982

4		AV.		0	0	0.00	1.67	12.77	3.84	1.71	84	0
									16.61			

#	SYM	NAME		CLASS	GROUP	PRICE	VAL.	GROWTH	YIELD	P/B	QUAL.	MKT V.
8	AHP	AHome		24	8	44.38	1.76	12.70	5.63	3.29	105	6883
28	BMY	BristM	*	24	8	68.63	1.39	12.82	3.35	2.33	100	4589
37	CBM	ChesPn		24	6	41.75	1.50+	12.26	4.60	2.06	90	1498
117	MKY	MaryK		24	6	53.75	1.16	24.14	0.52	5.84	87	776
141	PG	ProctG	*	24	6	118.88	1.37	11.09	4.04	2.12	98	9854
146	REV	Revlon	*	24	6	31.13	1.42+	11.89	5.91	1.25	76	1078
153	RBD	Rubbrm		24	6	27.00	0.96+	12.64	2.52	2.18	84	418
169	STY	SterlD		24	8	24.00	1.65+	11.42	4.83	1.48	97	1454

AMEX
OTC

249	NOXLB	Noxell	*	24	6	45.88	1.36	13.04	2.88	2.04	94	224

12-04-1982

9		AV.		0	0	0.00	1.40	13.55	3.81	2.51	92	0
									17.36			

#	SYM	NAME		CLASS	GROUP	PRICE	VAL.	GROWTH	YIELD	P/B	QUAL.	MKT V.
20	BLL	BallCp		25	6	28.25	1.50-	10.90	4.04	1.21	81	309
54	DSY	Dorsey	*	25	6	30.13	1.90+	13.26	3.98	0.90	70	124
76	FHP	FtHowP	*	25	7	48.75	1.09-	11.55	2.46	2.53	100	1316
159	SEE	SealdA	*	25	6	25.50	1.76+	14.50	2.67	1.26	87	85
185	UCC	UCamp		25	7	61.00	1.04+	7.81	4.92	1.22	80	1484
194	W	Wstvac		25	7	24.75	1.50+	9.19	5.17	0.83	83	658

AMEX
OTC
12-04-1982

6		AV.		0	0	0.00	1.47	11.20	3.87	1.32	83	0
									15.07			

#	SYM	NAME		CLASS	GROUP	PRICE	VAL.	GROWTH	YIELD	P/B	QUAL.	MKT V.
14	ADM	ArchrD		26	11	29.38	0.97+	13.30	0.65	1.66	87	2239
24	BRY	BeatFd		26	11	24.13	1.81	9.75	6.63	1.02	80	2429
31	CPC	CPC		26	11	36.50	2.06-	9.85	6.03	1.19	91	1767
81	GIS	GenMil		26	11	49.75	1.46+	11.73	4.02	1.79	85	2502
90	HNZ	Heinz		26	11	35.75	1.65	10.46	4.92	1.47	80	1683
92	HSY	Hershy		26	11	53.75	1.77	12.30	4.09	1.39	84	842
142	OAT	QuakOt		26	11	46.88	1.74+	10.46	4.69	1.30	85	919

AMEX
OTC
12-04-1982

7		AV.		0	0	0.00	1.64	11.12	4.43	1.40	85	0
									15.55			

#	SYM	NAME		CLASS	GROUP	PRICE	VAL.	GROWTH	YIELD	P/B	QUAL.	MKT V.
38	CHU	Church		27	15	38.13	1.70+	14.23	3.04	1.84	94	483
64	ECK	EckrdJ	*	27	15	25.00	1.67+	13.02	4.48	1.62	99	933
103	KM	KMart		27	15	26.00	1.25+	13.02	4.23	1.13	67	3223
110	LDG	LongDr	*	27	15	39.25	1.57+	13.27	2.96	1.85	108	415
113	LKS	LuckyS	*	27	15	17.25	1.41+	9.37	6.96	1.55	70	872
119	MCD	McDnld		27	15	60.63	1.28	15.12	1.71	1.91	80	3674
145	RDS	Revco		27	15	45.63	1.00+	13.51	2.19	2.91	96	936
148	RAD	RiteAd	*	27	15	48.25	1.24	15.87	1.91	2.67	90	677
160	S	Sears	*	27	15	31.50	0.87+	8.72	4.83	1.22	75	10959
165	SLC	Soutln		27	15	41.63	1.33	12.12	3.08	1.24	70	988
173	SVU	SuprVl	*	27	15	25.38	1.21+	15.29	2.52	2.82	78	929
175	SYY	Sysco		27	15	37.88	0.81	15.19	0.95	3.22	84	790

AMEX
OTC

223	CFSC	CFSCon	*	27	15	34.50	0.82+	13.40	1.62	1.64	60	181
258	SHON	Shoney		27	15	26.50	0.89+	18.69	0.75	3.40	78	381

12-04-1982

14		AV.		0	0	0.00	1.22	13.63	2.94	2.07	82	0
									16.57			

#	SYM	NAME	CLASS	GROUP	PRICE	VAL.	GROWTH	YIELD	P/B	QUAL.	MKT V.
33	CCB	CapCit *	28	17	124.50	0.99+	16.31	0.16	2.56	87	1633
57	DJ	DowJn	28	17	66.25	0.92+	17.64	1.81	5.39	94	2082
77	GCI	Gannet *	28	17	62.00	0.69-	10.39	2.90	3.25	91	3289
102	JOS	Josten *	28	5	26.50	1.36	11.99	3.77	2.26	92	334
106	LEE	LeeEnt	28	17	36.00	1.33-	15.68	3.44	3.27	80	247
AMEX											
208	MEG.A	MediaG *	28	17	44.25	1.56-	12.95	2.44	1.25	87	307
OTC											
244	MMED	Multmd	28	17	44.75	0.95+	14.42	1.79	2.48	80	456
262	WILL	WileyJ	28	17	23.75	1.58+	10.42	4.04	1.51	86	88
12-04-1982											
8		AV.	0	0	0.00	1.17	13.72	2.55	2.75	87	0
							16.27				

#	SYM	NAME	CLASS	GROUP	PRICE	VAL.	GROWTH	YIELD	P/B	QUAL.	MKT V.
43	CMY	ComPsy	29	8	37.75	0.69	17.45	1.06	4.55	73	414
129	OCR	Omnicr *	29	8	47.00	0.79+	14.44	1.87	3.78	87	327
AMEX											
OTC											
12-04-1982											
2		AV.	0	0	0.00	0.74	15.94	1.47	4.16	80	0
							17.41				

#	SYM	NAME	CLASS	GROUP	PRICE	VAL.	GROWTH	YIELD	P/B	QUAL.	MKT V.
46	GLW	CornGl	30	18	60.75	1.00+	11.89	4.28	1.21	71	1287
61	EGG	EG&G *	30	18	28.38	1.16+	18.09	1.27	3.97	99	828
73	FSI	FlistS *	30	17	25.38	1.19	20.68	0.79	3.25	80	372
AMEX											
OTC											
12-04-1982											
3		AV.	0	0	0.00	1.12	16.89	2.11	2.81	83	0
							19.00				

#	SYM	NAME	CLASS	GROUP	PRICE	VAL.	GROWTH	YIELD	P/B	QUAL.	MKT V.
84	GEN	GenRad	31	18	29.88	0.68+	17.80	0.40	2.33	70	264
93	HWP	HewltP *	31	18	72.50	0.95	17.87	0.39	3.27	99	9041
136	PKN	PerknE	31	18	27.88	0.88+	11.58	2.15	2.12	89	1193
166	SPY	SpecPh *	31	18	21.00	0.54+	15.40	0.00	1.41	67	98
177	TEK	Tektrn *	31	18	54.50	0.91+	9.22	2.20	1.47	89	1025
179	TER	Teradn	31	18	32.38	0.41+	16.54	0.00	2.55	56	272
AMEX											
205	FKM	FlukeJ *	31	18	26.38	0.57+	13.62	0.00	2.24	76	189
207	MAX	Matrix *	31	8	40.00	0.70-	26.52	0.00	5.68	85	175
OTC											
215	AVAK	Avantk	31	18	23.88	0.77	25.91	0.00	4.92	95	435
12-04-1982											
9		AV.	0	0	0.00	0.71	17.16	0.57	2.89	81	0
							17.73				

#	SYM	NAME	CLASS	GROUP	PRICE	VAL.	GROWTH	YIELD	P/B	QUAL.	MKT V.
49	DGN	DataGe *	32	19	37.75	0.89+	14.24	0.00	0.91	81	409
52	DEC	DigitE *	32	19	105.00	1.06+	14.19	0.00	1.64	96	5799
74	FLP	FloatP *	32	19	24.50	1.61-	29.85	0.00	3.77	82	214
98	IBM	IBM	32	19	86.50	1.82+	14.51	4.62	2.23	101	51638
140	PRM	PrimeC *	32	19	35.88	0.97+	23.77	0.00	4.27	71	1069
170	STK	StorTc	32	19	26.13	1.43	19.96	0.00	1.36	70	872
196	XRX	Xerox	32	19	38.75	1.66-	8.18	7.74	0.80	80	3275
AMEX											
202	CCS	CompCn	32	19	34.88	0.64-	22.65	0.00	4.78	78	188
211	WAN.B	Wang *	32	19	59.75	0.72+	21.79	0.33	4.80	76	3612
OTC											
221	CCTC	C&CT *	32	19	14.50	1.09+	19.06	0.00	1.47	79	105
224	CPTC	CPT	32	19	17.75	1.37+	22.48	0.00	2.73	77	289
260	TNDM	Tandem *	32	19	30.38	1.14+	30.62	0.00	3.59	86	1122
12-04-1982											
12		AV.	0	0	0.00	1.20	20.11	1.06	2.70	81	0
							21.17				

#	SYM	NAME		CLASS	GROUP	PRICE	VAL.	GROWTH	YIELD	P/B	QUAL.	MKT V.
78	GOI	Gearht	*	33	9	11.88	0.76-	15.78	3.03	0.97	68	183
156	SLB	Schlmb	*	33	9	39.25	2.92-	18.77	2.85	1.75	105	11520
AMEX
OTC
12-04-1982

#	SYM	NAME		CLASS	GROUP	PRICE	VAL.	GROWTH	YIELD	P/B	QUAL.	MKT V.
2		AV.		0	0	0.00	1.84	17.28	2.94	1.36	87	0
									20.22			

#	SYM	NAME		CLASS	GROUP	PRICE	VAL.	GROWTH	YIELD	P/B	QUAL.	MKT V.
2	AMD	AdvMcr		34	18	25.00	0.45+	18.67	0.00	3.88	67	650
12	AMP	AMPInc	*	34	18	66.88	0.79-	12.84	2.24	3.00	101	2401
16	AUG	Augat	*	34	18	32.50	0.81+	12.45	1.23	3.35	85	499
30	BDC	Burndy	*	34	18	21.00	0.94-	12.45	4.00	1.71	89	257
126	NSM	NtSemi		34	18	24.25	0.59-	14.10	0.00	1.64	78	567
180	TXN	TexIns	*	34	18	135.38	1.31+	17.40	1.48	2.06	95	3199
AMEX
199	AHA	AlphaI	*	34	18	34.25	1.10+	22.15	0.29	3.20	83	119
OTC
236	INTC	Intel	*	34	18	38.13	0.65+	18.85	0.00	2.85	85	1669
243	MOLX	Molex		34	18	58.38	0.97	17.55	0.21	3.37	87	386
12-04-1982
9		AV.		0	0	0.00	0.85	16.78	1.05	2.79	85	0
									17.83			

#	SYM	NAME		CLASS	GROUP	PRICE	VAL.	GROWTH	YIELD	P/B	QUAL.	MKT V.
17	AUD	AutoDt	*	35	19	35.13	0.81+	13.08	1.59	2.89	92	1198
44	CVN	Comvis	*	35	19	34.25	0.78+	23.14	0.00	4.28	77	936
47	CULD	Cullin	*	35	19	50.50	0.99-	32.47	0.00	7.59	85	338
65	EDS	EDS		35	19	49.75	0.70	15.81	1.37	5.75	91	1435
184	TYM	Tymshr		35	19	25.00	0.30	9.96	0.00	1.60	68	294
AMEX
OTC
228	ESCC	Ev&Sut	*	35	19	41.88	0.87-	30.46	0.00	5.74	85	364
235	ISCS	ISCSys		35	19	17.50	1.31+	29.69	0.00	4.79	85	252
237	INGR	Interg		35	19	38.50	1.29+	41.35	0.00	7.00	80	446
245	NDTA	NatDat		35	19	21.00	0.92	17.56	2.10	3.72	80	240
253	REYNA	ReyRey		35	19	26.13	1.26+	11.67	4.59	1.41	86	124
257	SMED	SharMd	*	35	19	49.88	0.75+	19.09	1.20	6.35	86	601
261	TRSC	TriadS	*	35	19	20.50	0.88+	17.91	0.00	2.30	85	148
12-04-1982
12		AV.		0	0	0.00	0.90	21.85	0.90	4.45	83	0
									22.75			

#	SYM	NAME		CLASS	GROUP	PRICE	VAL.	GROWTH	YIELD	P/B	QUAL.	MKT V.
68	ESY	ESystm		36	1	43.88	0.85	16.00	1.60	2.95	77	626
111	LOR	LoralC		36	1	38.25	1.07	13.81	2.09	2.25	87	391
144	RTN	Raythn	*	36	1	45.25	1.57-	13.04	3.31	1.90	101	3812
193	WJ	WatJhn		36	1	47.25	0.73	12.47	1.35	1.73	74	151
AMEX
OTC
255	SCIS	SCISys		36	1	29.13	0.62+	17.81	0.00	4.10	72	166
12-04-1982
5		AV.		0	0	0.00	0.97	14.62	1.67	2.59	82	0
									16.30			

#	SYM	NAME		CLASS	GROUP	PRICE	VAL.	GROWTH	YIELD	P/B	QUAL.	MKT V.
176	TAN	Tandy		37	15	53.00	1.07-	21.14	0.00	5.05	95	5505
AMEX
OTC
12-04-1982
1		AV.		0	0	0.00	1.07	21.14	0.00	5.05	95	0
									21.14			

#	SYM	NAME		CLASS	GROUP	PRICE	VAL.	GROWTH	YIELD	P/B	QUAL.	MKT V.
6	ADT	ADT		38	17	44.75	1.24+	10.75	3.84	1.30	80	277
AMEX
OTC
256	SNSR	Sensor	*	38	18	38.75	0.74	25.42	0.21	5.70	76	610
12-04-1982
2		AV.		0	0	0.00	0.99	18.09	2.03	3.50	78	0
									20.11			

#	SYM	NAME		CLASS	GROUP	PRICE	VAL.	GROWTH	YIELD	P/B	QUAL.	MKT V.
88	HRS	Harris		39	12	37.25	1.09+	11.38	2.75	1.63	81	1089
114	MAI	MACOM	*	39	21	23.50	0.80+	17.64	0.85	2.73	76	920
124	MLT	Mitel		39	21	28.88	0.74+	28.83	0.00	3.46	65	1076
132	PDN	Pardyn	*	39	21	47.25	1.03-	27.49	0.00	2.75	75	683
152	RM	RolmCp	*	39	21	45.25	0.69-	19.96	0.00	4.29	71	795
157	SFA	SciAtl	*	39	18	14.75	0.93+	12.77	0.81	1.93	90	345

AMEX
OTC

#	SYM	NAME		CLASS	GROUP	PRICE	VAL.	GROWTH	YIELD	P/B	QUAL.	MKT V.
220	COMM	ComunI		39	21	27.50	0.73	16.58	1.02	4.62	90	224
232	GSCC	GraphS	*	39	21	20.38	0.56+	27.73	0.00	3.84	51	346
246	NSCO	NetwkS		39	21	35.88	0.65+	35.45	0.00	8.34	76	348

12-04-1982

#		NAME		CLASS	GROUP	PRICE	VAL.	GROWTH	YIELD	P/B	QUAL.	MKT V.
9		AV.		0	0	0.00	0.80	21.98	0.60	3.73	75	0
									22.58			

#	SYM	NAME		CLASS	GROUP	PRICE	VAL.	GROWTH	YIELD	P/B	QUAL.	MKT V.
104	KMG	KerrM		40	10	25.75	1.98+	9.79	4.66	0.74	78	1359
137	P	Petrol	*	40	21	13.00	2.19-	12.84	4.62	1.18	83	676

AMEX
OTC
12-04-1982

#		NAME		CLASS	GROUP	PRICE	VAL.	GROWTH	YIELD	P/B	QUAL.	MKT V.
2		AV.		0	0	0.00	2.08	11.31	4.64	0.96	81	0
									15.95			

#	SYM	NAME		CLASS	GROUP	PRICE	VAL.	GROWTH	YIELD	P/B	QUAL.	MKT V.
15	ARC	AtlRic	*	41	10	38.75	2.49	10.61	6.71	0.88	75	9409
69	XON	Exxon	*	41	10	28.00	2.45-	6.89	10.71	0.79	86	24310
167	SD	StOCl		41	10	30.38	2.37+	7.63	7.90	0.76	91	10392
168	SN	StOInd		41	10	38.75	2.23-	9.24	7.23	0.90	84	11443
186	UCL	UnOCal		41	10	26.75	2.05-	10.78	4.11	0.87	80	4645

AMEX
OTC
12-04-1982

#		NAME		CLASS	GROUP	PRICE	VAL.	GROWTH	YIELD	P/B	QUAL.	MKT V.
5		AV.		0	0	0.00	2.32	9.03	7.33	0.84	83	0
									16.36			

#	SYM	NAME		CLASS	GROUP	PRICE	VAL.	GROWTH	YIELD	P/B	QUAL.	MKT V.
19	BKO	BakrIn	*	42	9	20.13	1.73-	12.91	4.97	1.03	88	1394
39	CBH	CBIInd		42	2	37.00	1.97-	11.97	4.32	1.30	90	646
48	DAN	Daniel		42	9	9.88	1.81-	14.46	2.03	0.79	80	86
87	HAL	Hallib	*	42	9	29.50	2.02-	10.21	5.42	0.91	95	3479
91	HP	HelmP		42	9	17.75	1.78-	14.32	2.03	1.08	87	446
95	HT	HughsT	*	42	9	18.00	1.78-	12.17	4.67	0.73	82	993
161	SII	SmithI	*	42	9	25.50	1.49-	12.21	4.08	0.84	93	583

AMEX

#	SYM	NAME		CLASS	GROUP	PRICE	VAL.	GROWTH	YIELD	P/B	QUAL.	MKT V.
203	CLB	CoreLb	*	42	9	11.38	0.90+	14.62	1.41	1.03	70	67

OTC
12-04-1982

#		NAME		CLASS	GROUP	PRICE	VAL.	GROWTH	YIELD	P/B	QUAL.	MKT V.
8		AV.		0	0	0.00	1.68	12.86	3.62	0.96	86	0
									16.47			

#	SYM	NAME		CLASS	GROUP	PRICE	VAL.	GROWTH	YIELD	P/B	QUAL.	MKT V.
172	SOC	SuprOl	*	43	10	26.50	0.87+	10.21	0.91	1.26	83	3375

AMEX
OTC
12-04-1982

#		NAME		CLASS	GROUP	PRICE	VAL.	GROWTH	YIELD	P/B	QUAL.	MKT V.
1		AV.		0	0	0.00	0.87	10.21	0.91	1.26	83	0
									11.11			

#	SYM	NAME		CLASS	GROUP	PRICE	VAL.	GROWTH	YIELD	P/B	QUAL.	MKT V.
94	HNG	HousNG	*	44	21	31.38	3.25-	13.92	5.74	0.88	87	1256
178	TGT	Tennco	*	44	21	31.63	2.09-	8.16	8.85	0.73	67	4083
181	TXO	TexO&G	*	44	21	30.50	1.82	19.64	1.05	2.44	82	2906

AMEX

#	SYM	NAME		CLASS	GROUP	PRICE	VAL.	GROWTH	YIELD	P/B	QUAL.	MKT V.
204	DGS	DorchG	*	44	21	10.38	0.70+	8.49	1.93	0.99	60	180

OTC
12-04-1982

#		NAME		CLASS	GROUP	PRICE	VAL.	GROWTH	YIELD	P/B	QUAL.	MKT V.
4		AV.		0	0	0.00	1.96	12.55	4.39	1.26	74	0
									16.94			

#	SYM	NAME		CLASS	GROUP	PRICE	VAL.	GROWTH	YIELD	P/B	QUAL.	MKT V.
115	MDA	MAPCO		45	9	23.50	1.77+	9.07	8.09	1.01	67	650

AMEX
OTC
12-04-1982

#	SYM	NAME		CLASS	GROUP	PRICE	VAL.	GROWTH	YIELD	P/B	QUAL.	MKT V.
1		AV.		0	0	0.00	1.77	9.07	8.09	1.01	67	0
									17.16			

#	SYM	NAME		CLASS	GROUP	PRICE	VAL.	GROWTH	YIELD	P/B	QUAL.	MKT V.
187	UNP	UnPac		46	20	44.38	1.50+	13.70	4.51	1.23	84	4276

AMEX
OTC
12-04-1982

#	SYM	NAME		CLASS	GROUP	PRICE	VAL.	GROWTH	YIELD	P/B	QUAL.	MKT V.
1		AV.		0	0	0.00	1.50	13.70	4.51	1.23	84	0
									18.21			

#	SYM	NAME		CLASS	GROUP	PRICE	VAL.	GROWTH	YIELD	P/B	QUAL.	MKT V.
7	AXP	AmExp	*	51	16	68.63	1.08	11.56	3.50	1.93	73	6572

AMEX
OTC
12-04-1982

#	SYM	NAME		CLASS	GROUP	PRICE	VAL.	GROWTH	YIELD	P/B	QUAL.	MKT V.
1		AV.		0	0	0.00	1.08	11.56	3.50	1.93	73	0
									15.06			

#	SYM	NAME		CLASS	GROUP	PRICE	VAL.	GROWTH	YIELD	P/B	QUAL.	MKT V.
3	AET	Aetna	*	52	16	39.75	1.90-	9.27	6.54	0.92	79	3226
83	GRN	GnRein	*	52	16	58.50	1.44	13.22	2.05	2.06	103	2554
100	JP	JefPlt		52	16	31.88	1.67+	8.17	5.52	0.72	88	684
109	LNC	LincNt		52	16	47.88	1.57+	8.71	6.68	0.71	75	1002
191	USH	USLIFE		52	16	24.25	1.48+	9.72	3.79	0.63	64	464

AMEX

#	SYM	NAME		CLASS	GROUP	PRICE	VAL.	GROWTH	YIELD	P/B	QUAL.	MKT V.
200	AVE	AVEMCO		52	16	13.00	1.47-	11.02	4.62	1.13	64	32

OTC

#	SYM	NAME		CLASS	GROUP	PRICE	VAL.	GROWTH	YIELD	P/B	QUAL.	MKT V.
213	AIGR	AIntGp	*	52	16	81.75	1.50+	17.08	0.69	1.70	82	4707
229	FGRP	FarmGp		52	16	37.75	1.48	10.11	3.60	1.46	101	1282

12-04-1982

#	SYM	NAME		CLASS	GROUP	PRICE	VAL.	GROWTH	YIELD	P/B	QUAL.	MKT V.
8		AV.		0	0	0.00	1.56	10.91	4.19	1.17	82	0
									15.10			

#	SYM	NAME		CLASS	GROUP	PRICE	VAL.	GROWTH	YIELD	P/B	QUAL.	MKT V.
10	T	ATT	*	53	21	60.00	1.77+	3.51	9.67	0.84	88	48906
149	RTC	RochTl		53	21	30.25	1.45+	7.07	7.27	1.13	78	305
189	UT	UniTel		53	21	20.50	1.84-	8.78	8.98	1.00	75	1544

AMEX
OTC

#	SYM	NAME		CLASS	GROUP	PRICE	VAL.	GROWTH	YIELD	P/B	QUAL.	MKT V.
241	MCIC	MCICom		53	21	39.00	1.06+	29.76	0.00	6.55	62	3802

12-04-1982

#	SYM	NAME		CLASS	GROUP	PRICE	VAL.	GROWTH	YIELD	P/B	QUAL.	MKT V.
4		AV.		0	0	0.00	1.53	12.28	6.48	2.38	76	0
									18.76			

#	SYM	NAME		CLASS	GROUP	PRICE	VAL.	GROWTH	YIELD	P/B	QUAL.	MKT V.
21	BAC	BnkAm	*	54	16	22.25	1.64-	8.39	6.83	0.72	77	3285
22	BBF	Barnet		54	16	30.75	1.59-	12.44	3.90	1.13	68	423
164	STB	SoetBk	*	54	16	20.88	1.31+	9.51	4.79	0.79	65	340
171	SU	SunBFl		54	16	21.50	1.67	10.67	5.40	0.96	70	222

AMEX
OTC
12-04-1982

#	SYM	NAME		CLASS	GROUP	PRICE	VAL.	GROWTH	YIELD	P/B	QUAL.	MKT V.
4		AV.		0	0	0.00	1.56	10.25	5.23	0.90	70	0
									15.48			

#	SYM	NAME		CLASS	GROUP	PRICE	VAL.	GROWTH	YIELD	P/B	QUAL.	MKT V.
118	MAS	Masco	*	55	2	52.50	1.13+	14.46	1.75	2.03	85	1377
134	PAY	PaylsC	*	55	2	42.50	0.87+	18.76	0.56	3.24	85	541
158	SHB	Scotty	*	55	2	28.38	0.83	12.73	2.40	2.23	79	187
195	WY	Weyerh		55	7	37.50	0.60+	12.23	3.47	1.71	66	4794

AMEX
OTC
12-04-1982

#	SYM	NAME		CLASS	GROUP	PRICE	VAL.	GROWTH	YIELD	P/B	QUAL.	MKT V.
4		AV.		0	0	0.00	0.86	14.54	2.05	2.31	79	0
									16.59			

#	SYM	NAME	CLASS	GROUP	PRICE	VAL.	GROWTH	YIELD	P/B	QUAL.	MKT V.
116	MMC	MarshM *	58	16	43.75	1.55-	11.98	5.49	2.33	106	1551

AMEX
OTC

12-04-1982

1		AV.	0	0	0.00	1.55	11.98	5.49	2.33	106	0
								17.47			

#	SYM	NAME	CLASS	GROUP	PRICE	VAL.	GROWTH	YIELD	P/B	QUAL.	MKT V.

AMEX
OTC

226	DBRSY	deBeer *	61	13	5.44	5.03+	10.52	8.82	0.46	80	1957

12-04-1982

1		AV.	0	0	0.00	5.03	10.52	8.82	0.46	80	0
								19.34			

#	SYM	NAME	CLASS	GROUP	PRICE	VAL.	GROWTH	YIELD	P/B	QUAL.	MKT V.
127	NEM	Newmt	62	13	45.50	0.37+	9.47	2.20	0.93	67	1230

AMEX
OTC

12-04-1982

1		AV.	0	0	0.00	0.37	9.47	2.20	0.93	67	0
								11.66			

10

The Market and Other Considerations

In the previous chapter, we discussed a few of the factors that determine whether you would be likely to achieve better investment results in one type of stock or another. In this chapter, we consider whether, at a particular time, one should be investing in stocks at all. Basically, an investor has three choices among financial instruments: stocks, bonds or short-term cash equivalents such as money market funds. The other possible areas are tangibles such as real estate, gold, silver, or diamonds; or collections such as paintings, antiques, coins, or stamps. Tangibles and collectibles are not in the purview of this book.

JUDGING THE PROSPECTS FOR THE MARKET

As discussed briefly earlier, stocks have a strong tendency to rise in price or decline in price together. When there is a violent move in the market in either direction, over 95% of the stocks normally move in the same direction. As we completed work on this book, we have just had one of the biggest and broadest bull moves in history. While a number of reasons have been given for the advance, it basically

resulted from the perception that inflation had declined
sharply from earlier peaks and was likely to stay down for a
time, and accordingly, interest rates would come down
and stay down for at least several years. This resulted in
massive amounts of money moving from tangibles, collectibles, and short-term investments into bonds and stocks.

Can one predict with any reliability the direction of the
market? The answer is a qualified "yes," as we will explain.
The following chart (Figure 10.1) shows a market indicator
we have developed, compared to the market.

Note that the market indicator, the solid line, usually led
the market over the 30-year span. However, there was a
substantial divergence between 1976 and the turn in the
market during the summer of 1982. The basic reason was
that energy stocks and other inflation beneficiaries domi-

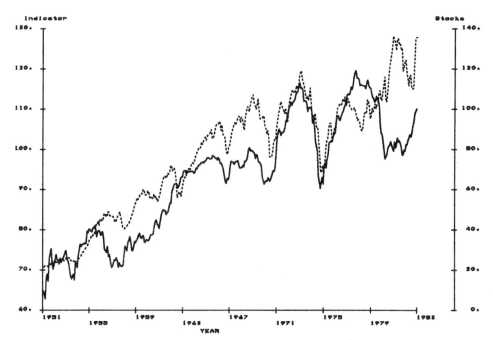

Figure 10.1   Market P/E Indicator —1951 —

nated the market. There was also a tremendous rise in interest rates, which depressed the interest sensitive stocks and nearly destroyed the bond market.

It appears that this indicator and the market are tracking together again; they will tend to move more or less in parallel unless there is another serious problem such as the OPEC-induced oil price rise. In any case, our indicator is based on common sense, and it is composed of four series. First is the government's "Leading Indicators of Business Activity" found in *Business Conditions Digest.* This forecasts whether the economy is likely to improve or decline. Second is the government's series entitled "Money and Financial Flows," also in *Business Conditions Digest.* This is composed of several series that show whether the economy is becoming more or less liquid. The third series is an index we have constructed from interest rate figures which show whether the bond market is rising or falling. The fourth series is an index we have constructed by dividing the government's figures for Earnings Adjusted for Inflation by Reported Earnings, as shown in the chart in Chapter 5, which discussed quality. In other words, if all four of these factors are favorable, stocks should and usually do rise in price because these are also the main determinants for the economy as a whole.

We continue to experiment with other statistical series that should have predictive characteristics. For example, the government publishes a series showing the Ratio of Non-Farm Prices to Unit Labor Costs. This indicates whether corporate profitability is likely to improve or decline, and seems to lead the stock market a good deal of the time. These matters involve financial forecasting, which is a different subject from the main thrust of this book. However, anyone with a personal computer can set up programs to store statistical data and perform mathematical operations on the data without much difficulty. We do not include the statistical programs we have developed because of space limitations. To do adequate justice to the subject of financial forecasting, we would have to write another book.

STOCKS VERSUS BONDS

When the economic indicators discussed above are favorable for stocks, they are usually also favorable for bonds. As shown in the chart on government yields, found in the previous chapter, interest rates have fallen sharply and bond prices have had one of the sharpest increases on record. For example, the Triple A IBM 9 3/8% bonds of 2004 were selling at 69 7/8 at the start of 1982, and are 91 3/8 as this was written. This is a gain of 21.5 points which added to the coupon of 9.375, gives a total return of 44.2%. This is based on a full year's income. In comparison, the Dow Jones Industrials show a total return for the year of 26.5% calculated the same way. Of course, some stocks have done much better than the averages. IBM common has gone from 56 7/8 to 84 1/4. This 27.37 points profit added to the dividend gives a total return of 54.2%.

The following chart shows a comparison of the Earnings Yield on Stocks projected through 1983, with the yield on high-grade corporate bonds. The Earnings Yield is the earnings divided by the price. The concept assumes that the earnings retained in the business is worth as much to the investor as the earnings paid out, which would give the dividend yield (Figure 10.2)

The solid line is the stock earnings yield: note the shifts that have occurred. Our conclusion is that bonds have been the better values recently, but that stocks and bonds are coming into equilibrium. We normally favor stocks for investors who do not need to emphasize income, as will be discussed in the next chapter, because if these are selected carefully, they will usually out-perform bonds.

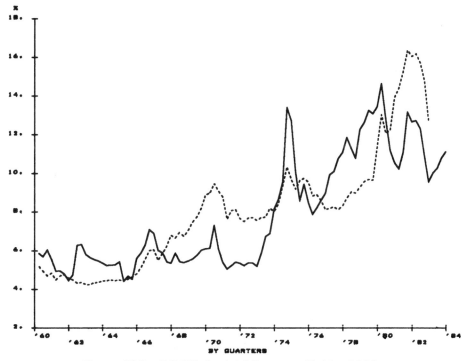

Figure 10.2   S & P Industrial Earnings Yield —1960—

SHORT-TERM RESERVES

It is usually prudent to have some short-term reserves in order to take advantage of buying opportunities as they occur. We use money market funds for the most part. There are occasions when the bulk of your funds should be in reserves. If both of the previous charts had been unfavorable, that is, the P/E Indicator had turned down and earnings yields on stocks were showing a widening negative spread, then reserves should be increased to a higher level than normal. It is difficult to be specific about how much reserves are called for without knowing the relevant facts about the investor, as will be discussed in the next chapter. We consider 50% in reserves, with the balance in high-grade bonds and quality stocks, as prudent for the average account during times when the indicators are negative.

OTHER MARKET INDICATORS

A look at any long-term chart of the market shows that bull markets and bear markets alternate with considerable regularity. The bull markets last longer and the bear markets are usually sharper, but there are exceptions. Since World War II, if one cut back on stocks after eight quarters of advancing prices in a row, and added to stocks after four quarters of declining prices, the results would have been quite good. However, there are better ways of anticipating market movements.

There are usually only a few weeks each year when a investor should buy stocks aggressively if he or she is looking for bargains. Examine the following pair of charts (Figures 10.3 and 10.4).

The top chart shows net upside or down-side volume. These figures are the weekly combined total of the New York Exchange, the American Exchange and Over-the-Counter. Sometimes you should look at the figures separately for each exchange. These figures are published weekly in *Barron's* and daily in the *Wall Street Journal.* The solid line is a 12-week moving average, and the dotted line a four-week moving average. Note that when both lines drop well below zero, at least to the minus 20 million mark, and then cross on the way back up, the market is usually a buy. However, also note that there were three selling climaxes in the bear market of 1981–82. The first two merely signalled a rally in a bear market, so you must interpret this type of data with care.

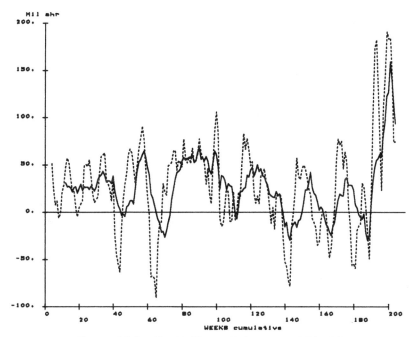

Figure 10.3   Net Up/Down Volume — 1979–82

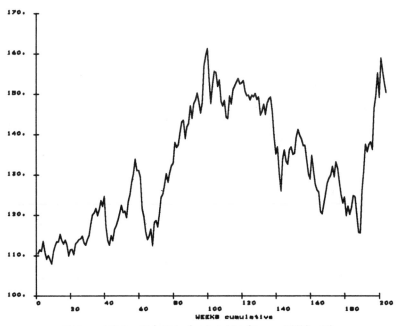

Figure 10.4   S & P Industrial Index — 1979–82

There are other helpful statistics on the market. The next pair of charts (Figure 10.5 and 10.6) shows member short-selling as a percent of total short-selling compared to the market. As mentioned earlier, stock exchange members have a real advantage over the average investor because they have access to information on buy orders under the market and sell orders over the market. These figures are published two weeks later, but are worth monitoring anyway. They are available in *Barron's* also.

The magic number seems to be about 85%, which is where the line is drawn. When member short-selling rises above that level for a time, it usually means trouble for the market. We are using a five-week moving average in this case, but the raw figures give a reasonably good picture. Note that this indicator is better at tops than at bottoms. The Wilshire Index is the market value of some 5,000 stocks.

MARKET LETTERS

There are a great many market letters available on a subscription basis. Over the years, we have taken trial subscriptions to most of them in order to examine their methods. While there were some interesting ideas in a number of these services, until now we have not found one that is consistently right on the market. The heroes come and go. For example, Granville has gone from being held in high esteem to becoming a joke. In his case, one friend tells us, Granville missed the 1982 bull market because he did not follow his own indicators. One service we are currently receiving has issued one sell signal after another during the rise in the market from August 1982. This service had been quite good for several years and had called the market turns with reasonable consistency. The problem is that methods that work well in one kind of stock market frequently fail in a different type of market.

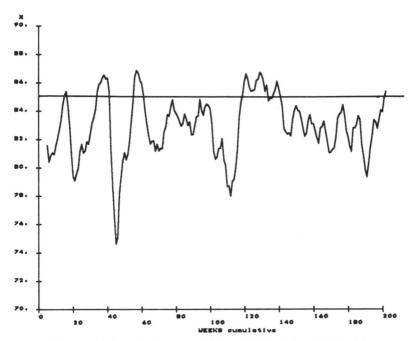

Figure 10.5 Member/Total Short (5 Wk Av) — 1979–82

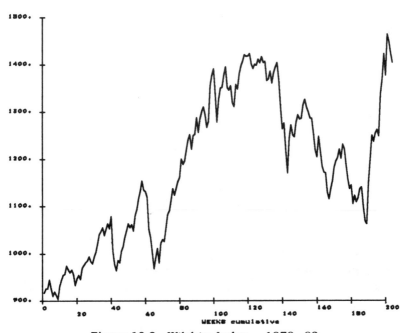

Figure 10.6 Wilshire Index — 1979–82

We do not recommend relying on any market letter, especially those that claim they can call the short-term swings in the market. If there is anyone who can do it 90% of the time, we would be surprised. Furthermore, it is a very bad habit to think in terms of trading the market. While the person who trades a great deal is perhaps quite popular with the broker, and at times with the tax collector, it is not the right approach to building up one's assets.

A TRUE STORY

Some readers of this book may be disappointed that we have not discussed stock charting, relative strength studies, and similar technical methods of selecting stocks based on the price action of the stock itself. Frankly, we do not believe in technical work. It may have some limited usefulness for traders, but that is about all. In the mid-sixties, some friends at a small but well-regarded institutional brokerage firm hired a math professor and a computer programmer to develop a computerized system of charting stocks and selecting the best ones to buy. They poured a great deal of time and money into it and came up with a system that seemed to work for a while in the bull market of those days. At lunch one day, a partner in that firm showed me a list of about 200 stocks, ranked in order of attractiveness according to that system. The top of the list was occupied by the popular speculations of the day, so I took a look at the bottom of the list—those least likely to succeed. There was Schlumberger, relatively new to the New York exchange and not well known, at the very bottom of the list. We had done some work on the company and had met some of the executives and, as a result of that lunch, began to accumulate the stock in accounts. Since then, the stock has been split, 3-for-2, eight times, and never sold lower than it's price then: about one on the present stock. That firm's system of picking stocks proved an expensive failure, and a "contrary opinion" approach was rewarding.

We know of no shortcuts to successful stock selection. Having a computer makes it possible to do many of the things that were impractical back in the days of slide rules and mechanical calculators. Accordingly, you can follow more stocks and use more elaborate analytical procedures now than then. Basically, you are looking at the same factors, however: quality, growth, and value. Those are the three essentials, and, in our opinion, these will not change.

To forestall an angry response from the technicians, we admit that watching the price of a stock is useful because it tells you what others are doing, and some of them may know something we do not. If a stock is suddenly weak, for example, it frequently means there is unfavorable news ahead, and thus it will pay to do some checking.

MODERN PORTFOLIO THEORY

Recent work analyzing stock price movements with a computer involves examining the characteristics of a stock as determined by its price action. For example, is a stock more or less volatile than the market? This work is generally referred to as "modern portfolio theory." The volatility factor is called Beta. This is a number assigned to each stock, which reflects how much it should go up or down relative to the market. If the market goes up or down 10% and the stock goes up or down the same amount, this is a Beta of one. If the stock moves 20% while the market is changing by 10%, this is a Beta of two. These stock characteristics are presumed to persist for a considerable period of time. In any large portfolio of stocks, the Beta factor does seem to average out about the same over time, while it may not for a particular stock or group of stocks. For example, oils have become more volatile than they were in the fifties and sixties. *Value Line* publishes figures on Beta, and some investors seem to be using Beta as the equivalent of quality. This is a mistake that may cause problems, since quality and volatility are very different attributes of stocks.

Extensions of this work now cover a number of other factors. For example, Alpha is supposed to measure another aspect of a stock—the industry or company factors that cause a stock to go up faster than the market but to go down at a slower rate. The William O'Neil chart service, mentioned earlier, gives Alpha values on stocks. These figures show how much a stock would have appreciated or depreciated on average each month over the last five years, assuming the market had done nothing. An Alpha of one means a stock would have risen 1% per month more than the market. Does Alpha persist for any extended period of time? It does not appear to. Accordingly, this work is of help in determining portfolio characteristics, but is not much help in achieving superior investment results. The Elton & Gruber book on modern portfolio theory, listed in the Bibliography, contains on page 118 the basic formula for calculating Alpha, Beta, and other data. This is simply a multiple correlation formula. As such, it is useful for various other purposes such as measuring how well a particular company's earnings track with various economic series. For example, you could calculate how General Motors sales correlate with the Gross National Product, and find out if "What's good for General Motors is good for the country," as many have claimed.

Our skepticism concerning the usefulness of these methods is based on limited experimentation. From a conceptual viewpoint, the question is how much valid information is contained in a stock's price fluctuations. In our opinion, it is not a lot. So much depends on such matters as how good the specialist is, whether some aggressive broker is pushing the stock, or whether the stock catches the fancy of the trading-oriented big institutions. Such influences come and go.

DIVERSIFICATION

Another matter of concern to investors is diversification. This is a concept misunderstood even by professionals, and needs some comment. Ten stocks can give adequate diversification if selected for their dissimilar investment characteristics, while 40 or 50 may give little actual diversification if all are the same type. For example, the energy stocks have all moved together recently. The same is frequently true in the case of the small technology stocks. Owning five airline stocks does not provide much more diversification than owning one. Diversification should be planned in relation to the financial requirement of the investor and the economic prospects for the economy, as discussed in the next chapter.

Modern portfolio theory puts major emphasis on portfolio diversification and balance. These investors examine such matters as diversifiable and nondiversifiable risk. However, we are not convinced that formulas for calculating how to construct the best portfolio mean very much. We spent a good deal of time on a complicated series of equations in one recent book on modern portfolio theory, before realizing that the equations simply proved that the best portfolio is the one in which the stocks appreciate the most. It seems quite likely that most investors have known that for some time. An outstandingly successful portfolio always contains at least one outstandingly successful stock. Therefore, the efforts that should prove the most rewarding are to find the best stocks in the best groups and to have a good fix on the general trend of the market. The important thing to remember about diversifying a portfolio is that, while it reduces the risk of loss, it also reduces the potential for profit.

11

Planning the Investment Program

Many successful people put less time and effort into planning an investment program that fits their requirements than they do in trying to improve their bridge game or their golf swing. Accordingly, their investments may not be well suited to their needs. When an investment counsellor takes on a new client, he or she asks questions about how much money the individual earns and can save, whether the person has any debts, and so forth. The answers to these questions determine what kind of investments are appropriate for that investor. The following two examples are at opposite extremes. Most investors need something in between.

THE GROWTH INVESTOR

The first example is a bright young doctor with a good practice in a prosperous community. The doctor is married, has children, and owns a home. Having inherited a

161

modest amount, this individual expects to inherit somewhat more in time. The doctor can save about $12,000 a year after taxes, which are paid quarterly. At this time, the doctor has $30,000 in inherited stocks, including some electric utilities, AT&T, municipal bonds, and some odds and ends of other stocks. Of course, a lot depends on the doctor's personality, cautiousness, and ability to be comfortable with a fair amount of risk. However, the doctor can well afford to emphasize maximum growth and very little income. We would advise selling all the present holdings in order to invest in six growth stocks of varying quality: two well-established big-growth companies, two of medium-size and quality having well-defined prospects for rapid growth, and two emerging growth companies in relatively new fields. However, the full amount should not be put into stocks immediately; about $4,000 in each stock would be appropriate initially, for a total of $24,000, leaving $6,000 for a money market fund. Then, each month, the doctor should buy, in rotation, $1,000 more of each stock. At the end of six months, $5,000 will have been invested in each stock, with a total of $6,000 at the end of a year. This procedure is called "dollar averaging." Since investors buy more shares for their money when the stock is down in price and fewer shares when the stock is up, the result is a low average cost.

If a market shakeout occurs, like the type discussed in the previous chapter, and the net volume figures give a buy signal, the investor might use some reserves to buy several stocks that month instead of one, and then not buy any until the reserves are restored. Also, if the market indicators turn unfavorable, the investor should stop the dollar averaging program for a time and accumulate reserves.

About once a year, the investor should review each stock to see if it is actually living up to the original growth expectations. If not, it should be replaced with another stock of similar size and quality that is achieving better results. In ten years, this person will have invested an additional $120,000, and the portfolio should be worth two or three times the total investment if the investor has used only reasonable judgment in making selections, and possibly much more if one of the stocks is a big winner.

THE INCOME INVESTOR

Now consider the case of an elderly widow of limited means. Assume she received $100,000 of insurance and securities when her husband died, and sold her home for $60,000 net and moved into an apartment. She has children, but they are making their own way and would have trouble providing much support for her. Her Social Security pays her rent with enough left over to meet the utility bills. She needs income, but cannot afford the risk of putting everything into long-term bonds, because if inflation became virulent again, she could be in trouble. In this case, about $60,000 should go into long-term, high-quality corporate bonds; $40,000 into short- and medium-term bonds; $5,000 into money market funds; and the balance into high grade stocks and convertible bonds. We used IBM, Procter & Gamble, AT&T, and 6% K-mart convertible debentures in such an account in 1981.

At this time, such a portfolio would provide about $13,000 a year of income and, in addition, should show reasonable appreciation if investment conditions continue to be favorable. If inflation shows signs of rekindling, the long-term bonds should be sold and the funds reinvested in short-term bonds and money market reserves. As in the first example, the holdings have to be reviewed from time to time, for the purpose of determining if they are still attractive investments and whether possible changes would improve the portfolio.

TRADING STRATEGIES

It is much easier to become a good investor in securities, that is, a buyer, than it is to become a good seller. There are all kinds of reasons for not selling securities. Some of these have a certain degree of validity, for example, if one has a large gain and would have to pay a tax. Others are not sensible, such as having a loss but not wanting to take it. Occasionally, there is one compelling reason for selling stocks or long bonds; that is, you know of another investment that should do better. An equally compelling reason is to build up reserves so that you will have funds when the next bargain sale in the market occurs, as it surely will.

Is there a formula for successful trading in the market? We do not know of one, but there are a number of helpful techniques you can use. For example, we mentioned dollar averaging. This is an especially useful method in meandering sideways markets where there is no clear trend. It is a good way to get a portfolio started, but is of less use afterward.

For individuals in high tax brackets, it probably pays to regularly take any short-term losses you may have near the end of each year. Some investors who wish to keep the position first double up and then sell the high-cost stock after 30 days. For individuals who concentrate a good deal of their investment funds in the emerging growth stock area of the market discussed before, stop-loss orders may be a good precaution. That is, an order is placed with the broker to sell the stock if the price drops to a predetermined level. Stop-loss orders are usually put in at 12% to 15% below the current market, or at some support level in the stock. If the stock rises, the stop-loss order price is accordingly increased.

Another technique is to sell call options against a stock when you think it has reached a level where it is no longer a really good value, but not at a price that makes it a clear-cut sale. A call option means that the seller contracts to sell a stock at an agreed-on price, at any time prior to an expiration date, in return for a cash payment. There are also puts, in which the seller agrees to buy a stock at an agreed-on price prior to an expiration date. The seller of puts and calls does well when stock prices do not change appreciably. These strategies are of limited usefulness for most investors. Stockbrokers will give investors a booklet entitled *Understanding the Risks and Uses of Listed Options* on request.

An effective strategy for the large portfolio was explained to me some years ago by a friend who had compiled an enviable record as a fund manager. Each month, he calculated the percent profit or loss in each holding of more than a year, and divided that number by the number of months he had held it. For example, he bought XYZ at 50 four years ago. It is now 98, so he made 1% per month on that stock. This is a little like Alpha in the modern portfolio theory discussed earlier. This procedure warns you when a good selection of some time back is no longer helping the portfolio. The problem is to always keep the list of holdings in tune with market and economic conditions. without overtrading.

THE SELECT ROUTINE

The method we use for selecting stocks by various investment characteristics was explained briefly earlier in the book. After you have data on a number of stocks of different types in the computer, start experimenting with this routine. Each time you reprice your stocks, see what looks attractive for your requirements, and also for current investment conditions.

For example, we will see what stocks would be possible candidates for the young doctor's portfolio discussed earlier. The following are three lists with different quality, total return, and other characteristics.

# SYM	NAME	CLASS	GROUP	PRICE	VAL.	GROWTH	YIELD	P/B	QUAL.	MKT V.
12-04-1982					0.90<	15.00<	0.2<	5.0>	90<	
Total return >= 17.00			2000<MARKET VALUE< 99000							
93 HWP	HewltP *	31	18	72.50	0.95	17.87	0.39	3.27	99	9041
156 SLB	Schlmb *	33	9	39.25	2.92-	18.77	2.85	1.75	105	11520
162 SKB	SmkB *	22	8	64.88	1.98-	15.33	4.32	2.66	105	5361
180 TXN	TexIns *	34	18	135.38	1.31+	17.40	1.48	2.06	95	3199
12-04-1982										
4	AV.	0	0	0.00	1.79	17.34	2.26	2.43	101	0
						19.60				

# SYM	NAME	CLASS	GROUP	PRICE	VAL.	GROWTH	YIELD	P/B	QUAL.	MKT V.
12-04-1982					0.80<	17.00<	0.0<	6.0>	75<	
Total return >= 20.00			500<MARKET VALUE< 2000							
117 MKY	MaryK	24	6	53.75	1.16	24.14	0.52	5.84	87	776
132 PDN	Pardyn *	39	21	47.25	1.03-	27.49	0.00	2.75	75	683
209 PLL	PallCP *	18	4	44.88	0.97+	19.30	1.16	4.67	85	605
260 TNDM	Tandem *	32	19	30.38	1.14+	30.62	0.00	3.59	86	1122
12-04-1982										
4	AV.	0	0	0.00	1.07	25.39	0.42	4.21	83	0
						25.81				

# SYM	NAME	CLASS	GROUP	PRICE	VAL.	GROWTH	YIELD	P/B	QUAL.	MKT V.
12-04-1982					0.50<	22.00<	0.0<	7.0>	60<	
Total return >= 22.00			0<MARKET VALUE< 500							
74 FLP	FloatP *	32	19	24.50	1.61-	29.85	0.00	3.77	82	214
199 AHA	AlphaI *	34	18	34.25	1.10+	22.15	0.29	3.20	83	119
202 CCS	CompCn	32	19	34.88	0.64-	22.65	0.00	4.78	78	188
207 MAX	Matrix *	31	8	40.00	0.70-	26.52	0.00	5.68	85	175
215 AVAK	Avantk	31	18	23.88	0.77	25.91	0.00	4.92	95	435
224 CPTC	CPT	32	19	17.75	1.37+	22.48	0.00	2.73	77	289
227 DYTC	Dynatc *	0	8	23.63	1.11-	22.52	0.00	3.47	80	110
228 ESCC	Ev&Sut *	35	19	41.88	0.87-	30.46	0.00	5.74	85	364
235 ISCS	ISCSys	35	19	17.50	1.31+	29.69	0.00	4.79	85	252
237 INGR	Intrs	35	19	38.50	1.29+	41.35	0.00	7.00	80	446
12-04-1982										
10	AV.	0	0	0.00	1.08	27.36	0.03	4.61	83	0
						27.39				

Obviously, there are quite a number of choices, particularly in the last category.

There follows a list of stocks suitible for the widow, as discussed above.

# SYM	NAME	CLASS	GROUP	PRICE	VAL.	GROWTH	YIELD	P/B	QUAL.	MKT V.
12-04-1982					1.00<	3.00<	5.0<	5.0>	85<	
Total return >= 12.00			1000<MARKET VALUE< 99000							
8 AHP	AHome	24	8	44.38	1.76	12.70	5.63	3.29	105	6883
10 T	ATT *	53	21	60.00	1.77+	3.51	9.67	0.84	88	48906
31 CPC	CPC	26	11	36.50	2.06-	9.85	6.03	1.19	91	1767
41 KO	CocaCl *	21	11	49.50	1.39-	10.11	5.25	2.25	105	6716
69 XON	Exxon *	41	10	28.00	2.45-	6.89	10.71	0.79	86	24310
87 HAL	Hallib *	42	9	29.50	2.02-	10.21.	5.42	0.91	95	3479
94 HNG	HousNG *	44	21	31.38	3.25-	13.92	5.74	0.88	87	1256
116 MMC	MarshM *	58	16	43.75	1.55-	11.98	5.49	2.33	106	1551
147 RJR	ReynIn	23	11	49.25	2.38-	10.04	6.50	1.03	89	5145
167 SD	StOCl	41	10	30.38	2.37+	7.63	7.90	0.76	91	10392
190 UPJ	UpJohn	22	8	44.75	1.36+	9.32	5.36	1.24	87	1351
12-04-1982										
11	AV.	0	0	0.00	2.03	9.65	6.70	1.41	93	0
						16.35				

Again, we have a number to choose from. If we lowered our quality requirement a little, we would have quite a few more.

The select routine shows only the summary valuations. Before making a decision to replace one holding in a portfolio with another, look at the valuation in detail to see if the earnings estimate on which the valuation is based assumes a strong improvement over the next few quarters, or whether it is essentially a continuation of present earnings trends. In any case, the earnings estimates and growth rates should be rechecked.

The stocks for the portfolio should be selected with due regard to the outlook for the market and the economy. As discussed in Chapter 9, you should decide how the funds should be divided among the economic groups. Another matter you should take into account is how well you know a particular company. In other words, do not simply buy the stock with the best valuation.

THE SCATTER DIAGRAMS

This routine plots any two valuation factors on a grid. For example, you can plot the Growth Rate against the P/E, or the Valuation against the Quality Rating. This will help in identifying stocks that have particular investment characteristics for further study. We have found that this routine stimulates further research. If you focus on particular relationships, it may lead to questioning some of the data in the valuation. For example, you might wonder, "Is stock A's growth rate really that much higher than stock B's?" It pays to remember that most of the data used in the valuations are opinions, not facts, and like any opinion, they can be wide of the mark.

12

Coming Events Cast
Their Shadows Before

PRIDE GOETH...

Everyone in the investment business has made egregious blunders and had humbling experiences. The one I remember best was also one of my first. It taught me something I have never forgotten, and did me a world of good. I graduated from the Harvard School of Business Administration in the spring of 1938. The previous fall the stock market had collapsed, down 50% in six months, and the economy was right back in the massive Depression. High-grade long-term bonds were yielding 2 1/2%. I went to work in the investment department of a life insurance company in Hartford, Connecticut. My assignment was to follow the railroad bonds in the portfolio. They were typically selling at half of par value or lower. The bonds of some of the bankrupt roads were selling at 10 or 15. The company had several bonds of the once mighty New York Central System, still solvent but barely so. I was told to write a report analyzing the railroad and our bond holdings. I knew little about railroads, but was given a helping hand by rail-bond analysts in bond houses, and learned a lot from bond buyers in other insurance companies. I had access to various services, which gave such information as the traffic density on the various divisions of the railroad. Also, the railroads were required by the Interstate Commerce Commision to publish all kinds of data on their operations. Such esoteric statistics as gross ton miles per train hour are one measure of efficiency. There are a host of others.

Well, to make a long story at least tolerable, I wrote a voluminous report on the New York Central and our bond holdings. It was 40 or 50 closely-typed pages, with 20 or 30 more pages of statistics, numerous maps, and other data. Another analyst in the company, a close friend to this day, said, "That is all I ever wanted to know about the New York Central and I am sorry we asked."

The professor of investments at the business school had asked our class to send him reports we wrote that might be used as case studies. With the permission of my boss I sent a copy to my former professor, a great and wonderful man. Shortly, I received a letter saying he was going to use my report. I was pretty set up by this, but pride goeth before a fall. I learned, somewhat later, that it was being used as an example of how not to write a report.

The way the case-study system works is the student is given a report on some subject, and is asked to write a critique and give opinions as to what he or she would do, and why. I learned later that the student who got the best mark on this case said that all the data in my report was essentially useless. The real question was whether or not World War II was going to break out, and if it did, what would happen to American railroads. He concluded that the experience in W W I was not germaine to the question. In that war, the government took over the railroads and nearly wrecked them. He said that all the railroads needed was more traffic to make a lot of money, since they were operating at 50% of capacity or less. His recommendation was that the insurance company should hold its bonds and perhaps buy more, the junkier the better. He was absolutely right. In other words, the answer to the question of what to do about our rail bond holdings was basically a macroeconomic and socio–political problem. If we analyzed those matters properly, the rest would follow. Things are always changing, and if we can recognize the probable direction of change, we have a good chance of being right in our investment decisions.

HABITS OF THOUGHT

It is not given to humans to foretell the future, but it is possible to at least know what is happening now and draw some conclusions from it. Unfortunately, the consensus view is usually wrong. The reason is that businesspersons and investors take actions that frequently have a contrary result. For example, if everyone expects raw material prices to rise, they stock up. Finally, things get out of hand, and they find they are overstocked. Then they cut back, and prices and business collapse. This has happened time and again. Also, government, business, and investors are usually "fighting the last war." Recently most people have been concerned about inflation and high interest rates. Well over a year ago, some observers began to recognize that the real question was, "Can we unwind inflation without going into a depression?"

As mentioned earlier, we have found that the habit of looking at the other side of a matter is often rewarding. In any case, we are convinced that the problems everyone is worrying about are not the ones that do the worst damage. The trick is not to get "blind-sided."

There is always a cause, or several causes, for every effect. In the case of stocks, it may be something trivial such as a broker messing up a large trade, or something much more serious. When a stock you are interested in has a significant price move on heavy volume, it usually means something and you should find out what is happening. More fundamental are unexpected changes in the earnings. Why did it happen? Is it the result of a nonrecurring event, or something more permanent? For example, IBM has just announced that it is changing their accounting to conform to a new method of reporting foreign earnings, and that it will add about 10% to 1981 and 1982 results. The stock reacted with a strong advance. Everyone who follows IBM knew that this was going to happen, and that it was only a question of when. Accordingly, the market reaction was not very sensible. Of course, as indicated earlier, the stock was an excellent value anyway.

SOME PROBLEMS

With so many problems in the world that need to be watched, it is a little foolish to get onto the subject, but we will mention a few. We are inclined to put the problems of international trade and foreign debt at the top of the list. Undeveloped and Communist countries owe over $500 billion to the industrialized countries, and a large part of it to the banks. This money was borrowed for the purpose of developing those countries, but much of it went into high living by a favored few. To pay it off, these countries have to be able to sell us something we want to buy. But many of these countries produce things we can produce ourselves. Accordingly, there are strong lobbies fighting to restrict imports. Sugar is a good example. The answer is quite clear: If we and other industrialized countries resort to protectionism, those foreign loans are going to default and there will be an international banking crisis.

Another problem that concerns us is how to help needy people without developing a permanent welfare class. Welfare encourages people to make less effort to provide for themselves. Studies show that the children of welfare families frequently grow up to go on welfare themselves. Other studies show that, because of social security, people have made fewer provisions for their retirement and old age. There is a limit to how much money can be taken from people who work and given to people who do not work. Also, if a smaller proportion of the population is producing goods and services, their productivity will have to go up or the total amounts of goods and services available will decline. The U.S. and most of the rest of the world have this problem; it is gradually destroying incentives and, unless reversed, will destroy the free-market economy.

ECONOMICS

The original meaning of the word was "the efficient management of a household." Now economics means something vague and somewhat forbidding having to do with national and international problems. When my son was in college, I read the book they assigned him in a freshman economics class and was so incensed that I made an issue of it and it was eventually changed. It was nothing but liberal propaganda that glorified the intervention of government and the role of unions, and painted our capitalistic system as corrupt and greedy. Unfortunately, many, perhaps most, people have little or no understanding of how the economy works, or how a particular event is likely to affect them. For example, governments, even the Republicans under Nixon, are always trying to control prices. They forget that a free price is necessary to bring supply in balance with demand. That is OPEC's problem now. They pushed prices so high that demand was severely curtailed. It is estimated that, in 1982, it takes 26% less oil to produce one unit of inflation-adjusted GNP in the industrialized countries than it did nine years earlier.

OPEC also failed to recognize that, when it succeeded in raising the price of oil, an inevitable consequence was that the prices of other materials would have to decline, thus helping to bring on the economic malaise the world has been going through. The reason, of course, is that to the degree that oil products are a necessity, people have to cut back on other expenditures to accommodate the effect on their budget. In the U.S. the worst price control effort has been in agricultural products. Price supports have been set so high for dairy products that few can afford butter and cheese anymore, so we give it to poor people and poor countries. Has the farmer benefitted? No; quite the contrary has occurred. We are in real danger of bankrupting all but the most efficient farmers. Price support efforts inevitably hurt those they were designed to help.

Efforts to hold prices down are just as damaging. The products disappear from the store shelves and a black market develops. A friend who has traveled off the beaten path says that the typical housewife in Communist countries spends 30 or 40 hours a week standing in line or hunting around to find food and other things her family needs.

Taxes are another matter that no one appears to understand. I talk with people I meet casually, including cab drivers, shoe-shiners, and so on. Very few are concerned about taxes, because they avoid some tax because they do a cash business and are in low brackets anyway. However, in one recent conversation with a cab driver who owned his own cab, which he had just bought for $11,000, I asked how much went for taxes. He mentioned the sales tax and other taxes adding up to about $700. I told him that, counting corporate taxes for the auto company, the steel company, and all the other companies that supplied parts and materials for the cab, as well as the taxes paid by the employees of those companies (which have to be considered in setting their wages or salaries), at least half the cost of the cab was taxes. I am not sure he believed me, but it is true.

The only way to cure unemployment is to increase the demand for goods and services. The best way to do that is to lower prices. The only way prices can be lowered is to reduce cost. Since labor costs, capital costs (interest rates), and taxes are the main components of cost, we have to attack all three. Labor rates are excessive in industries such as steel and auto. Taxes are excessive right across the board, and interest rates should be lower, as they will be if we handle the other two elements of cost properly.

In selecting companies for investment, it pays to consider such matters. For example, we do not invest in companies with labor cost disadvantages or union problems.

PERSPECTIVE

There have been times in recent years when it seemed that the whole fabric of western civilization was coming unraveled. We should occasionally ask, where are we? Are we past the peak and in a down-hill slide? Is this the equivalent of Athens under Pericles or Rome after the Punic Wars? There are interesting parallels today to the time of Sulla, who restored the Roman Republic, only to have it disappear 30 years later under Julius Caesar. The answer is basically involved with an appraisal of the good sense of the citizens and the wisdom of the leaders. A world view is not very reassuring. In Europe, some countries are getting rid of socialist governments, while others are electing socialists. Their economic problems are worse than ours. England may muddle through, but even Germany, the post-war economic miracle, is in trouble. They have an even heavier welfare and social security burden than the U.S. The Soviets are dangerously paranoid, and in an effort to control their subjects, may do serious mischief. Most of Asia is beyond our understanding, and perhaps beyond hope. In Africa, the former colonies have proved incapable of running their own affairs. Much of Central and South America is either dictator controlled or wracked by revolution, first one and then the other. The Middle

East, with half the world's oil, is like a volcano in the early stages of eruption. The big blow-up may be still to come. In other words, civilization is on the edge of disaster, but then it nearly always has been. Perhaps the threats can be averted or postponed. While it pays to take the long view, this means several years, not several centuries.

Investors should be more aware than most that the concept of private property and free enterprise is the mainspring of human progress and well-being. Our corporate enterprise system, together with science and invention, works better than any other economic system that has been used in the past or present. State control is a dismal failure and always will be, because it destroys incentive and initiative. The reason the free enterprise system is under attack all over the world is that it does not distribute goods and services equally. It is human nature for people who are not very capable or are unfortunate, and therefore not able to do much for themselves, to want to get some of the good things away from those who have them. This is where capitalism tends to break down.

Winston Churchill said, "The inherent vice of capitalism is the unequal sharing of the blessings; the inherent virtue of socialism is the equal sharing of miseries." This is entirely true, but many people do not seem to understand it.

If capitalism and our free enterprise system fail, then democracy will fail with it. Many people over the years have distrusted the whole concept of democracy. Plato said, nearly 2,500 years ago, "Democracy ... never giving a thought to the pursuits which make a statesman, and promoting to honor anyone who professes to be the people's friend." He continued, "These and other kindred characteristics are proper to democracy, which is a charming form of government, full of variety and disorder, and dispensing a sort of equality to equals and unequals alike."

It is appalling how lightly people take the right to vote, how little effort they make to learn the qualifications of the candidates, and how little they understand the fundamental issues. Perhaps the right to vote should be restricted to those who can establish that they can vote wisely. In any case, a better understanding of how to meet reasonable economic and social goals should be part of the education process. Perhaps courses in economic history should be offered more widely in colleges and universities. People have tried almost every type of social and economic system at one time or another, and the record of what works and doesn't work is clear.

Alexander Tyler, the famous British historian who studied our American democracy in the first half of the 1800s had this to say, "A democracy ... can only exist until the voters discover that they can vote themselves largess from the public treasury. From that moment on, the majority votes for the candidate promising the most benefits from the public treasury, with the result that a democracy collapses over loose fiscal policy ... always followed by a dictatorship." Give this serious thought.

SUMMING UP

Successful investment involves making decisions based on good information, on how much of one's assets should be in stocks, what groups are likely to do best, and which stocks in each group will excel. This is a mandatory procedure for successful professionals and a very desirable one for even the small investor. Taking care with small investments now will mean taking care of large investments later on.

Investors should remember that portfolios should be changed as conditions change. Otherwise, their investments will "march up the hill and then march down again."

Professional investors have their own styles and ways of doing things. As with professional golfers, no two play it exactly the same way. Some do very well in bull markets. Some handle bear markets better than most. Some prosper in up-and-down choppy markets. The approach described in this book works well in any kind of a market, but much will depend on how carefully it is implemented. For the inexperienced investor, here are a few rules (This is like telling a new golfer to keep his or her head down).

Don't try to follow too many stocks at first.

Do follow at least a few from each of the five major groups.

Look after the bad news on your investments and let the good news alone.

Don't be fully invested all the time. Raise buying power reserves when stocks are strong for the frequent "fire sales."

Make changes to improve your list after a drop in the market of 15% to 20% from the previous high. This saves on taxes, and there are usually bargains around.

Earnings are the only thing that matter in the long run. If the earnings prospects are not good, it does not matter how low the price of a stock is.

Keep the average quality of your investments up.

Keep the average growth rate of your stocks high.

Keep the average valuation of your stocks well above the market average.

For income, buy bonds or high-grade preferreds, and a few common stocks such as AT&T.

Keep the valuation figures up to date, and try to find more than one good source of information on each stock.

The methods described in this book are practical and they work. Good investing!

Stock Selection Software

Appendix A-1

```
10  ' "SETUP"
20              'STOCK SELECTION SOFTWARE    VERSION 1.0    IBM PC
30              'ROBERT W JENKS   7/15/82   MOD 5/9/83
40      CLS:KEY OFF:SCREEN 0,0,0:CLOSE
50      PRINT TAB(27),"SETUP Program"
60      PRINT
70      PRINT "This Program sets up a working stock diskette.
80      PRINT
90      PRINT "Its Purpose is to create the necessary data files in the ";
100     PRINT "required format."
110     PRINT
120     PRINT "You must start with a diskette containing the IBM ";
130     PRINT "Operating System (FORMAT with /S option) and BASIC.COM"
140     PRINT "which will be dedicated as a STOCK SELECTION disk."
150     PRINT
160     PRINT "   Designate the drive (A,B,C,D,E,F) to be used"
170     PRINT "   (ENTER defaults to drive A)   ";
180     GOSUB 970    'GET DRIVE
190     IF R$<"A" THEN SD$="A:" ELSE SD$=R$+":"
200     PRINT
210     PRINT "   Place the diskette to be used in drive ";SD$
220     PRINT "   Press ENTER when ready, or  Esc  to escape ";:LOCATE ,,1
230     GOSUB 1240
240     IF R$=CHR$(27) THEN PRINT:END
250     IF R$<>CHR$(13) THEN 230
260     PRINT:PRINT
270          REM  ** CURRENT DATE
280     N$="CURDATE.SYD":GOSUB 1160:IF F9 THEN 310
290     OPEN SD$+N$ FOR OUTPUT AS #1:WRITE #1,DATE$,TIME$:CLOSE #1
300          REM  ** STOCK INDEX
310     N$="STOCK.INX":W1=50:NL=6:L1=NL+9:S1=53
320     S$=SPACE$(L1):MID$(S$,NL+1,2)=CHR$(0)+CHR$(0)
330     GOSUB 1160:IF F9 THEN 410
340     MID$(S$,1,1)="*"
```

Abbreviations used in the Programs are:

MR = Major/Outer Menu Routine

MS = Major/Outer Menu Subroutine

S = Subroutine

Appendix A-1   (Continued)

```
350    GOSUB 1030    'WRITE NEW INDEX
360    GOSUB 1080    'OPEN AND CLEAR
370    MID$(S$,1,1)="#":LSET SB$=S$: PUT #1,1    'IDENTIFY AMEX
380    MID$(S$,1,1)="=":LSET SB$=S$: PUT #1,2    'IDENTIFY OTC
390    CLOSE #1
400         REM  ** SCATTER DIAGRAM
410    MID$(S$,1,1)=" "
420    N$="GRUPGRPH.SYD"
430    GOSUB 1160:IF F9 THEN 460
440    GOSUB 1030
450         REM  ** STOCK INDEX ALPHABETIC LIST
460    N$="LETTERS.SYD"
470    GOSUB 1160:IF F9 THEN 520
480    A$=SPACE$(7)
490    OPEN SD$+N$ FOR OUTPUT AS #1
500    FOR E=1 TO 3:FOR C=1 TO 26:WRITE #1,A$:NEXT C:NEXT E:CLOSE #1
510         REM  ** DEFLATOR CONSTANTS
520    N$="DEFLATOR.SYD"
530    GOSUB 1160:IF F9 THEN 590
540    RESTORE 1300
550    OPEN SD$+N$ FOR OUTPUT AS #1
560    FOR X=1 TO 14:READ D:WRITE #1,D:NEXT X
570    CLOSE #1
580         REM  ** SYMBOLS FILE
590    N$="SYMBOLS.SYD":GOSUB 1160:IF F9 THEN 620
600    OPEN SD$+N$ FOR OUTPUT AS #1:CLOSE #1
610         REM  ** PRICES FILE
620    N$="PRICES.SYD":GOSUB 1160:IF F9 THEN 650
630    OPEN SD$+N$ FOR OUTPUT AS #1:CLOSE #1
640         REM  ** DISK DRIVES
650    P$="":D$=""
660    GOSUB 790    'PROGRAM DRIVE
670    GOSUB 860    'DATA DRIVE
680         REM  SAVE DRIVE INFO
690    OPEN SD$+"DRIVES.SYD" FOR OUTPUT AS #1
700    IF P$<>"" THEN WRITE #1,P$
710    IF D$<>"" THEN WRITE #1,D$
720    CLOSE #1
730         REM  ** EXIT PROGRAM
740    PRINT:PRINT "Esc  for STARTUP program ";:GOSUB 1240
750    IF R$=CHR$(27) THEN CHAIN SD$+"STARTUP"
760    END
770         REM  *****
780         REM  ** STOCK FILE PROGRAM DRIVE  S
790    PRINT
800    PRINT "The default disk drive for stock PROGRAMS and SYSTEM FILES is A:"
810    GOSUB 940    'GET LETTER
820    IF R$=CHR$(13) THEN P$="A:" ELSE P$=R$+":"
830    PRINT P$:P$="STOCKPROGS="+P$
840    RETURN
850         REM  ** STOCK FILE DATA DRIVE  S
860    PRINT
870    PRINT "The default disk drive for stock DATA files is B:"
880    GOSUB 940    'GET LETTER
890    IF R$=CHR$(13) THEN D$="B:" ELSE D$=R$+":"
900    PRINT D$:D$="STOCKDATA="+D$
910    RETURN
920         REM  *****
930         REM  GET DRIVE LETTER  S
940    PRINT "You may designate a different drive."
950    PRINT "Input new drive (A,B,C,D,E,F) or press ENTER: ";
960         REM  S
```

Appendix A-1   (Continued)

```
970   R$="":LOCATE ,,1
980   WHILE NOT(R$>="A" AND R$<="F" OR R$=CHR$(13)):R$=INKEY$:WEND
990   IF R$>" " THEN PRINT R$ ELSE PRINT
1000  RETURN
1010        REM  *****
1020        REM  WRITE STOCK INDEX FILE DATA FORMAT   S
1030  GOSUB 1080
1040  FOR M=1 TO S1:PUT #1,M:NEXT M
1050  CLOSE #1:RETURN
1060        REM  *****
1070        REM  OPEN STOCK INDEX FORMAT FILE FOR WRITE   S
1080  OPEN SD$+N$ AS #1 LEN=W1
1090  FIELD #1,L1 AS SB$,4 AS PB$,4 AS VB$,4 AS GB$,4 AS RB$,4 AS BB$,4 AS QB$,4
AS MB$
1100  LSET SB$=S$
1110  LSET PB$=MKS$(0):LSET VB$=MKS$(0):LSET GB$=MKS$(0)
1120  LSET RB$=MKS$(0):LSET BB$=MKS$(0):LSET QB$=MKS$(0):LSET MB$=MKS$(0)
1130  RETURN
1140        REM  *****
1150        REM  TEST IF FILE ALREADY EXISTS   S
1160  F9=-1:ON ERROR GOTO 1270
1170  OPEN SD$+N$ FOR INPUT AS #1
1180  ON ERROR GOTO 0
1190  CLOSE #1
1200  IF F9 THEN PRINT "File ";N$;" already exists" ELSE PRINT "Creating ";N$
1210  RETURN
1220        REM  *****
1230        REM  INPUT CHARACTER    S
1240  R$="":WHILE R$="":R$=INKEY$:WEND:RETURN
1250        REM  *****
1260        REM  TOGGLE FLAG IF ERROR OCCURRED
1270  F9=NOT F9:RESUME NEXT
1280        REM  *****
1290        REM  DEFLATOR CONSTANTS UP TO 1983
1300  DATA .96,1,1.058,1.16,1.372,1.338,1.416,1.521,1.628,1.774,1.925
1310  DATA 2.05,2.17,83
1320  END 'PROGRAM
```

Appendix A-2

```
10  ''"STARTUP"
20           'STOCK SELECTION SOFTWARE    VERSION 1.0    IBM PC
30           'ROBERT W JENKS  8/27/82    MOD 5/9/83
40           'HOUSEKEEPING CHORES
50    SCREEN 0,0,0:KEY OFF:CLS:WIDTH 80:CLOSE
60    COMMON PD$
70    DEF FNE$(X$,L)=RIGHT$("0"+MID$(STR$(INT(ABS(VAL(MID$(X$,L))))),2),2)
80    PRINT TAB(20),"STARTUP program":PRINT
90           '*** GET PROGRAM DRIVE FROM FILE
100   PD$=""
110   EROR=0:ON ERROR GOTO 810
120   OPEN "DRIVES.SYD" FOR INPUT AS #1
130   ON ERROR GOTO 0
140   IF EROR THEN 250
150   WHILE NOT EOF(1) AND PD$=""
160      INPUT #1,R$
170      L=INSTR(R$,"=")
180      IF L<>0 THEN IF LEFT$(R$,L-1)="STOCKPROGS" THEN PD$=MID$(R$,L+1)
190   WEND:CLOSE #1
200   IF PD$="" THEN 250
210          'CHECK IF ON LINE
220   GOSUB 840    'CHECK FOR MANAGER
230   IF NOT EROR THEN 320
240          'FIND PROGRAM DRIVE BY SEARCHING DISKS  A: TO F:
250   PRINT "Searching for system drive..."
260   P=0
270   P=P+1
280   IF P=7 THEN 900
290   PD$=CHR$(64+P)+":"
300   GOSUB 840    'CHECK FOR MANAGER
310   IF EROR THEN 270
320   PRINT "System drive ";PD$
330          'LOCK IN CAPS
340   PRINT:PRINT "Upper-case set"
350   TESTBIT=&H40:R$="U":GOSUB 990
360          'GOTO 740      'BYPASS SET DATE/TIME
370          'GET DATE AND TIME
380   EROR=0:ON ERROR GOTO 810
390   OPEN PD$+"CURDATE.SYD" FOR INPUT AS 1:ON ERROR GOTO 0
400   IF EROR THEN 910
410   D1$="01-01-80":T$="00:00:00":EROR=0
420   IF EOF(1) THEN 450
430   INPUT #1,D1$
440   IF NOT EOF(1) THEN INPUT #1,T$
450   CLOSE #1
460          'NEW DATE
470   M$=MID$(D1$,1,2):D$=MID$(D1$,4,2):Y$=MID$(D1$,7)
480   PRINT
490   PRINT "  Input date, or (P) if Previous, ENTER if Current date is correct
..."
500   PRINT "Previous date was  ";D1$
510   PRINT "Current    date is ? ";DATE$
520   ROW=CSRLIN
530   INPUT "New      date    > ",A$
540   IF A$="" THEN 660
550   IF A$="P" THEN DATE$=D1$:GOTO 660
560   A1=1:GOSUB 940    '- / ?
570   D$=FNE$(A$,A+1)
580   IF A<>0 THEN M$=FNE$(A$,1)
590   A1=A1+1:GOSUB 940    '- / ?
600   IF A<>0 THEN Y$=FNE$(A$,A+1)
610   A$=M$+"-"+D$+"-"+Y$
```

Appendix A-2   (Continued)

```
620    EROR=0:ON ERROR GOTO 810:DATE$=A$:ON ERROR GOTO 0
630    IF EROR THEN LOCATE ROW,1:PRINT TAB(79):LOCATE ,1,1:GOTO 530
640    PRINT TAB(20);DATE$
650         'NEW TIME
660    PRINT
670    PRINT "    Input time, or press ENTER if current time is correct..."
680    PRINT "Previous time was  ";T$
690    PRINT "Current  time is ? ";TIME$
700    ROW=CSRLIN
710    INPUT "New        time    > ",B$
720    IF B$="" THEN 760
730    EROR=0:ON ERROR GOTO 810:TIME$=B$:ON ERROR GOTO 0
740    IF EROR THEN LOCATE ROW,1:PRINT TAB(79):LOCATE ,1,1:GOTO 710
750         'SAVE DATE/TIME
760    OPEN PD$+"CURDATE.SYD" FOR OUTPUT AS 1
770    WRITE #1,DATE$,TIME$
780    CLOSE #1
790    CHAIN PD$+"MANAGER",20
800         'ERROR TRAP
810    EROR=-1:RESUME NEXT
820         '*******
830         'CHECK FOR MANAGER  S
840    EROR=0:ON ERROR GOTO 810
850    OPEN PD$+"MANAGER.BAS" FOR INPUT AS #1:CLOSE #1
860    ON ERROR GOTO 0
870    RETURN
880         '*******
890         'CRASH
900    PRINT "Program disk not found":END
910    PRINT "System files not set up on drive ";PD$;".  Use SETUP program":END
920         '*******
930         'TEST DATE FOR - / S
940    A=INSTR(A1,A$,"-"):IF A=0 THEN A=INSTR(A1,A$,"/")
950    A1=A:RETURN
960         '********************
970         'CHANGE KEYBOARD MODE  S
980         'KBS=KEYBOARD STATUS, KBLA=KBS LOW ADDRESS, R$:LOWER/UPPER CASE
990    DEF SEG=&H40:KBLA=&H17:KBS=PEEK(KBLA)
1000   STATE=(KBS AND TESTBIT)=TESTBIT
1010   IF NOT STATE AND R$="U" OR STATE AND R$="L" THEN POKE KBLA,KBS XOR TESTBIT
1020   DEF SEG:RETURN
1030   END 'PROGRAM
```

Appendix A-3

```
10      CHAIN "STARTUP"
20    ''"MANAGER"
30            'STOCK SELECTION SOFTWARE   VERSION 1.0   IBM PC
40            'ROBERT W JENKS  10/2/82   MOD 5/9/83
50            'STOCK PROGRAMS MANAGER     USES FILE "DRIVES.SYD"
60      CLS:KEY OFF:WIDTH 80:LOCATE ,,0
70      COMMON FKEY$(),PD$,DD$
80            '*** GET DATA DRIVE
90      IF DD$<>"" THEN 200
100     EROR=0:ON ERROR GOTO 1120
110     OPEN PD$+"DRIVES.SYD" FOR INPUT AS #1
120     ON ERROR GOTO 0
130     IF EROR THEN DD$="B:":GOTO 200
140     WHILE NOT EOF(1) AND DD$=""
150       INPUT #1,R$
160       L=INSTR(R$,"=")
170       IF L=0 THEN DD$="B:" ELSE IF LEFT$(R$,L-1)="STOCKDATA" THEN DD$=MID$(R$,
L+1)
180       WEND:CLOSE #1
190            '*** PICTOGRAPH
200     GOSUB 960  'FKEY$ FOR DISPLAY
210     GOSUB 760  'GET PROMPTS
220            '*** DISPLAY
230            'HEADING
240     T$=STRING$(30,177):T1$=STRING$(2,177)
250     PRINT TAB(25);T$;TAB(60);FKEY$(7)
260     PRINT TAB(25);T1$;" Stock Selection Software ";T1$;
270     PRINT TAB(60);FKEY$(8);" to DOS"
280     PRINT TAB(25);T$;TAB(60);FKEY$(9)
290     PRINT TAB(36);"MANAGER"
300            'KEY
310     X1=33
320     FOR Y=3 TO 15 STEP 3
330       LOCATE Y+2,X1:PRINT FKEY$(0)
340       LOCATE Y+3,X1:PRINT FKEY$(Y\3)
350       LOCATE Y+4,X1:PRINT FKEY$(6)
360       NEXT
370            'PROMPT
380     Y1=3
390     FOR Y=1 TO 5:Y1=Y1+3:FOR X=0 TO 1
400       FOR Q=0 TO 1:LOCATE Y1-Q,1+47*X:PRINT PROMPT$(Y,X,Q):NEXT
410       NEXT:NEXT
420            '*** SELECTION
430     LOCATE 20,39,0:PRINT " ";CHR$(29);
440     R$="":WHILE R$="":R$=INKEY$:WEND:PRINT CHR$(219);CHR$(29);
450     LOCATE ,,1
460     PRL=LEN(R$):R$=RIGHT$(R$,1)
470     IF PRL=1 THEN IF R$=CHR$(27) THEN 610 ELSE 430
480     VR=ASC(RIGHT$(R$,1))-58:IF VR<1 THEN 430
490     ON VR GOTO 540,550,560,570,580,430,430,430,430,430
500     VR=VR-25:IF VR<1 THEN 430
510     ON VR GOTO 430
520     GOTO 430
530            'ACTION
540     CHAIN "STOKINDX",20
550     CHAIN "STOCKPGM",20
560     CHAIN "SCATTER",20
570     CHAIN "ESTIMATE",20
580     CHAIN "LOGTREND",20
590            'SHIFTED
600            '*** END WITH RETURN TO DOS
610     CLS:SYSTEM
```

Appendix A-3 (Continued)

```
620        '*** RESTORE FUNCTION KEYS & END (OPTIONAL EXIT)
630   KEY 1,"LIST .-"+CHR$(13)
640   KEY 2,"RUN"+CHR$(13)
650   KEY 3,"LOAD"+CHR$(34)
660   KEY 4,"SAVE"+CHR$(34)
670   KEY 5,"CONT"+CHR$(13)
680   KEY 6,","+CHR$(34)+"LPT1:"+CHR$(34)+CHR$(13)
690   KEY 7,"TRON"+CHR$(13)
700   KEY 8,"TROFF"+CHR$(13)
710   KEY 9,"KEY"
720   KEY 10,"SCREEN 0,0,0"+CHR$(13)
730   CLS:KEY ON
740   END
750        '***** GET PROMPTS   S
760   DIM PROMPT$(5,1,1)
770   T$=SPACE$(30):T1$=CHR$(24):RESTORE 850
780   FOR Y=1 TO 5:FOR X=0 TO 1:KEY Y+Y+X-1,"":FOR Z=0 TO 1:PROMPT$(Y,X,Z)=T$
790     READ N$:IF LEN(N$)=0 THEN 810
800     IF Z=1 THEN IF X=1 THEN N$=T1$+" "+N$ ELSE N$=N$+" "+T1$
810     IF X=0 THEN RSET PROMPT$(Y,X,Z)=N$ ELSE LSET PROMPT$(Y,X,Z)=N$
820     NEXT:NEXT:NEXT
830   RETURN
840        'DATA
850   DATA "STOCK INDEX Program",""
860   DATA "STOCK FILES Program",""
870   DATA "SCATTER DIAGRAM Program",""
880   DATA "STOCK ESTIMATES Program",""
890   DATA "LOG TREND Program",""
900   DATA "",""
910   DATA "",""
920   DATA "",""
930   DATA "",""
940   DATA "",""
950        '***** SET UP KEY DISPLAY   S
960   DIM FKEY$(9)
970   N$=STRING$(4,205)
980   A=0:B=201:C=187:D=7:GOSUB 1080
990   A=6:B=200:C=188:D=9:GOSUB 1080
1000  T$=CHR$(186):FKEY$(8)=T$+" ESC"+T$+" Exit"
1010  N$=T$+"  F  "+T$:X1=0
1020  FOR X=1 TO 5
1030    X1=X1+1:GOSUB 1100:T$=N$
1040    X1=X1+1:GOSUB 1100:FKEY$(X)=T$+" "+N$
1050  NEXT
1060  RETURN
1070       '***** TOP, BOTTOM   S
1080  T$=CHR$(B)+N$+CHR$(C):FKEY$(D)=T$:FKEY$(A)=T$+" "+T$:RETURN
1090       '***** NUMBER TO STRING   S
1100  MID$(N$,4)=MID$(STR$(X1),2):RETURN
1110       '***** ERROR TRAP
1120  EROR=-1:RESUME NEXT
1130  END 'PROGRAM
```

Appendix A-4

```
10      CHAIN "STARTUP"
20  ''"STOKINDX"
30          'STOCK SELECTION SOFTWARE   VERSION 1.0   IBM PC
40          'ROBERT W JENKS  1978    MOD 5/9/83
50          'USES FILES "STOCK.INX" "LETTERS.SYD", "GRUPGRPH.SYD"
60          '"SYMBOLS.SYD" AND "PRICES.SYD"
70          '**********
80          'INITIALIZE
90          '**********
100     KEY OFF:SCREEN 0,0,0:WIDTH 80:CLS
110     GOSUB 6750   'OUTPUT TO SCREEN
120     COMMON PD$,DD$
130     IF PD$="" THEN PD$="A:"   'PROGRAM DISK DRIVE DEFAULT
140     NL=6    'CODE NAME LENGTH
150     W2=NL+9 'INDEX ENTRY STRING SIZE
160     W1=50   'INDEX RECORD WIDTH
170     S3=10   'GROUPING FOR REPRICE
180     S4=20   'GROUPING FOR DISPLAY
190     S1=999  'LIMIT TO # OF STOCKS IN INDEX
200     LGRP=21 'LAST VALID GROUP
210     DIM P1(S3),V1(S3),G1(S3),R1(S3),B1(S3),Q1(S3),MKT1(S3),F$(S3),A$(3,26)
220     DEF FNESC(I$)=I$=CHR$(27)                    'TEST FOR ESCAPE
230     DEF FNUL(I$,E$)=I$=E$ OR I$=CHR$(ASC(E$)+32)  'UPPER/LOWER CASE
240          '**********
250          'INDEX MENU
260          '**********
270     GOSUB 850   'BUILD PROMPTS
280     CLS
290          'HEADING
300     LOCATE 1,1
310     T$=STRING$(25,177):T1$=STRING$(2,177)
320     PRINT TAB(27);T$;TAB(58);FKEY$(7)
330     PRINT TAB(27);T1$;" STOCK INDEX Program ";T1$;TAB(58)
340     PRINT FKEY$(8);" to MANAGER"
350     PRINT TAB(27);T$;TAB(58);FKEY$(9)
360     PRINT
370          'KEY
380     X1=33
390     FOR Y=3 TO 15 STEP 3
400        LOCATE Y+2,X1:PRINT FKEY$(0)
410        LOCATE Y+3,X1:PRINT FKEY$(Y\3)
420        LOCATE Y+4,X1:PRINT FKEY$(6)
430        NEXT
440          'PROMPT
450     Y1=3
460     FOR Y=1 TO 5:Y1=Y1+3:FOR X=0 TO 1
470        FOR Q=0 TO 1:LOCATE Y1-Q,1+47*X:PRINT PROMPT$(Y,X,Q):NEXT
480        NEXT X,Y
490          'HOUSE CLEANING
500     FREE=FRE("")
510     X=0:Y=0:Z=0:L=0:M=0:P2=0:V2=0:G2=0:R2=0:B2=0:Q2=0:MKT2=0:M1$=""
520          '***** SELECTION
530     LOCATE 20,39,0:PRINT " ";CHR$(29);
540     R$="":WHILE R$="":R$=INKEY$:WEND:PRINT CHR$(219);CHR$(29);
550     PRL=LEN(R$):R$=RIGHT$(R$,1)
560     IF FNESC(R$) THEN 640
570     LOCATE ,,1
580     VR=ASC(R$)-58:IF PRL=1 OR VR<1 THEN 530
590     ON VR GOTO 650,660,670,680,690,700,710,720,730,740
600     VR=VR-25:IF VR<1 THEN 530
610     ON VR GOTO 760,530,770,530,780,790,800,810,820,530
620     GOTO 530
```

Appendix A-4   (Continued)

```
630            'ACTION
640      CLOSE:CHAIN PD$+"MANAGER",20   'EXIT
650      CLS:M$="I":GOSUB 1140:GOTO 280    'INSERT
660      CLS:M$="R":GOSUB 1530:GOTO 280    'READ
670      CLS:M$="M":GOSUB 2110:GOTO 280    'MOVE
680      CLS:M$="G":GOSUB 2820:GOTO 280    'GROUP
690      GOSUB 3740:GOTO 280               'ALPHABETIC
700      CLS:M$="L":GOSUB 2820:GOTO 280    'CLASS
710      CLS:GOSUB 4500:GOTO 280           'REPRICE ALL
720      CLS:M$="S":GOSUB 2120:GOTO 280    'CODE NAME
730      CLS:GOSUB 5560:GOTO 280           'LOAD TOKENS FOR REPRICE
740      GOSUB 4030:GOTO 280               'SELECT
750            'SHIFTED
760      CLS:M$="W":GOSUB 1150:GOTO 280    'WRITE
770      CLS:M$="D":GOSUB 2100:GOTO 280    'DELETE
780      CLS:GOSUB 3460:GOTO 280           'CREATE ALPH
790      CLS:M$="L1":GOSUB 2820:GOTO 280   'CLASS DECADE
800      CLS:GOSUB 5100:GOTO 280           'REPRICE *
810      CLS:M$="T":GOSUB 2090:GOTO 280    'TICKER
820      CLS:GOSUB 5750:GOTO 280           'ENTER REMOTE PRICES
830            '****************
840            '***** GET PROMPTS    S
850      DIM PROMPT$(5,1,1)
860      T$=SPACE$(30):T1$=CHR$(24):RESTORE 940
870      FOR Y=1 TO 5:FOR X=0 TO 1:KEY Y+Y+X-1,"":FOR Z=0 TO 1:PROMPT$(Y,X,Z)=T$
880        READ N$:IF LEN(N$)=0 THEN 900
890        IF Z=1 THEN IF X=1 THEN N$=T1$+" "+N$ ELSE N$=N$+" "+T1$
900        IF X=0 THEN RSET PROMPT$(Y,X,Z)=N$ ELSE LSET PROMPT$(Y,X,Z)=N$
910      NEXT Z,X,Y
920      RETURN
930            'PROMPTS
940      DATA "Insert stock","Overwrite index"
950      DATA "Read Index",""
960      DATA "Move stock","Delete stock"
970      DATA "List by group",""
980      DATA "List first stock alphabetic","Create alphabetic list"
990      DATA "List by class","List by class decade"
1000     DATA "Reprice by decade","Reprice * stocks"
1010     DATA "Search for code name","Search for ticker symbol"
1020     DATA "Store symbols (modem pricing)","Read modem prices"
1030     DATA "Select by criteria",""
1040           '*********************************************
1050           'ALL MENU SUBROUTINES RETURN THROUGH THESE LINES
1060           '*********************************************
1070     PRINT SPC(79)
1080     IF CSRLIN>1 THEN LOCATE CSRLIN-1,1,1 ELSE PRINT
1090     GOSUB 6700    'PROMPT
1100     M$="":CLOSE #1,#2:LOCATE ,,0:RETURN
1110           '****************
1120           'WRITE TO INDEX   MS
1130           '****************
1140     PRINT "Insert";:GOTO 1160
1150     PRINT "Overwrite";
1160     INPUT " at stock location: ",R$:IF VAL(R$)<=0 THEN 1100 ELSE L=VAL(R$)
1170     GOSUB 6030    'OPEN STOCK INDEX
1180     Z=L
1190     GET #1,Z:GOSUB 6080    'ASSIGN TO STANDARD VARIABLES
1200     IF LEFT$(S$,1)="*" THEN 1490
1210     GOSUB 6320    'DISPLAY HEADING, ENTRY
1220     PRINT USING "###";Z;
1230     S$=SPACE$(W2)
1240     INPUT " Stock code, or (END) to exit routine= ",R$:MID$(S$,1,NL)=R$
```

Appendix A-4   (Continued)

```
1250    IF LEFT$(S$,3)="END" OR LEFT$(S$,3)="end" THEN 1490
1260    IF LEFT$(S$,1)=" " THEN 1220
1270    INPUT "Ticker symbol : ",R$:MID$(S$,NL+5,5)=R$
1280    INPUT "Classification: ",R$
1290    IF VAL(R$)<=0 OR VAL(R$)>255 THEN R$=CHR$(0) ELSE R$=CHR$(VAL(R$))
1300    MID$(S$,NL+1,1)=R$
1310    INPUT "Group number  = ",G3
1320    IF G3<0 OR G3>LGRP THEN 1310 ELSE MID$(S$,NL+2,1)=CHR$(G3)
1330    PRINT "Star stock (Y)? ";:GOSUB 6630
1340    IF R$="Y" THEN MID$(S$,NL+3,1)="*"
1350    INPUT "Price          : ",R$:IF VAL(R$)<=0 THEN P2=0 ELSE P2=VAL(R$)
1360    IF M$<>"W" THEN IF M$="I" THEN 1390 ELSE 2610
1370    PRINT "Options"
1380    PRINT "(C) Clear data field, ";
1390    PRINT "Esc  Escape update? ";:GOSUB 6630
1400    IF FNESC(R$) THEN 1220
1410    IF M$="I" THEN 2610
1420    LSET SB$=S$:LSET PB$=MKS$(P2)
1430    FOR DO=R$="C" TO -1
1440      LSET VB$=MKS$(0):LSET GB$=MKS$(0):LSET RB$=MKS$(0)
1450      LSET BB$=MKS$(0):LSET QB$=MKS$(0):LSET MB$=MKS$(0)
1460      NEXT
1470    PUT #1,Z
1480    Z=Z+1:GOTO 1190
1490    GOTO 1100
1500        '*****************
1510        'DISPLAY THE INDEX    MS
1520        '*****************
1530    INPUT "Read from stock number: ",R$:L=VAL(R$):IF L<=0 THEN 1100
1540    PRINT
1550    PRINT "Options"
1560    PRINT "(G)  Store for SCATTER graph"
1570    PRINT "(A)  Averages"
1580    PRINT "(P)  Printout"
1590    PRINT "Esc  Escape from routine"
1600    PRINT "? ";:GOSUB 6630:M1$=R$
1610    IF FNESC(M1$) THEN 1100
1620    T=1:T2=0
1630    CLS
1640    IF M1$="G" THEN GOSUB 6140    'OPEN GRUPGRPH FILE
1650    IF M1$="P" THEN GOSUB 6760    'OUTPUT TO PRINTER
1660    GOSUB 6030    'OPEN STOCK INDEX
1670    X=INT(L/S4)
1680    IF M1$<>"P" THEN CLS
1690    GOSUB 6270    'PRINT HEADING
1700        '*** DISPLAY 20 LINES
1710    FOR Y=1 TO S4
1720      Z=S4*X+Y:IF Z<L THEN 1820
1730      GET #1,Z:GOSUB 6080    'ASSIGN TO VARIABLES
1740      FIRST$=LEFT$(S$,1)
1750      IF FIRST$="*" THEN 1880
1760      IF FIRST$="#" THEN 2030 ELSE IF FIRST$="=" THEN 2040
1770      T2=T2+1:V2=V2+V:G2=G2+G:R2=R2+R:B2=B2+B:Q2=Q2+Q
1780      IF M1$="A" THEN 1820
1790      IF M1$="G" THEN GOSUB 6190:T=T+1:PUT #2,T    'ASSIGN
1800      GOSUB 6350    'PRINT A LINE FROM INDEX
1810      IF T>=51 THEN 1990
1820      NEXT
1830    IF M1$="A" OR M1$="G" OR M1$="P" THEN R$=INKEY$:GOTO 1860
1840    PRINT "Continue, or not  Esc? ";
1850    GOSUB 6580
1860    IF FNESC(R$) THEN SUPPRESS=-1:GOTO 1890
```

Appendix A-4   (Continued)

```
1870  X=X+1:GOTO 1680
1880  PRINT #3,"End of index";TAB(79):PRINT #3,
1890  IF M1$="P" THEN GOSUB 6750    'OUTPUT TO SCREEN
1900  IF M1$=CHR$(13) THEN GOSUB 6700    'PROMPT
1910  CLOSE #1
1920  IF M1$="G" THEN 1980
1930  IF M1$<>"A" THEN 1100
1940  S$=SPACE$(W2):MID$(S$,1,3)="AV.":MID$(S$,NL+1,2)=CHR$(0)+CHR$(0)
1950  Z=T2:P=0:V=V2/T2:G=G2/T2:R=R2/T2:B=B2/T2:Q=INT(Q2/T2):MKT=0
1960  GOSUB 6350    'DISPLAY LINE
1970  GOTO 1090
1980         '***   CLOSE GRAPH FILE
1990  S$="STOCKS":P=T:V=V2/T:G=G2/T:R=R2/T:B=B2/T:Q=Q2/T:MKT=0
2000  GOSUB 6190    'ASSIGN TO FIELDS
2010  PUT #2,1:GOTO 1100
2020         '***   MARKET SEPARATORS
2030  PRINT #3,"End of NYSE, beginning of AMEX";:GOTO 2050
2040  PRINT #3,"End of AMEX, beginning of OTC";
2050  PRINT TAB(79):PRINT:C5=C5+1:GOTO 1820
2060         '****************
2070         'SEARCH FOR STOCK   MS
2080         '****************
2090  INPUT "Ticker symbol: ",C$:GOTO 2130
2100  PRINT "Delete ";
2110  IF M$="M" THEN PRINT "Move ";
2120  INPUT "stock code name: ",C$
2130  IF C$="" THEN 1100
2140  C$=LEFT$(C$+SPACE$(NL),NL)
2150  IF M$<>"M" THEN 2180
2160  INPUT "Insert prior to entry #: ",R$
2170  L1=VAL(R$):IF L1<=0 THEN 1100
2180  GOSUB 6030    'OPEN STOCK INDEX
2190  X=1:S$=" "
2200  WHILE LEFT$(S$,1)<>"*"
2210    GET #1,X
2220    S$=SB$
2230    IF M$="T" THEN S1$=RIGHT$(S$,5)+SPACE$(NL-5) ELSE S1$=LEFT$(S$,NL)
2240    IF S1$=C$ THEN GOTO 2290
2250    X=X+1:WEND
2260  PRINT "Stock not found":PRINT
2270  GOTO 1070
2280         '***   NAME MATCH
2290  GOSUB 6090    'FIELDS TO STANDARD VARIABLES
2300  Z=X:GOSUB 6320    'DISPLAY HEADING & LINE
2310  IF M$="D" OR M$="M" THEN 2500
2320  R$=" "
2330  WHILE R$<>CHR$(27) AND R$<>CHR$(13)
2340    PRINT "Change (S)ymbol, Star Stock (Y/N), (C)lass, (G)roup, (P)rice? ";
2350    GOSUB 6630
2360    IF R$="P" THEN INPUT "Price= ",P:GOSUB 6320
2370    IF R$="G" THEN INPUT "Group= ",C3:MID$(S$,NL+2,1)=CHR$(C3):GOSUB 6320
2380    IF R$="C" THEN INPUT "Class= ",C3:MID$(S$,NL+1,1)=CHR$(C3):GOSUB 6320
2390    IF R$="S" THEN INPUT "Symbol: ",R$:MID$(S$,NL+5,5)=R$+"     ":GOSUB 6310
2400    IF R$="Y" THEN MID$(S$,NL+3,1)="*":GOSUB 6320
2410    IF R$="N" THEN MID$(S$,NL+3,1)=" ":GOSUB 6320
2420    WEND
2430  PRINT "Esc  Escape update? ";:GOSUB 6580
2440  IF NOT FNESC(R$) THEN LSET SB$=S$:LSET PB$=MKS$(P):PUT #1,X
2450  CLOSE #1
2460  SUPPRESS=-1:GOTO 1070
2470         '***********
2480         'DELETE STOCK
2490         '***********
```

Appendix A-4   (Continued)

```
2500    L=X:S5=S1:S1$=S$:P2=P:V2=V:G2=G:R2=R:B2=B:Q2=Q:MKT2=MKT
2510    IF M$<>"M" THEN 2540
2520    IF X=L1 OR X=L1-1 THEN 2270
2530    IF X>L1 THEN L=L1:S5=X:S$=S1$:GOTO 2620 ELSE L1=L1-1:S5=L1
2540    WHILE LEFT$(S$,1)<>"*" AND X<S5
2550      GET #1,X+1:S$=SB$:PUT #1,X
2560      X=X+1:WEND
2570    IF M$="M" THEN L=L1:S5=L1:S$=S1$:GOTO 2620 ELSE 2460
2580            '************
2590            'INSERT STOCK
2600            '************
2610    S5=S1
2620    GET #1,L
2630    T$=SB$:P1=CVS(PB$):V1=CVS(VB$):G1=CVS(GB$):R1=CVS(RB$):B1=CVS(BB$)
2640    Q1=CVS(QB$):MKT1=CVS(MB$)
2650    LSET SB$=S$
2660    LSET PB$=MKS$(P2):LSET VB$=MKS$(V2):LSET GB$=MKS$(G2):LSET RB$=MKS$(R2)
2670    LSET BB$=MKS$(B2):LSET QB$=MKS$(Q2):LSET MB$=MKS$(MKT2)
2680    PUT #1,L
2690    X=L+1
2700    WHILE LEFT$(S$,1)<>"*" AND X<=S5
2710      GET #1,X:GOSUB 6080    'ASSIGN TO STANDARD VARIABLES
2720      LSET SB$=T$
2730      LSET PB$=MKS$(P1):LSET VB$=MKS$(V1):LSET GB$=MKS$(G1):LSET RB$=MKS$(R1)
2740      LSET BB$=MKS$(B1):LSET QB$=MKS$(Q1):LSET MB$=MKS$(MKT1)
2750      PUT #1,X
2760      T$=S$:P1=P:V1=V:G1=G:R1=R:B1=B:Q1=Q:MKT1=MKT
2770      X=X+1:WEND
2780    GOTO 1900
2790            '*********************************************
2800            'EXTRACT STOCKS BY GROUP OR CLASSIFICATION   MS
2810            '*********************************************
2820    IF M$="G" THEN PRINT "Group <0 -";LGRP;">: ";:INPUT "",R$
2830    IF M$="L" THEN INPUT "Classification <0-255>: ",R$
2840    IF M$="L1" THEN INPUT "Classification decade <0-6>: ",R$
2850    IF R$="" THEN 1100 ELSE G4=VAL(R$)
2860    IF M$="G" THEN IF G4>LGRP THEN 2820
2870    IF M$="L1" THEN IF G4>25 THEN 2840
2880    IF G4<0 OR G4>255 THEN 2820
2890            '** MODE
2900    PRINT
2910    PRINT "Options"
2920    PRINT "(G)   Store for SCATTER graph"
2930    PRINT "(A)   Add prices to these stocks"
2940    PRINT "(P)   Printout"
2950    PRINT "Esc   Escape from routine"
2960    GOSUB 6630:M2$=R$
2970    IF FNESC(M2$) THEN 1100
2980    IF M2$="G" THEN GOSUB 6140    'OPEN GRUPGRPH FILE
2990    CLS
3000    IF M2$="P" THEN GOSUB 6760
3010    GOSUB 6270    'HEADING
3020    T=0:T1=0:V1=0:G1=0:R1=0:B1=0:Q1=0
3030    IF M$="L1" THEN D3=10 ELSE D3=1
3040    GOSUB 6030    'OPEN STOCK INDEX
3050    Z=1:S$=" "
3060    WHILE LEFT$(S$,1)<>"*"
3070      GET #1,Z:GOSUB 6080    'ASSIGN TO STANDARD VARIABLES
3080      G3=ASC(MID$(S$,NL+2,1))
3090      IF G3<1 OR G3>LGRP THEN GOSUB 6500:GOTO 3120    'MARKET SEPARATOR
3100      IF M$<>"G" THEN G3=INT(ASC(MID$(S$,NL+1,1))/D3)
3110      IF G3=G4 THEN GOSUB 3250
```

Appendix A-4   (Continued)

```
3120     Z=Z+1:WEND
3130     IF M2$="A" OR T1=0 THEN 3220
3140     S$=SPACE$(W2):MID$(S$,1,3)="AV.":MID$(S$,NL+1,2)=CHR$(0)+CHR$(0)
3150     Z=T1:P=T1:V=V1/T1:G=G1/T1:R=R1/T1:B=B1/T1:Q=INT(Q1/T1):MKT=0
3160     IF M2$="G" THEN GOSUB 6190:PUT #2,1
3170     PRINT #3,TAB(4);DATE$
3180     P=0:GOSUB 6350        'DISPLAY LINE
3190     PRINT #3,USING SPACE$(49)+"#####.##";G+R
3200     PRINT #3,
3210     IF M2$="P" THEN GOSUB 6750        'OUTPUT TO SCREEN
3220     GOTO 1070
3230            '*****************
3240            '***   GROUP/CLASSIFICATION MATCH   S
3250     GOSUB 6350        'DISPLAY LINE
3260     IF M2$="A" THEN 3380
3270     IF V=0 THEN 3300
3280     T1=T1+1:V1=V1+V:G1=G1+G:R1=R1+R:B1=B1+B:Q1=Q1+Q
3290     IF M2$="G" THEN GOSUB 6190:PUT #2,T1+1
3300     T=T+1:IF T<20 THEN RETURN
3310            '***   20 DISPLAYED
3320     T=0:IF M2$="P" THEN RETURN
3330     IF M2$="G" THEN GOSUB 6270:RETURN         'HEADING
3340     PRINT "Continue, or not  Esc? ";
3350     IF FNESC(INPUT$(1)) THEN S$="*"
3360     PRINT:RETURN
3370            '***   RE-PRICE MODE
3380     PRINT "Price: ";:GOSUB 5350    'GET PRICE
3390     PRINT
3400     IF FNESC(R$) THEN GOSUB 3340:IF S$="*" THEN RETURN ELSE 3380
3410     IF R$<>"" THEN P=VAL(R$):LSET PB$=MKS$(P):PUT #1,Z
3420     RETURN
3430            '**********************
3440            'CREATE ALPHABETIC LIST    MS
3450            '**********************
3460     PRINT "This routine locates alphabetic pointers to STOCK.INX"
3470     PRINT "Creating alphabetic list":LOCATE ,,0
3480     GOSUB 6030    'OPEN STOCK INDEX
3490     X=1:GET #1,X:T$=SB$
3500     C2=ASC(T$):FIRST$=CHR$(C2):Z=1
3510     IF FIRST$="#" THEN Z=2:GOTO 3540
3520     IF FIRST$="=" THEN Z=3:GOTO 3540
3530     IF C2<>42 THEN GOSUB 3690
3540     WHILE C2<>42
3550       X=X+1
3560       C1=C2
3570       GET #1,X:T$=SB$
3580       C2=ASC(T$):FIRST$=CHR$(C2)
3590       IF FIRST$="#" THEN Z=2:GOTO 3620
3600       IF FIRST$="=" THEN Z=3:GOTO 3620
3610       IF FIRST$>="A" AND FIRST$<="Z" AND C1<>C2 THEN GOSUB 3690
3620     WEND
3630            '** WRAP UP
3640     CLOSE #1:PRINT
3650     OPEN PD$+"LETTERS.SYD" FOR OUTPUT AS #2
3660     FOR E=1 TO 3:FOR C=1 TO 26:WRITE #2,A$(E,C):NEXT C,E
3670     GOTO 1100
3680            '** ENTER INTO ALPHABETIC INDEX   S
3690     T1$=STR$(X)+SPACE$(3):T1$=MID$(T1$,2):T1$=LEFT$(T1$,3)
3700     A$(Z,C2-64)=T1$+" "+LEFT$(T$,6):PRINT ".";:RETURN
3710            '**********************
3720            'DISPLAY ALPHABETIC LIST    MS
3730            '**********************
```

Appendix A-4   (Continued)

```
3740  CLS
3750  PRINT "Pointers to STOCK.INX"
3760  IF LETTERSREAD=0 THEN GOSUB 3970
3770  FOR E=1 TO 3
3780    PRINT
3790    ON E GOSUB 3920,3930,3940
3800    PRINT TAB(14);
3810    C5=1
3820    FOR C=1 TO 26
3830      ENTRY$=A$(E,C)
3840      IF ENTRY$=SPACE$(LEN(ENTRY$)) THEN ENTRY$="   "+CHR$(C+64)+"
3850      IF C5/5=INT(C5/5) THEN PRINT
3860      C5=C5+1
3870      PRINT "  ";ENTRY$;
3880      NEXT:PRINT
3890    NEXT
3900  PRINT:GOTO 1070
3910        'EXCHANGE HEADINGS
3920  PRINT "NYSE";:RETURN
3930  PRINT "AMEX";:RETURN
3940  PRINT "OTC";;:RETURN
3950        '*****
3960        'READ LETTERS FILE   S
3970  OPEN PD$+"LETTERS.SYD" FOR INPUT AS #2
3980  FOR E=1 TO 3:FOR C=1 TO 26:INPUT #2,A$(E,C):NEXT C,E
3990  CLOSE #2:LETTERSREAD=-1:RETURN
4000        '*******************************
4010        'EXTRACT STOCKS MEETING CRITERIA    MS
4020        '*******************************
4030  CLS
4040  PRINT "Select by criteria"
4050  PRINT
4060  PRINT "  Input limits for multi-way selection from STOCK.INX"
4070  INPUT "Valuation    limit: ",V2
4080  INPUT "Growth       limit: ",G2
4090  INPUT "Yield        limit: ",R2
4100  INPUT "Total Return limit: ",T3
4110  INPUT "Price/Book   limit: ",B2
4120  IF B2<=0 THEN SUPPRESS=-1:GOTO 1070
4130  INPUT "Quality      limit: ",Q2
4140  PRINT "  Enter market value limits in $ millions"
4150  INPUT "Low          limit: ",MKT1
4160  INPUT "High         limit: ",MKT2
4170  IF MKT2<=0 THEN MKT2=999999!
4180  IF MKT2<MKT1 THEN SWAP MKT2,MKT1
4190  IF T3<G2+R2 THEN T3=G2+R2
4200  PRINT
4210  PRINT "Options"
4220  PRINT "(G)  Store for SCATTER graph"
4230  PRINT "(P)  Printout"
4240  PRINT "Esc  Escape routine"
4250  PRINT "? ";:GOSUB 6630:M2$=R$
4260  IF FNESC(M2$) THEN SUPPRESS=-1:GOTO 1070 ELSE CLS
4270  IF M2$="P" THEN GOSUB 6760
4280  GOSUB 6270    'HEADING
4290  PRINT #3,DATE$;TAB(42);
4300  PRINT #3,USING "###.##< ";V2;
4310  PRINT #3,USING "###.##<";G2;
4320  PRINT #3,USING "###.#<";R2;
4330  PRINT #3,USING "###.#>";B2;
4340  PRINT #3,USING "####<";Q2
4350  PRINT #3,USING "Total return >=####.##";T3;
```

Appendix A-4   (Continued)

```
4360    PRINT #3,USING "    ######<= Market value <=######";MKT1;MKT2
4370    GOSUB 6030    'OPEN STOCK INDEX
4380    IF M2$="G" THEN GOSUB 6140    'OPEN GRUPGRPH
4390    T=0:T1=0:V1=0:G1=0:R1=0:B1=0:Q1=0
4400    Z=1:S$=" "
4410    WHILE LEFT$(S$,1)<>"*"
4420      GET #1,Z:GOSUB 6080
4430      T4=V>=V2 AND G>=G2 AND R>=R2 AND G+R>=T3 AND B<=B2 AND Q>=Q2
4440      IF T4 AND MKT>=MKT1 AND MKT<=MKT2 THEN GOSUB 3250
4450      Z=Z+1:WEND
4460    GOTO 3130
4470            '****************************
4480            'ENTER PRICES INTO THE INDEX    MS
4490            '****************************
4500    PRINT "Manual pricing by decade"
4510    PRINT "During routine, Esc to escape group of ten."
4520    PRINT
4530    INPUT "Enter prices from stock number: ",R$
4540    N=VAL(R$):IF N=0 THEN 1100
4550    GOSUB 6030    'OPEN STOCK INDEX
4560    FEND=0
4570    Y=INT(N/S3)
4580            '** FILL BUFFER
4590    FOR X=1 TO S3
4600      IF FEND THEN 4670
4610      LOCATION=X+S3*Y
4620      GET #1,LOCATION
4630      S$=SB$:IF LEFT$(S$,1)="*" THEN FEND=-1:TOX=X
4640      F$(X)=S$
4650      P=CVS(PB$):P1(X)=P:V1(X)=CVS(VB$):G1(X)=CVS(GB$)
4660      R1(X)=CVS(RB$):B1(X)=CVS(BB$):Q1(X)=CVS(QB$):MKT1(X)=CVS(MB$)
4670    NEXT
4680    CLS
4690    IF FEND AND TOX=1 THEN 5060
4700            '** ENTER PRICES
4710    GOSUB 5490    'HEADING
4720    FOR X=1 TO S3
4730      IF FEND AND X>=TOX THEN GOTO 4860
4740      S$=F$(X):P=P1(X)
4750      IF ASC(S$)<65 THEN GOSUB 6500:GOTO 4850    'MARKET SEPARATOR
4760      PRINT USING "###    ";INT(X+S3*Y);
4770      PRINT LEFT$(S$,NL);
4780      PRINT USING "  ####.##   :";P;
4790      GOSUB 5350    'GET PRICE
4800      IF FNESC(R$)THEN 4860
4810      IF R$="" THEN 4840
4820      P1(X)=VAL(R$)
4830      IF P<>0 THEN PRINT TAB(32);:PRINT USING "####.#%";100*(P1(X)-P)/P;
4840      PRINT
4850    NEXT
4860    Z=X-1
4870    PRINT:PRINT "Any price errors (Y), Esc Exit? ";
4880    GOSUB 6630
4890    IF R$<>"Y" THEN 4980
4900    PRINT "Which local # (1 TO";S3;")";:";:INPUT "",R$
4910    IF R$="" THEN 4980 ELSE X=VAL(R$)
4920    IF X<1 OR X>S3 THEN 4900
4930    PRINT USING LEFT$(F$(X),6)+"  ####.##   ";P1(X);:GOSUB 5350
4940    IF NOT FNESC(R$) AND R$<>"" THEN P=VAL(R$)
4950    IF P>0 THEN P1(X)=P
4960    GOTO 4870
4970            '** WRITE PRICES BACK TO INDEX
```

Appendix A-4   (Continued)

```
4980   FOR X=1 TO Z:LOCATION=X+S3*Y
4990     LSET SB$=F$(X)
5000     LSET PB$=MKS$(P1(X)):LSET VB$=MKS$(V1(X)):LSET GB$=MKS$(G1(X))
5010     LSET RB$=MKS$(R1(X)):LSET BB$=MKS$(B1(X)):LSET QB$=MKS$(Q1(X))
5020     LSET MB$=MKS$(MKT1(X))
5030     PUT #1,LOCATION
5040     NEXT
5050   IF NOT FNESC(R$) AND NOT FEND THEN Y=Y+1:GOTO 4590
5060   GOTO 1100
5070        '*****************************
5080        'ENTER STAR STOCK PRICES ONLY   MS
5090        '*****************************
5100   PRINT "Enter (E) at end of line to indicate error, allow changes"
5110   PRINT "Esc to escape routine.
5120   PRINT TAB(3);:GOSUB 5490     'HEADING
5130   GOSUB 6030     'OPEN STOCK INDEX
5140   X=1:S$=" "
5150   WHILE LEFT$(S$,1)<>"*"
5160     GET #1,X:S$=SB$:P=CVS(PB$)
5170     IF ASC(S$)<65 THEN GOSUB 6500:GOTO 5190     'MARKET SEPARATOR
5180     IF MID$(S$,NL+3,1)="*" THEN GOSUB 5230
5190     X=X+1:WEND
5200   PRINT:GOTO 1070
5210        '**************
5220        '** ENTER PRICE   S
5230   PRINT USING "###   ";INT(X);
5240   PRINT LEFT$(S$,NL);"   *   ";
5250   PRINT USING "####.## :";P;
5260   GOSUB 5350     'GET PRICE
5270   IF FNESC(R$) THEN GOSUB 5520:IF FNESC(R$) THEN S$="*":SUPPRESS=-1:RETURN E
LSE 5230
5280   IF R$="" THEN PRINT:RETURN
5290   P3=VAL(R$)
5300   IF P<>0 THEN PRINT TAB(40):PRINT USING "####.#%   ";100*(P3-P)/P;
5310   PRINT "(E)? ";:GOSUB 6580:IF FNUL(R$,"E") THEN 5230
5320   LSET PB$=MKS$(P3):PUT #1,X
5330   RETURN
5340          '** INPUT PRICE   S
5350   R$="":DP=0:LOCATE ,,1
5360   R1$=INPUT$(1)
5370   IF R1$>="0" AND R1$<="9" THEN R$=R$+R1$:PRINT R1$;:GOTO 5360
5380   IF R1$="." THEN IF DP THEN 5360 ELSE DP=-1:R$=R$+R1$:PRINT R1$;:GOTO 5360
5390   IF R1$=CHR$(13) THEN RETURN
5400   IF R1$=CHR$(8) THEN GOSUB 5440     'ERASE CHAR
5410   IF FNESC(R1$) THEN R$=CHR$(27):RETURN
5420   GOTO 5360
5430          'ERASE CHARACTER   S
5440   IF R$="" THEN RETURN
5450   IF RIGHT$(R$,1)="." THEN DP=0
5460   R$=LEFT$(R$,LEN(R$)-1)
5470   LOCATE ,POS(0)-1:PRINT " ";:LOCATE ,POS(0)-1:RETURN
5480          '** REPRICE HEADING   S
5490   PRINT TAB(26);"Price   ENTER if same"
5500   RETURN
5510          '** VERIFY ESCAPE   S
5520   PRINT:PRINT "Esc   Escape routine? ";:GOTO 6580
5530        '*******************************************
5540        'STORE TICKER SYMBOLS FOR REMOTE REPRICING   MS
5550        '*******************************************
5560   PRINT "This routine stores ticker symbols in file SYMBOLS.SYD"
5570   PRINT "Esc  to escape STORE SYMBOLS routine ";
5580   GOSUB 6580:IF FNESC(R$) THEN 1100
```

Appendix A-4   (Continued)

```
5590  PRINT 'Storing symbols':LOCATE ,,0
5600  OPEN PD$+"PRICES.SYD" FOR OUTPUT AS #2:CLOSE #2
5610  GOSUB 6030    'OPEN STOCK INDEX
5620  OPEN PD$+"SYMBOLS.SYD" FOR OUTPUT AS #2
5630  X=1:S$=" "
5640  WHILE LEFT$(S$,1)<>"*"
5650    GET #1,X:S$=SB$:S1$=MID$(SB$,NL+5,5)
5660    IF S1$<"A" OR S1$>"ZZZZZ" THEN 5700
5670    L=INSTR(S1$," ")
5680    IF L<>0 THEN S1$=LEFT$(S1$,L-1)
5690    PRINT #2,S1$:PRINT ".";
5700    X=X+1:WEND
5710  PRINT:GOTO 1100
5720        '*********************
5730        'READ REMOTE PRICE LIST   MS
5740        '*********************
5750  PRINT "This routine transfers remote prices from PRICES.SYD file to STOCK
INX"
5760  PRINT "Esc  to escape READ MODEM PRICES routine ";
5770  GOSUB 6580:IF FNESC(R$) THEN 1100
5780  PRINT "Loading prices":LOCATE ,,0
5790  CLOSE #3
5800  GOSUB 6030    'OPEN STOCK INDEX
5810  OPEN PD$+"SYMBOLS.SYD" FOR INPUT AS #2
5820  OPEN PD$+"PRICES.SYD" FOR INPUT AS #3
5830  X=1:S$=" "
5840  WHILE LEFT$(S$,1)<>"*" AND NOT EOF(2) AND NOT EOF(3)
5850    GET #1,X:S$=SB$:S1$=MID$(SB$,NL+5,5)
5860    IF S1$<"A" OR S1$>"ZZZZZ" THEN 5930
5870    L=INSTR(S1$," ")
5880    IF L<>0 THEN S1$=LEFT$(S1$,L-1)
5890    INPUT #2,S2$
5900    IF S2$<>S1$ THEN 5960
5910    INPUT #3,P
5920    IF P>0 THEN LSET PB$=MKS$(P):PUT #1,X:PRINT ".";
5930    X=X+1:WEND
5940  PRINT:GOSUB 6750:GOTO 1100    'OUTPUT TO SCREEN
5950        'ERROR MESSAGE
5960  PRINT "Forced exit due to ticker symbol out of order."
5970  INPUT "Run STORE SYMBOLS FOR PRICING routine and reprice by modem. ",R$
5980  GOTO 5940
5990        '*********************
6000        'DISK I/O
6010        '*********************
6020        'OPEN STOCK INDEX FILE   S
6030  OPEN PD$+"STOCK.INX" AS #1 LEN=W1
6040  FIELD #1,W2 AS SB$,4 AS PB$,4 AS VB$,4 AS GB$,4 AS RB$,4 AS BB$,4 AS QB$,
      AS MB$
6050  RETURN
6060        '**********************************************
6070        'ASSIGN INDEX FIELDS TO STANDARD VARIABLES   S
6080  S$=SB$
6090  P=CVS(PB$):V=CVS(VB$):G=CVS(GB$):R=CVS(RB$):B=CVS(BB$):Q=CVS(QB$)
6100  MKT=CVS(MB$)
6110  RETURN
6120        '*******************
6130        'OPEN GRUPGRPH FILE   S
6140  OPEN PD$+"GRUPGRPH.SYD" AS #2 LEN=W1
6150  FIELD #2,W2 AS SG$,4 AS PG$,4 AS VG$,4 AS GG$,4 AS RG$,4 AS BG$,4 AS QG$,
      AS MG$
6160  RETURN
6170        '*****************************
```

Appendix A-4   (Continued)

```
6180          'ASSIGN VALUES TO GRUPGRPH FIELDS   S
6190   LSET SG$=S$
6200   LSET PG$=MKS$(P):LSET VG$=MKS$(V):LSET GG$=MKS$(G):LSET RG$=MKS$(R)
6210   LSET BG$=MKS$(B):LSET QG$=MKS$(Q):LSET MG$=MKS$(MKT)
6220   RETURN
6230          '***************  .
6240          'OUTPUT
6250          '***************
6260          'DISPLAY HEADING    S
6270   PRINT #3,"        #  Sym    Name      Class Group Price   ";
6280   PRINT #3,"Val.  Growth   Yield   P/B Qual. Mkt V."
6290   RETURN
6300          '****************
6310          'HEADING AND LINE , S
6320   GOSUB 6270
6330          '************
6340          'DISPLAY LINE     S
6350   PRINT #3,USING "   ###  ";Z;
6360   PRINT #3,MID$(S$,NL+5,5);" ";LEFT$(S$,NL);" ";MID$(S$,NL+3,1);
6370   PRINT #3,USING "#####";ASC(MID$(S$,NL+1,1));
6380   PRINT #3,USING "#####";ASC(MID$(S$,NL+2,1));
6390   PRINT #3,USING "#####.##";P;
6400   PRINT #3,USING "###.##";V;
6410   PRINT #3,MID$(S$,NL+4,1);
6420   PRINT #3,USING "####.##";G;
6430   PRINT #3,USING "###.##";R;B;
6440   PRINT #3,USING "####";INT(Q);
6450   PRINT #3,USING "  ######";MKT
6460   C5=C5+1
6470   RETURN
6480          '****************
6490          'MARKET SEPARATORS    S
6500   FIRST$=LEFT$(S$,1)
6510   IF FIRST$="#" THEN PRINT #3,"AMEX"
6520   IF FIRST$="=" THEN PRINT #3,"OTC"
6530   RETURN
6540          '**************************
6550          'KEYBOARD INPUT
6560          '**************************
6570          'SIMULATE 1 CHARACTER INPUT    S
6580   LOCATE ,,1:R$="":WHILE R$="":R$=INKEY$:WEND
6590   IF R$>" " THEN PRINT R$ ELSE PRINT
6600   RETURN
6610          '*******************************************
6620          '1 CHARACTER INPUT   & CONVERT TO UPPER CASE    S
6630   GOSUB 6580
6640          '******************
6650          'LOWER CASE TO UPPER    S
6660   IF R$>="a" AND R$<="z" THEN R$=CHR$(ASC(R$)-32)
6670   RETURN
6680          '****************
6690          'PAUSE FOR VIEWING    S
6700   C5=0
6710   IF SUPPRESS THEN SUPPRESS=0:RETURN
6720   PRINT "Press any key to continue ";:R$=INPUT$(1):PRINT:RETURN
6730          '*************
6740          'OUTPUT SELECT    S
6750   CLOSE #3:OPEN "SCRN:" FOR OUTPUT AS #3:RETURN    'TO SCREEN
6760   PRINT "Directing output to printer.  Please wait..."
6770   CLOSE #3:OPEN "LPT1:" FOR OUTPUT AS #3:RETURN    'TO PRINTER
6780   END 'PROGRAM
```

Appendix A-5

```
10      CHAIN 'STARTUP'
20    ''STOCKPGM'
30            'STOCK SELECTION SOFTWARE   VERSION 1.0   IBM PC
40            'ROBERT W JENKS  1978  MOD 5/9/83
50            'USES FILES 'STOCK.INX', 'DEFLATOR.SYD' AND THE STOCK FILES
60      KEY OFF:SCREEN 0,0,0:WIDTH 80:CLS:CLOSE
70      GOSUB 8470     'OUTPUT TO SCREEN
80      COMMON PD$,DD$
90      IF PD$='' THEN PD$='A:'  'PROGRAM DISK DRIVE DEFAULT
100     IF DD$='' THEN DD$='B:'  'DATA DISK DRIVE DEFAULT
110     LGRP=21       'LAST VALID GROUP
120     NL=6          'CODE NAME LENGTH
130     W2=NL+9       'INDEX ENTRY STRING LENGTH
140     W1=50         'INDEX RECORD WIDTH
150     CSR1=11       'START LINE FOR REGULAR CURSOR MONOCHROME BOARD
160     CSR2=12       'END LINE FOR REGULAR CURSOR MONOCHROME BOARD
170     INSS=6        'START OF CURSOR FOR INSERT MODE  MONOCHROME BOARD
180     CSR1=7        'START LINE FOR REGULAR CURSOR COLOR BOARD
190     CSR2=7        'END LINE FOR REGULAR CURSOR COLOR BOARD
200     INSS=4        'START OF CURSOR FOR INSERT MODE  COLOR BOARD
210     NLB=&H20      'NUM LOCK MASK
220     DIM Q(16,9),G(12,3),V(15),D1(14),GROUPS(LGRP)
230     E$=SPACE$(79):H$=E$:F$=SPACE$(67)
240     DEF FNESC(CHAR$)=CHAR$+CHR$(27)
250            '** GET DEFLATOR CONSTANTS
260     OPEN PD$+'DEFLATOR.SYD' FOR INPUT AS #1
270     X=1:WHILE NOT EOF(1):INPUT #1,D1(X):X=X+1:WEND
280     CLOSE #1:D1=D1(14)-12
290            '***********************
300            '*  STOCK PROGRAM MENU  *
310            '***********************
320     GOSUB 790     'GET PROMPTS
330     GOTO 360
340     PRINT 'Press any key to continue ';
350     R$=INPUT$(1):PRINT
360     CLS
370            'HEADING
380     LOCATE 1,1
390     T7=28
400     T$=STRING$(24,177):T1$=STRING$(2,177)
410     PRINT TAB(T7);T$;TAB(55);FKEY$(7)
420     PRINT TAB(T7);T1$;' STOCK FILE program ';T1$;
430     PRINT TAB(55);FKEY$(8);' to MANAGER'
440     PRINT TAB(T7);T$;TAB(55);FKEY$(9)
450     PRINT
460            'KEY
470     X1=33
480     FOR Y=3 TO 15 STEP 3
490       LOCATE Y+2,X1,1:PRINT FKEY$(0)
500       LOCATE Y+3,X1,1:PRINT FKEY$(Y\3)
510       LOCATE Y+4,X1,1:PRINT FKEY$(6)
520       NEXT
530            'PROMPT
540     Y1=3
550     FOR Y=1 TO 5:Y1=Y1+3:FOR X=0 TO 1
560       FOR Q=0 TO 1:LOCATE Y1-Q,1+47*X:PRINT PROMPT$(Y,X,Q):NEXT
570       NEXT X,Y
580            'HOUSE CLEANING
590     FREE=FRE('')
600            '*** SELECTION
610     LOCATE 20,39,0:PRINT ' ';CHR$(29);
```

Appendix A-5   (Continued)

```
620    R$="":WHILE R$="":R$=INKEY$:WEND:PRINT CHR$(219);CHR$(29);
630    LOCATE ,,1
640    PRL=LEN(R$):R$=RIGHT$(R$,1)
650    IF PRL=1 THEN IF R$=CHR$(27) THEN 720 ELSE 610
660    VR=ASC(RIGHT$(R$,1))-58:IF VR<1 THEN 610
670    ON VR GOTO 730,740,750,760,770,610,610,610,610,610
680    VR=VR-25:IF VR<1 THEN 610
690    ON VR GOTO 610
700    GOTO 610
710          'ACTION
720    CLOSE:CHAIN PD$+"MANAGER",20
730    CLS:GOTO 3130    'DISPLAY
740    CLS:GOTO 1000    'NEW FILE
750    CLS:GOTO 4210    'VALUATIONS
760    CLS:GOSUB 3960:GOTO 360    'DEFLATOR CONSTANTS
770    CLS:GOSUB 4970:GOTO 360    'DATA DISK FILES
780          '***** GET PROMPTS   S
790    DIM PROMPT$(5,1,1)
800    T$=SPACE$(30):T1$=CHR$(24):RESTORE 880
810    FOR Y=1 TO 5:FOR X=0 TO 1:KEY Y+Y+X-1,"":FOR Z=0 TO 1:PROMPT$(Y,X,Z)=T$
820      READ N$:IF LEN(N$)=0 THEN 840
830      IF Z=1 THEN IF X=1 THEN N$=T1$+" "+N$ ELSE N$=N$+" "+T1$
840      IF X=0 THEN RSET PROMPT$(Y,X,Z)=N$ ELSE LSET PROMPT$(Y,X,Z)=N$
850      NEXT Z,X,Y
860    RETURN
870          'DATA
880    DATA "Stock display",""
890    DATA "Set up new file",""
900    DATA "Do group valuations",""
910    DATA "Change deflator constants",""
920    DATA "List data disk files",""
930    DATA "","","","","","","","","",""
940          '
950          '*******************************
960          '*                             *
970          '*   ENTER INITIAL STOCK DATA  MR
980          '*                             *
990          '*******************************
1000   FOR X=1 TO 16:FOR Y=0 TO 9:Q(X,Y)=0:NEXT Y,X
1010   INPUT "Stock code for new file: ",S$:IF S$="" THEN 360
1020   S$=S$+SPACE$(NL):S$=LEFT$(S$,NL)
1030   GOSUB 8130    'OPEN STOCK INDEX AND ASSIGN FIELDS
1040   X=1:S2$=" "
1050   WHILE LEFT$(S2$,1)<>"*"
1060     GET #2,X:S2$=SB$
1070     IF LEFT$(S2$,NL)=S$ THEN 1110
1080     X=X+1:WEND
1090   CLOSE #2:GOSUB 8080:PRINT "Stock ";SF$;" not found in index":GOTO 340
1100         '
1110   CLOSE #2
1120   GOSUB 8080    'SPACE TEST
1130   ON ERROR GOTO 1180
1140   OPEN DD$+SF$+".DAT" FOR INPUT AS #1:CLOSE #1:ON ERROR GOTO 0
1150   PRINT "File already exists, Esc  Exit? ";
1160   GOSUB 8260
1170   IF FNESC(R$) THEN 360 ELSE 1250
1180   IF ERR<>71 THEN RESUME 1230
1190   PRINT "Check drive, Esc Exit? ";
1200   GOSUB 8260
1210   IF FNESC(R$) THEN RESUME 360 ELSE RESUME 1130
1220   RESUME 1230
1230   ON ERROR GOTO 0
```

Appendix A-5   (Continued)

```
1240          '** HEADING
1250    H$=S$+"-"
1260    PRINT "Stock heading (input company name, group, etc.):"
1270    PRINT H$;:INPUT "",A1$
1280    H$=H$+A1$:H$=LEFT$(H$,79)
1290          '** GET QUARTERLY DATA
1300    GOSUB 1770
1310          '** ENTER GROWTH & BALANCE SHEET DATA
1320    CLS:D$=""
1330    PRINT
1340    INPUT "4 yr $  Earnings estimate= ",G(1,0)
1350    INPUT "5 yr $  Earnings estimate= ",G(2,0)
1360    INPUT "Est 1 %   Growth estimate= ",G(4,0)
1370    INPUT "Est 2 %   Growth estimate= ",G(5,0)
1380    IF D$<>"" THEN 1460
1390    PRINT
1400    PRINT "   Enter values in millions"
1410    INPUT "Cash                     = ",G(8,0)
1420    INPUT "Working capital          = ",G(9,0)
1430    INPUT "Debt                     = ",G(10,0)
1440    INPUT "Convertibles outstanding = ",G(11,0)
1450    INPUT "Shares                   = ",G(12,0)
1460    PRINT
1470    PRINT "Any errors in the (G)rowth or (B)alance sheet figures? ";
1480    GOSUB 8310:D$=R$
1490    IF D$="G" THEN 1330 ELSE IF D$="B" THEN 1390
1500    GOSUB 5440   'CALCULATE GROWTH FIGURES
1510          '** ENTER VALUATION DATA & FOOTNOTE
1520    CLS:D$=""
1530    PRINT
1540    INPUT "S&P Quality rating= ",V(1)
1550    INPUT "V.L Quality rating= ",V(2)
1560    INPUT "C.D (Constant dollar) rating= ",V(3)
1570    PRINT S$;:INPUT "- price= ",V(8)
1580    GOSUB 6010   'CALCULATE VALUATION FIGURES
1590    IF D$<>"" THEN 1620
1600    PRINT
1610    PRINT "Footnotes (67 characters max.):":INPUT "",A1$:F$=A1$
1620    PRINT
1630    PRINT "Any errors in (V)aluation or (F)ootnotes? ";:LOCATE ,,1
1640    GOSUB 8310:D$=R$
1650    IF D$="V" THEN 1530 ELSE IF D$="F" THEN 1600
1660    GOSUB 7750   'YEAR SKEW
1670    GOSUB 3380   'GET BACK EARNINGS FOR DEFLATOR
1680          '** DISPLAY AND SAVE
1690    GOSUB 2320   'DISPLAY
1700    PRINT "Esc  Escape update of file ";S$;"? ";
1710    GOSUB 8310
1720    IF NOT FNESC(R$) THEN GOSUB 7910
1730    GOTO 360
1740          '**********************
1750          'ENTER QUARTERLY DATA  S
1760          '**********************
1770    INPUT "First year for data= ",Y1
1780    IF Y1>2100 THEN 1770 ELSE Y1=Y1 MOD 100
1790    INPUT "First quarter end month (2,3,4)= ",M1
1800    IF M1<2 OR M1>4 THEN 1790
1810          '** ENTER YEAR
1820    FOR X=1 TO 16:Q(X,0)=Y1+INT((X-1)/4):NEXT
1830    IF M1<4 THEN 1880
1840          '** ADJUST YEAR
1850    FOR X=2 TO 16:Q(X-1,0)=Q(X,0):NEXT
```

Appendix A-5   (Continued)

```
1860    Q(16,0)=Q(16,0)+1
1870         '** ENTER MONTHS
1880    IF M1>3 THEN M2=M1-3 ELSE M2=M1+9
1890    FOR Y=1 TO 3
1900       T=M1+3*(Y-1)
1910       FOR X=0 TO 3:Q(X*4+Y,1)=T
1920       NEXT X,Y
1930    FOR X=0 TO 3:Q(X*4+4,1)=M2:NEXT
1940    '
1950    INPUT "Quarter in which fiscal year ends (1-4)= ",Q
1960    IF Q<1 OR Q>4 THEN 1950
1970         '** GET EARNINGS, DIVIDENDS, BOOK
1980    Y=1
1990    FOR Z=1 TO 4
2000       D$=""
2010       PRINT
2020       FOR X=Y TO Y+3
2030          PRINT Q(X,0);:PRINT USING "###";Q(X,1);
2040          INPUT " Quarterly earnings= ",Q(X,2)
2050          NEXT
2060       IF D$<>"" THEN 2160
2070       PRINT
2080       FOR X=Y TO Y+3
2090          PRINT Q(X,0);:PRINT USING "###";Q(X,1);
2100          INPUT " Quarterly dividends= ",Q(X,5)
2110          NEXT
2120       IF D$<>"" THEN 2160
2130       PRINT
2140       X=Y+Q-1
2150       PRINT Q(X,0);:PRINT USING "###";Q(X,1);:INPUT " Book value= ",Q(X,8)
2160       PRINT:PRINT "Any errors in (E)arnings, (D)ividends, (B)ook? ";
2170       GOSUB 8310:D$=R$
2180       IF D$="E" THEN 2010
2190       IF D$="D" THEN 2070
2200       IF D$="B" THEN 2130
2210       Y=Y+4
2220       PRINT "(Esc) Exit from quarterly data input? ";
2230       GOSUB 8260
2240       IF FNESC(R$) THEN 2260
2250       NEXT
2260    GOSUB 5120    'CALC. QUARTERLY FIGURES
2270    RETURN
2280         '
2290         '************************
2300         'DISPLAY COMPANY DATA  S
2310         '************************
2320    GOSUB 5640    'CALC. DEFLATOR
2330    CLS
2340    IF D$="P" THEN GOSUB 8480    'OUTPUT TO PRINTER
2350    PRINT #3,H$    'HEADING
2360    PRINT #3,DATE$
2370    PRINT #3,"          Earnings    %    Dividends    ";
2380    PRINT #3,"    % Retained/  Growth         Earns"
2390    PRINT #3,"Yr Mo    Qt.  Cum. Growth  Qt.    Cum.  ";
2400    PRINT #3,"Book  prior yr Calculations    vs Defl"
2410    PRINT #3,TAB(71);:PRINT #3,USING "Base ####";BY
2420         '** DISPLAY EACH LINE OF QUARTERLY DATA
2430    FOR X=1 TO 12
2440       ON X GOSUB 2830,2840,2850,2860,2880,2890,2900,2910,2930,2940,2950,2960
2450       NEXT
2460         '** DISPLAY THE VALUATION FIGURES
2470    X=16:WHILE Q(X,4)=0 AND X>0:X=X-1:WEND
```

Appendix A-5   (Continued)

```
2480    GOSUB 3030    'TEST '+,-, '
2490    PRINT #3,"Qual: S&P";:PRINT #3,USING "#### VL#### CD####";V(1);V(2);V(3);
2500    S1=0:N1=0
2510    FOR T=1 TO 3:IF V(T)<>0 THEN S1=S1+V(T):N1=N1+1
2520      NEXT
2530    PRINT #3," Av:";
2540    IF N1<>0 THEN PRINT #3,USING "####";S1/N1; ELSE PRINT #3,"    0";
2550    T=16:WHILE Q(T,8)=0 AND T>0:T=T-1:WEND
2560    IF T=0 THEN B1=0 ELSE B1=V(8)/Q(T,8)
2570    PRINT #3,USING " +## +## +## = ####%";V(4);V(5);V(6);V(7);
2580    PRINT #3,USING " P/B ###.##";B1;:PRINT #3,TAB(76) MID$(S2$,10,1)
2590    PRINT #3,USING "Val.: Price ####.##    Yield ##.#";V(8);V(9);
2600    PRINT #3,USING "+Gr ####=#####*Q.R##.##=##.##";V(10);V(11);V(12);V(13);
2610    PRINT #3,USING "/PE ###.##=###.##";V(14);V(15)
2620    IF D$="P" THEN FOR X=1 TO 10:PRINT #3,;:NEXT:GOSUB 8470    'TO SCREEN
2630    RETURN
2640            '****** S
2650            'PRINT A ROW OF QUARTERLY DATA
2660    PRINT #3,USING "##"        ;Q(X+4,0);
2670    PRINT #3,USING "###"        ;Q(X+4,1);
2680    PRINT #3,USING "###.##"    ;Q(X+4,2);Q(X+4,3);
2690    PRINT #3,USING "#####.#"    ;Q(X+4,4);
2700    PRINT #3,USING "###.##"    ;Q(X+4,5);Q(X+4,6);
2710    PRINT #3,USING "####.##"    ;Q(X+4,8);
2720    PRINT #3,USING "####.#    ";Q(X+4,9);
2730    RETURN
2740            'GROWTH & DEFL
2750    GOSUB 2660    'ROW OF QUARTERLY DATA
2760    PRINT #3,PR$;
2770    PRINT #3,USING "#####.##  "  ;G(LCTR,0);
2780    PRINT #3,USING "######.#"    ;G(LCTR,3):RETURN
2790    PRINT #3,USING "#########.###";G(LCTR-2,0);
2800    PRINT #3,USING "########.#"  ;G(LCTR,3):RETURN
2810            '******
2820            'LINE FORMAT AFTER QUARTERLY DATA
2830    PR$="  4 yr $":LCTR=1:GOTO 2750
2840    PR$="  5 yr $":LCTR=2:GOTO 2750
2850    PR$="  4 yr %":LCTR=3:GOTO 2750
2860    PR$=" Est 1 %":LCTR=4:GOSUB 2750
2870    PRINT #3,TAB(53) " Est 2 %";:LCTR=5:GOTO 2770
2880    PR$="% Retain":LCTR=6:GOTO 2750
2890    PR$="Average ":LCTR=7:GOTO 2750
2900    GOSUB 2660:PRINT #3,TAB(71):LCTR=8:GOTO 2780
2910    GOSUB 2660:PRINT #3,        "Quality factor Mil";:LCTR=9:GOSUB 2780
2920    PRINT #3,TAB(53)          "Cash";:LCTR=10:GOTO 2790
2930    GOSUB 2660:PRINT #3,        "Work";:LCTR=11:GOTO 2790
2940    GOSUB 2660:PRINT #3,        "Debt";:LCTR=12:GOTO 2790
2950    GOSUB 2660:PRINT #3,USING "Conv#########.###    Mkt Val";G(11,0):RETURN
2960    GOSUB 2660:PRINT #3,USING "Shares#######.###";G(12,0);
2970    PRINT #3,USING "########";G(12,0)*V(8)
2980    PRINT #3,TAB(5) F$:RETURN    'FOOTNOTES
2990            '
3000            '*****************
3010            'TEST FOR '+,-, '  S
3020            '*****************
3030    IF LEN(S2$)<10 THEN S2$=S2$+SPACE$(10)
3040    IF Q(X,4)>1.1*V(10) THEN MID$(S2$,10,1)="+":RETURN
3050    IF Q(X,4)<.9*V(10) THEN MID$(S2$,10,1)="-" ELSE MID$(S2$,10,1)=" "
3060    RETURN
3070
```

Appendix A-5   (Continued)

```
3080          '************************
3090          '*                      *
3100          '*   MODIFY STOCK DATA   MR
3110          '*                      *
3120          '************************
3130     INPUT 'Stock code for display: ',S$:S$=S$+SPACE$(NL):S$=LEFT$(S$,NL)
3140     GOSUB 7640    'READ FILE
3150     IF F9=1 THEN 360
3160     D$=''
3170     GOSUB 2320    'DISPLAY
3180     IF D$='P' OR D$='p' THEN D$='P':GOTO 3160
3190          '** MENU
3200     LOCATE 23,1,1
3210     PRINT '(N)umeric, (H)eading, (F)ootnotes, (S)plit, (Y)ear update, ';
3220     PRINT '(D)eflator? ';
3230     GOSUB 8310:D$=R$
3240     IF D$='N' THEN 6310
3250     IF D$='H' THEN 3820
3260     IF D$='F' THEN 3880
3270     IF D$='S' THEN 3530
3280     IF D$='Y' THEN 3690
3290     IF D$='D' THEN 3380
3300     LOCATE CSRLIN-1,,1:PRINT E$:LOCATE CSRLIN-1,,1
3310     PRINT '(W)rite to disk, (P)rintout, Esc  Exit? ';
3320     GOSUB 8310:D$=R$
3330     IF D$='W' THEN GOSUB 7910    'WRITE TO STOCK FILE
3340     IF FNESC(D$) OR D$='W' AND F9=0 THEN 360
3350     GOTO 3170
3360          '********************
3370          'CHANGE BACK EARNINGS
3380     CLS
3390     FOR X=1 TO 12:G(X,1)=D1(X+D2):NEXT
3400     INPUT 'New base year for deflator calculations: ',Y1
3410     WHILE Y1>99:Y1=Y1-100:WEND
3420     IF Y1<D1+D2 THEN 3170
3430     PRINT 'You may change back earnings or bypass an entry with ENTER alone'
3440     FOR X=1 TO 12:PRINT X+D1+D2-1;:PRINT USING '#####.##';G(X,2);
3450       INPUT '  Earnings:',R$:IF R$<>'' THEN G(X,2)=VAL(R$)
3460       NEXT
3470     FOR X=1 TO 12:G(X,3)=G(X,1)/G(Y1-D1+D2-1,1):NEXT
3480     FOR X=1 TO 12:G(X,1)=G(X,3):NEXT
3490     GOSUB 5440    'CALC GROWTH
3500     GOTO 3170
3510          '***********
3520          'STOCK SPLIT
3530     N=-100
3540     WHILE N<=-100
3550       INPUT; 'New shares added as a percentage of stock outstanding: ',N
3560       WEND
3570     IF N=0 THEN 6530
3580     M=100/(100+N)
3590     FOR X=1 TO 16
3600       Q(X,2)=Q(X,2)*M:Q(X,3)=Q(X,3)*M:Q(X,5)=Q(X,5)*M:Q(X,6)=Q(X,6)*M
3610       Q(X,8)=Q(X,8)*M
3620       NEXT
3630     G(1,0)=G(1,0)*M:G(2,0)=G(2,0)*M:G(12,0)=G(12,0)/M
3640     FOR X=1 TO 12:G(X,2)=G(X,2)*M:NEXT
3650     V(8)=V(8)*M
3660     GOTO 6530
3670          '***********
3680          'YEAR UPDATE
3690     LOCATE CSRLIN-1,1,1:PRINT SPC(79):LOCATE ,1,1
```

Appendix A-5   (Continued)

```
3700    PRINT "Esc  Escape Year Update routine? ";
3710    GOSUB 8260:IF FNESC(R$) THEN 6530
3720    FOR X=1 TO 12:FOR Y=0 TO 9:Q(X,Y)=Q(X+4,Y):NEXT Y,X
3730    FOR X=13 TO 16:Q(X,0)=Q(X-4,0)+1:Q(X,1)=Q(X-4,1):NEXT
3740    FOR X=13 TO 16:FOR Y=2 TO 9:Q(X,Y)=0:NEXT Y,X
3750    FOR X=0 TO 11:G(X,1)=G(X+1,1):G(X,2)=G(X+1,2):NEXT
3760    G(12,1)=0:G(12,2)=0
3770    G(1,0)=G(2,0):G(2,0)=0
3780    D1=D1+1
3790    GOTO 6530
3800          '**************
3810          'CHANGE HEADING
3820    GOSUB 7310    'STRING INSTRUCTIONS
3830    LOCATE 1,1,1
3840    H$=H$+E$:L4=79:A1$=LEFT$(H$,L4):X=1:GOSUB 7360:H$=A1$
3850    GOTO 3200
3860          '***************
3870          'CHANGE FOOTNOTES
3880    GOSUB 7310    'STRING INSTRUCTIONS
3890    LOCATE 20,5,1
3900    F$=F$+E$:L4=67:A1$=LEFT$(F$,L4):X=1:GOSUB 7360:F$=A1$
3910    GOTO 3200
3920          '
3930          '********************************
3940          '*  CHANGE DEFLATOR CONSTANTS  MS
3950          '********************************
3960    F2=0
3970    CLS:PRINT
3980    FOR X=1 TO 14:PRINT D1(X):NEXT
3990    PRINT "Bypass entry with ENTER alone"
4000    LOCATE 1,1
4010    PRINT "(Y)ear update all constants, (W)rite to disk, Esc  Exit? ";
4020    GOSUB 8310
4030    IF R$="W" THEN 4100
4040    IF FNESC(R$) THEN 4140
4050    IF R$="Y" THEN FOR X=1 TO 12:D1(X)=D1(X+1):NEXT:D1(14)=D1(14)+1:GOTO 3970
4060    X=1
4070    WHILE X<15:INPUT "",R$:IF R$<>"" THEN D1(X)=VAL(R$):F2=1
4080      X=X+1:WEND
4090    GOTO 3970
4100    IF NOT F2 THEN 4140    'NO CHANGES
4110    OPEN PD$+"DEFLATOR.SYD" FOR OUTPUT AS #1
4120    FOR X=1 TO 14:WRITE #1,D1(X):NEXT
4130    CLOSE #1
4140    CLS:RETURN
4150          '
4160          '********************************
4170          '*                              *
4180          '*  CALCULATE GROUP VALUATIONS  MR
4190          '*                              *
4200          '********************************
4210    P1=0:LINE INPUT "Do valuations on group numbers: ",R$
4220    IF R$="" THEN 360 ELSE GP$=R$
4230    FOR X=0 TO LGRP:GROUPS(X)=0:NEXT
4240    FOR X=1 TO LEN(R$):IF MID$(R$,X,1)=" " THEN MID$(R$,X,1)=","
4250      NEXT
4260    GOSUB 4910    'EXTRACT GROUP
4270    X=INSTR(R$,","):IF X<>0 THEN R$=MID$(R$,X+1):GOTO 4260
4280    GF=0:FOR X=0 TO LGRP:IF GROUPS(X) THEN GF=-1
4290      NEXT
4300    IF NOT GF THEN 360
4310          '*** MODE
```

Appendix A-5   (Continued)

```
4320    PRINT "Valuations on whole group (G), star stocks (*), single stock (S)? "
;
4330    GOSUB 8310:V1$=R$
4340    IF V1$="G" OR V1$="*" THEN 4380
4350    IF V1$="S" THEN INPUT "Stock name:",S1$ ELSE 360
4360    IF S1$="" THEN 360 ELSE S1$=S1$+SPACE$(6):S1$=LEFT$(S1$,6)
4370            '*** MAIN LOOP
4380    GOSUB 8130    'OPEN STOCK INDEX AND ASSIGN FIELDS
4390    X1=1:S2$=" "
4400    WHILE LEFT$(S2$,1)<>"*"
4410      GET #2,X1:S2$=SB$:P=CVS(PB$)
4420      S$=LEFT$(S2$,NL)
4430      G2=ASC(MID$(S2$,NL+2))
4440      IF GROUPS(G2) THEN G1=G2:GOTO 4500
4450      X1=X1+1:WEND
4460    BEEP:PRINT "Group valuations on ";GP$;" done"
4470    CLOSE #2:GOTO 340
4480            '**************************
4490            'GROUP MATCH
4500    IF (V1$="S" AND S$<>S1$) OR (V1$="*" AND MID$(S2$,NL+3,1)<>"*") THEN 4450
4510    R$=INKEY$:IF FNESC(R$) THEN 4840
4520    GOSUB 7640  'READ FILE
4530    IF F9=1 THEN 4870
4540            '*** UPDATE FILE
4550    V(8)=P
4560    GOSUB 5440    'CALCULATE GROWTH FIGURES
4570    GOSUB 6010    'CALCULATE VALUATION FIGURES
4580    GOSUB 3030    'TEST "+,-, "
4590    IF LEFT$(H$,NL)<>S$ THEN 4880
4600    GOSUB 7910    'WRITE FILE
4610    IF F9<>1 THEN 4660
4620    PRINT "(R) Retry or (Esc) Exit? ";
4630    GOSUB 8310
4640    IF FNESC(R$) THEN 4470 ELSE 4600
4650            '*** UPDATE INDEX
4660    V=V(15):G=V(10):R=V(9):Q=V(7)
4670    T=16:WHILE Q(T,8)=0 AND T>0:T=T-1:WEND
4680    IF T=0 THEN E=0 ELSE E=V(8)/Q(T,8)
4690    MKT=G(12,0)*V(8)
4700    IF P1=0 THEN PRINT TAB(24);"Price Valuation Growth   Yield    P/B    Qualit
y Mkt V."
4710    PRINT USING "Group ## \        \     ";G1;H$;
4720    PRINT USING "#####.##";P;V;:PRINT MID$(S2$,NL+4,1);
4730    PRINT USING "#####.##";G;R;E;Q;
4740    PRINT USING " ######";MKT
4750    IF P1>19 THEN P1=0 ELSE P1=P1+1
4760    GOSUB 8180    'ASSIGN VALUES AND PUT
4770            '
4780    IF V1$="G" OR V1$="*" THEN 4450
4790    PRINT "Continue with group valuations (G)? ";
4800    GOSUB 8310:V1$=R$
4810    IF V1$="G" THEN 4450
4820    CLOSE #2:GOTO 360
4830            '*** ERROR MSGS
4840    PRINT "Esc   Escape from do valuations at stock ";S$;"? ";
4850    GOSUB 8310
4860    IF FNESC(R$) THEN GOTO 4470 ELSE 4520
4870    PRINT "Error in reading file: ";S$:GOTO 4450
4880    PRINT "Code name mismatch ";LEFT$(H$,NL);" <> ";S$:GOTO 4450
4890            '******
4900            'EXTRACT GROUP FROM STRING   S
4910    G1=VAL(R$):IF G1>0 AND G1<=LGRP THEN GROUPS(G1)=-1
```

Appendix A-5   (Continued)

```
4920   RETURN
4930   '
4940        '*******************
4950        'LIST DATA FILES   MS
4960        '*******************
4970   ON ERROR GOTO 5050:FILES DD$+"*.DAT":ON ERROR GOTO 0
4980   PRINT "Option to delete files.  Input code name or ENTER when done..."
4990   R$=" "
5000   WHILE R$<>""
5010     INPUT "Delete stock: ",R$:IF R$="" THEN 5030
5020     ON ERROR GOTO 5060:KILL DD$+R$+".DAT":ON ERROR GOTO 0
5030     WEND
5040   RETURN
5050   RESUME 5040
5060   RESUME NEXT
5070        '*******************
5080        '** CALCULATIONS **
5090        '*************************
5100        'CALCULATE QUARTERLY FIGURES   S
5110        '*** CUMULATIVE EARNINGS
5120   FOR X=4 TO 16:Q(X,3)=0:NEXT
5130   FOR X=4 TO 16
5140     FOR Y=X TO X-3 STEP -1
5150       IF Q(X,2)<>0 THEN Q(X,3)=Q(X,3)+Q(Y,2)
5160       NEXT
5170     NEXT
5180        '*** % GROWTH
5190   FOR X=4 TO 16
5200     IF Q(X-4,3)<=0 OR Q(X,3)<=0 THEN Q(X,4)=0:GOTO 5240
5210     Q(X,4)=100*(Q(X,3)/Q(X-4,3)-1)
5220     IF Q(X,4)>99999! THEN Q(X,4)=99999!
5230     IF Q(X,4)<-9999 THEN Q(X,4)=-9999
5240     NEXT
5250        '*** CUMULATIVE DIVIDENDS
5260   FOR X=1 TO 16:Q(X,6)=0:Q(X,9)=0:NEXT
5270   T=0
5280   FOR X=5 TO 8:IF Q(X,8)<>0 THEN T=X-4
5290     NEXT
5300   Y=T
5310   FOR Z=4+T TO 12+T STEP 4
5320     FOR X=Y+1 TO Y+4
5330       Q(Z,6)=Q(Z,6)+Q(X,5)
5340       NEXT
5350     Y=Y+4
5360     NEXT
5370        '*** % RETAINED
5380   FOR Z=5 TO 16
5390     IF Q(Z-4,8)>0 AND Q(Z,3)>0 THEN Q(Z,9)=100*(Q(Z,3)-Q(Z,6))/Q(Z-4,8)
5400     NEXT
5410   RETURN
5420        '************************
5430        'CALCULATE GROWTH FIGURES   S
5440   IF G(2,0)>0 AND Q(16,3)>0 THEN 5470
5450   IF G(1,0)<=0 OR Q(12,3)<=0 THEN G(3,0)=0:GOTO 5480
5460   G(3,0)=EXP(LOG(G(1,0)/Q(12,3))/4)*100-100:GOTO 5480
5470   G(3,0)=EXP(LOG(G(2,0)/Q(16,3))/4)*100-100
5480   FOR X=16 TO 9 STEP -1
5490     IF Q(X,9)<>0 THEN GOTO 5510
5500     NEXT
5510   G(6,0)=Q(X,9)
5520   IF G(3,0)<0 THEN G(3,0)=0
5530   IF G(6,0)<0 THEN G(6,0)=0
```

Appendix A-5   (Continued)

```
5540          '*** AVERAGE GROWTH
5550     G(7,0)=0:Y=0
5560     FOR X=3 TO 6
5570       IF G(X,0)<=0 THEN 5590
5580       G(7,0)=G(7,0)+G(X,0):Y=Y+1
5590       NEXT
5600     IF Y<>0 THEN G(7,0)=G(7,0)/Y
5610     RETURN
5620          '****************
5630          'DEFLATOR ROUTINE   S
5640     BY=0
5650     GOSUB 7750    'YEAR SKEW
5660     FOR X=1 TO 16:IF Q(X,0)=D1(14) THEN 5690
5670       NEXT
5680     REASON=1:GOTO 5910
5690     FOR Y=X TO X-4 STEP -1:IF Q(Y,8)<>0 THEN 5710
5700       NEXT
5710     IF Y>X-5 THEN G(11,2)=Q(Y,3)
5720     Y=X
5730     FOR X=16 TO 1 STEP -1:IF Q(X,3)<>0 THEN 5750
5740       NEXT
5750     IF X<Y THEN X=Y+3
5760     IF X>16 THEN X=16
5770     G(12,2)=Q(X,3)
5780     FOR Y=1 TO 12:G(Y,3)=D1(Y):NEXT
5790     FOR Y=1 TO 12:IF G(Y,1)=1 THEN 5830
5800       NEXT
5810     REASON=2:GOTO 5910
5820          '* BASE YEAR FOUND
5830     G(12,1)=G(12,3)/G(Y,3)
5840     IF G(Y,2)=0 THEN REASON=3:GOTO 5910
5850     BY=D1+Y
5860     FOR X=1 TO 12
5870       IF G(X,1)<>0 THEN G(X,3)=100*G(X,2)/(G(Y,2)*G(X,1))
5880       NEXT
5890     RETURN
5900          '** IMPROPER DEFLATOR DATA MESSAGES
5910     CLS:PRINT "Deflator calulations cannot be completed"
5920     PRINT "because ";
5930     IF REASON=1 THEN PRINT "of a quarterly and deflator end years disparity."
5940     IF REASON=2 THEN PRINT "a base year has not been found."
5950     IF REASON=3 THEN PRINT "there are no base year earnings."
5960     PRINT "Press any key to continue ";:R$=INPUT$(1):PRINT
5970     RETURN
5980          '****************************
5990          'CALCULATE VALUATION FIGURES   S
6000          '*** ADJUSTED QUALITY
6010     S1=0:N1=0
6020     FOR T=1 TO 3
6030       IF V(T)<>=0 THEN S1=S1+V(T):N1=N1+1
6040       NEXT
6050     IF G(8,0)>G(10,0) THEN V(4)=5 ELSE V(4)=0
6060     IF G(9,0)>G(10,0) THEN V(5)=5 ELSE V(5)=0
6070     IF G(11,0)>0 THEN V(6)=-5 ELSE V(6)=0
6080     IF N1=0 THEN V(7)=0 ELSE V(7)=S1/N1+V(4)+V(5)+V(6)
6090          '*** YIELD
6100     FOR X=16 TO 1 STEP -1
6110       IF V(8)<>0 THEN V(9)=4*Q(X,5)/V(8)*100:IF Q(X,5)<>0 THEN GOTO 6140
6120       NEXT
6130          '*** ADJUSTED TOTAL RETURN
6140     V(10)=G(7,0)    'GROWTH
6150     V(11)=V(9)+V(10)    'TOTAL RETURN
6160     V(12)=V(7)/100    'QUALITY
```

Appendix A-5 (Continued)

```
6170  V(13)=V(11)*V(12)
6180          '*** P/E
6190  FOR X=16 TO 1 STEP -1
6200    IF Q(X,3)<>0 THEN GOTO 6230
6210    NEXT
6220  GOTO 6250
6230  V(14)=V(8)/Q(X,3)
6240          '*** VALUATION
6250  IF V(14)>0 THEN V(15)=V(13)/V(14) ELSE V(15)=0
6260  RETURN
6270          '**************
6280          '** EDITING **
6290          '**************
6300          'CHANGE NUMERIC  S
6310  LOCATE CSRLIN-1,1,1
6320  PRINT "   Esc to exit. ";CHR$(24);CHR$(25);CHR$(26);CHR$(27);
6330  PRINT ", Tab, Shift Tab, Home, End and ";CHR$(17);CHR$(217);
6340  PRINT " move cursor. ";CHR$(17);" deletes."
6350  PRINT "Modes 1:Ins to accept data,";CHR$(17);CHR$(217);" to enter. ";
6360  PRINT "2: Top row numerics, cursor keys enter.";:LOCATE CSRLIN-1,,1:PRINT
6370  LOCATE 1,1,1:C=1:Y=1:NUM$=""
6380  TESTBIT=NLB:R$="L":GOSUB 8390     'SHIFT NUM PAD TO CC
6390          'INPUT LOOP
6400  B$="":WHILE B$="":B$=INKEY$:WEND
6410  B=ASC(RIGHT$(B$,1))
6420  ON LEN(B$) GOTO 6430,6490
6430  IF B=9 THEN 6590
6440  IF B=13 THEN 6580
6450  IF B=32 THEN IF C>78 THEN 6400 ELSE C=C+1:PRINT B$;:GOTO 6400
6460  IF B=27 THEN 6530
6470  IF B>47 AND B<58 OR B=45 OR B=46 THEN NUM$=CHR$(B):GOTO 6680
6480  GOTO 6400
6490  IF B>70 THEN 6510
6500  IF B=15 THEN 6600 ELSE 6400
6510  ON B-70 GOTO 6370,6610,6400,6400,6620,6400,6630,6400,6640,6650,6400,6670
6520  GOTO 6400
6530  GOSUB 5120     'CALC QUARTERLY
6540  GOSUB 5440     'CALC GROWTH
6550  GOSUB 6010     'CALC VALUATION
6560  GOTO 3170
6570          '** MOVE CURSOR
6580  IF Y>23 THEN 6400 ELSE C=1:Y=Y+1:LOCATE Y,C,1:GOTO 6400      ''CR
6590  IF C>74 THEN 6400 ELSE C=C+5:LOCATE ,C,1:GOTO 6400      'TAB = +5
6600  IF C<6 THEN 6400 ELSE C=C-5:LOCATE ,C,1:GOTO 6400      'SHIFT TAB = -5
6610  IF Y<2 THEN 6400 ELSE Y=Y-1:LOCATE Y,,1:GOTO 6400      'CSR UP
6620  IF C<2 THEN 6400 ELSE C=C-1:LOCATE ,C,1:GOTO 6400      'CSR LEFT
6630  IF C>78 THEN 6400 ELSE C=C+1:LOCATE ,C,1:GOTO 6400      'CSR RIGHT
6640  C=79:LOCATE ,C,1:GOTO 6400     'CSR TO END OF LINE
6650  IF Y>23 THEN 6400 ELSE Y=Y+1:LOCATE Y,,1:GOTO 6400      'CSR DOWN
6660          '** MAP DATA
6670  NUM$=""
6680  X=80*Y+C:GOSUB 7250
6690  IF C=1 OR C=2 THEN 6920
6700  IF C>2 AND C<6 THEN 6950
6710  IF Y=22 THEN 6780
6720  IF Y=21 THEN 6790
6730  IF C>5 AND C<12 THEN 6890
6740  IF C>24 AND C<31 THEN 6900
6750  IF C>36 AND C<44 THEN 6910
6760  IF C>60 AND C<69 THEN 6840 ELSE 6400
6770          '
6780  IF X>1771 AND X<1780 THEN GOSUB 7030:V(8)=U1:GOTO 6400 ELSE 6400
6790  IF X>1689 AND X<1694 THEN GOSUB 7030:V(1)=U1:GOTO 6400
```

Appendix A-5   (Continued)

```
6800    IF X>1696 AND X<1701 THEN GOSUB 7030:V(2)=U1:GOTO 6400
6810    IF X>1703 AND X<1708 THEN GOSUB 7030:V(3)=U1:GOTO 6400
6820    GOTO 6400
6830        '
6840    IF Y>5 AND Y<11 THEN ON Y-5 GOTO 6860,6860,6400,6860,6860
6850    IF Y>14 AND Y<20 THEN 6870 ELSE 6400
6860    GOSUB 7030:G(Y-5,0)=U1:GOTO 6400
6870    GOSUB 7030:G(Y-7,0)=U1:GOTO 6400
6880        '
6890    IF U2=0 THEN 6400 ELSE GOSUB 7030:Q(Y-U2,2)=U1:GOTO 6400
6900    IF U2=0 THEN 6400 ELSE GOSUB 7030:Q(Y-U2,5)=U1:GOTO 6400
6910    IF U2=0 THEN 6400 ELSE GOSUB 7030:Q(Y-U2,8)=U1:GOTO 6400
6920    IF U2=0 THEN 6400 ELSE GOSUB 7030:U1=U1-U2
6930    IF U1>2100 THEN 6400 ELSE U1=U1 MOD 100
6940    FOR X=0 TO 3:FOR Y=1 TO 4:Q(4*X+Y,0)=U1+X:NEXT Y,X:GOTO 6530
6950    IF U2=0 THEN 6400
6960    GOSUB 7030:T=Q(4*U2+U3,1)-U1
6970    FOR X=1 TO 16
6980        Q(X,1)=Q(X,1)-T
6990        IF Q(X,1)<1 THEN Q(X,1)=Q(X,1)+12 ELSE IF Q(X,1)>12 THEN Q(X,1)=Q(X,1)-1
2
7000        NEXT
7010    GOTO 6530
7020        '**** GET DATA   S
7030    IF NUM$<>"" THEN 7110
7040        'MODE 1 INPUT
7050    TESTBIT=NLB:R$="U":GOSUB 8390     'SHIFT NUM PAD TO NUMERIC
7060    IF POS(0)>1 THEN LOCATE ,POS(0)-1,1
7070    INPUT "^",NUM$
7080    R$="L":GOSUB 8390      'SHIFT NUM PAD TO CC
7090    GOTO 7220
7100        'MODE 2 INPUT
7110    PRINT NUM$;
7120    B$="":WHILE B$="":B$=INKEY$:WEND
7130    B=ASC(RIGHT$(B$,1))
7140    IF LEN(B$)=2 THEN 7220
7150    IF B=46 OR B>47 AND B<58 THEN NUM$=NUM$+CHR$(B):PRINT CHR$(B);:GOTO 7120
7160    IF B<>8 THEN 7120
7170        'DELETE
7180    IF LEN(NUM$)>1 THEN NUM$=LEFT$(NUM$,LEN(NUM$)-1):GOTO 7200
7190    IF LEN(NUM$)=1 THEN NUM$="" ELSE 7120
7200    LOCATE ,POS(0)-1,1:PRINT " ";:LOCATE ,POS(0)-1,1:GOTO 7120
7210        'INPUT COMPLETE
7220    U1=VAL(NUM$):NUM$="":LOCATE Y,C,1:RETURN
7230        '****** S
7240        'LOCATOR FOR QUARTERLY DATA ARRAY
7250    U2=0:U3=0
7260    IF Y>5 AND Y<10 THEN U2=1:U3=Y-5:RETURN
7270    IF Y>10 AND Y<15 THEN U2=2:U3=Y-10:RETURN
7280    IF Y>15 AND Y<20 THEN U2=3:U3=Y-15:RETURN ELSE RETURN
7290        '***********************
7300        'STRING EDIT INSTRUCTIONS   S
7310    LOCATE CSRLIN-1
7320    PRINT CHR$(26);", ";CHR$(27);",Ins, Del are active, Esc exits";TAB(79)
7330    RETURN
7340        '***********
7350        'STRING EDIT   S
7360    FLG=0
7370    TESTBIT=NLB:R$="L":GOSUB 8390     'SHIFT NUM PAD TO CC
7380    B$="":WHILE B$="":B$=INKEY$:WEND
7390    B=ASC(RIGHT$(B$,1))
7400    IF LEN(B$)=2 THEN 7480
```

Appendix A-5   (Continued)

```
7410    IF B=27 THEN LOCATE ,,,CSR1,CSR2:RETURN
7420    IF X=L4 THEN 7380
7430    IF B<32 OR B>126 THEN 7380
7440    IF FLG AND X>=L4 THEN FLG=NOT FLG
7450    IF NOT FLG THEN MID$(A1$,X,1)=B$:PRINT B$;:X=X+1:GOTO 7380
7460    MID$(A1$,X)=B$+MID$(A1$,X,LEN(A1$)-X-1):PRINT B$;:X=X+1
7470    GOSUB 7590:GOTO 7380
7480    IF B=75 AND X>1 THEN X=X-1:LOCATE ,POS(0)-1,1:GOTO 7570
7490    IF B=77 AND X<L4 THEN X=X+1:LOCATE ,POS(0)+1,1:GOTO 7570
7500    IF B<>82 THEN 7540      'INS
7510    FLG=NOT FLG
7520    IF FLG THEN LOCATE ,,,INSS,CSR2 ELSE LOCATE ,,,CSR1,CSR2
7530    GOTO 7380
7540    IF B<>83 THEN 7380      'DEL
7550    IF X<L4 THEN MID$(A1$,X)=MID$(A1$,X+1)
7560    MID$(A1$,LEN(A1$),1)=" ":GOSUB 7590
7570    FLG=0:GOTO 7520
7580        '** PRINT REST OF LINE  S
7590    TMP=POS(0):PRINT MID$(A1$,X);:LOCATE ,TMP,1:RETURN
7600        '**************
7610        '** DISK I/O **
7620        '*******************
7630        'READ STOCK DATA FILE  S
7640    GOSUB 8080:IF SF$="" THEN F9=1:RETURN      'SPACE TEST
7650    F9=0:ON ERROR GOTO 7850
7660    OPEN DD$+SF$+".DAT" FOR INPUT AS #1
7670    IF F9=1 THEN ON ERROR GOTO 0:RETURN
7680    ON ERROR GOTO 7840
7690    INPUT #1,H$:ON ERROR GOTO 0:IF F9=1 THEN CLOSE #1:RETURN
7700    FOR X=1 TO 16:FOR Y=0 TO 9:INPUT #1,Q(X,Y):NEXT Y,X
7710    FOR X=1 TO 12:FOR Y=0 TO 2:INPUT #1,G(X,Y):NEXT Y,X
7720    FOR X=1 TO 15:INPUT #1,V(X):NEXT
7730    INPUT #1,F$:CLOSE #1
7740        '*** DEFLATOR SKEW  S
7750    D2=1
7760    IF Q(16,0)=D1(14)+1 AND Q(16,1)=1 THEN RETURN
7770    FOR X=16 TO 1 STEP -1
7780      IF Q(X,0)=D1(14) THEN RETURN
7790      IF Q(X,0)=D1(14)-1 THEN GOTO 7810
7800      NEXT
7810    D2=0
7820    RETURN
7830        'ERROR MSGS
7840    PRINT "Heading expected, no data in file ";LEFT$(S$,Y):GOTO 7870
7850    IF ERR=53 THEN  PRINT "File ";LEFT$(S$,Y);" is not on line":GOTO 7870
7860    PRINT "Unable to access file ";LEFT$(S$,Y);" - check drive"
7870    PRINT "Press any key to continue ";:R$=INPUT$(1):PRINT
7880    F9=1:RESUME NEXT
7890        '*************************
7900        'WRITE DATA TO STOCK FILE  S
7910    F9=0:S$=LEFT$(H$,NL)
7920    GOSUB 8080    'SPACE TEST
7930    IF SF$="" THEN 8040
7940    ON ERROR GOTO 7850
7950    OPEN DD$+SF$+".DAT" FOR OUTPUT AS #1
7960    ON ERROR GOTO 0:IF F9=1 THEN RETURN
7970    WRITE #1,H$
7980    FOR X=1 TO 16:FOR Y=0 TO 9:WRITE #1,Q(X,Y):NEXT Y,X
7990    FOR X=1 TO 12:FOR Y=0 TO 2:WRITE #1,G(X,Y):NEXT Y,X
8000    FOR X=1 TO 15:WRITE #1,V(X):NEXT
8010    WRITE #1,F$
8020    CLOSE #1:RETURN
```

Appendix A-5   (Continued)

```
8030          '** ERROR MESSAGE
8040     CLS:PRINT "Cannot write file - no code name in heading ";:R$=INPUT$(1)
8050     PRINT:F9=1:RETURN
8060          '*****************************
8070          'ELIMINATE SPACES IN STOCK NAME   S
8080     Y=1:WHILE Y<NL+1 AND MID$(S$,Y,1)<>" ":Y=Y+1:WEND:Y=Y-1
8090     SF$=LEFT$(S$,Y)
8100     RETURN
8110          '**********************
8120          'OPEN STOCK INDEX FILE   S
8130     OPEN PD$+"STOCK.INX" AS #2 LEN=W1
8140     FIELD #2,W2 AS SB$,4 AS PB$,4 AS VB$,4 AS GB$,4 AS RB$,4 AS BB$,4 AS QB$,4
AS MB$
8150     RETURN
8160          '****************************
8170          'ASSIGN INDEX VALUES AND PUT   S
8180     LSET SB$=S2$:LSET PB$=MKS$(P):LSET VB$=MKS$(V):LSET GB$=MKS$(G)
8190     LSET RB$=MKS$(R):LSET BB$=MKS$(E):LSET QB$=MKS$(Q):LSET MB$=MKS$(MKT)
8200     PUT #2,X1
8210     RETURN
8220          '********************
8230          '** KEYBOARD INPUT **
8240          '**********************
8250          'SINGLE CHARACTER INPUT   S
8260     LOCATE ,,1:R$=INPUT$(1)
8270     IF R$<" " THEN PRINT ELSE PRINT R$
8280     RETURN
8290          '****************************
8300          'SINGLE CHARACTER & CONVERT   S
8310     GOSUB 8260
8320          '********************
8330          'CONVERT TO UPPER CASE   S
8340     IF R$>="a" AND R$<="z" THEN R$=CHR$(ASC(R$)-32)
8350     RETURN
8360          '********************
8370          'CHANGE KEYBOARD MODE   S
8380          'KBS=KEYBOARD STATUS, KBLA=KBS LOW ADDRESS, R$:LOWER/UPPER CASE
8390     DEF SEG=&H40:KBLA=&H17:KBS=PEEK(KBLA)
8400     STATE=(KBS AND TESTBIT)=TESTBIT
8410     IF NOT STATE AND R$="U" OR STATE AND R$="L" THEN POKE KBLA,KBS XOR TESTBIT
8420     DEF SEG:RETURN
8430          '***********
8440          '** OUTPUT **
8450          '****************************
8460          'OUTPUT TO SCREEN OR PRINTER   S
8470     CLOSE #3:OPEN "SCRN:" FOR OUTPUT AS 3:RETURN    'TO SCREEN
8480     PRINT "Directing output to printer.  Please wait..."
8490     CLOSE #3:OPEN "LPT1:" FOR OUTPUT AS 3:RETURN    'TO PRINTER
8500     END 'PROGRAM
```

Appendix A-6

```
10      CHAIN "STARTUP"
20    ''"SCATTER"
30            'STOCK SELECTION SOFTWARE   VERSION 1.0   IBM PC
40            'ROBERT W JENKS  1978  MOD 5/9/83
50            'DISPLAY A SCATTER DIAGRAM ON SCREEN BASED ON "STOCK.INX" DATA
60            'READS FILE "GRUPGRPH.SYD". DATA SUPPLIED BY "STOKINDX.BAS"
70      KEY OFF:SCREEN 0,0,0:WIDTH 80:CLS
80      COMMON PD$,DD$
90      IF PD$="" THEN PD$="A:"    'PROGRAM DISK DRIVE DEFAULT
100     NL=6      'CODE NAME LENGTH
110     W2=NL+9   'STRING LENGTH
120     W1=50     'INDEX SPACING
130     T9=30     'TAB
140     GOSUB 1610     'TITLE
150     NPROMPTS=9
160     DIM D(53,NPROMPTS),A1$(53),C$(53),P1$(NPROMPTS)
170     FOR X=0 TO NPROMPTS:READ P1$(X):NEXT
180     DATA ""
190     DATA "(1) Price","(2) Value","(3) Growth","(4) Yield"
200     DATA "(5) Price/Book","(6) Quality","(7) Market Value"
210     DATA "(8) Total Return","(9) Price/Earnings"
220     C1$="ABCDEFGHIJKLMNOPQRSTUVWXYZabcdefghijklmnopqrstuvwxyz"
230     FOR X=1 TO 52:C$(X)=MID$(C1$,X,1):NEXT
240     L$=STRING$(79,"-")
250            '** GET DATA
260     PRINT:PRINT "Loading data..."
270     GOSUB 1760     'OPEN GRUPGRPH
280     V=0:GOSUB 1820     'GET DATA
290     A$=A1$(0):T1=D(0,1)-1:D(0,1)=0
300     IF T1<0 THEN CLOSE #2:GOTO 1550
310     IF T1>52 THEN T1=52
320     T=0:T3=0
330     FOR V=1 TO T1
340        GOSUB 1820
350        D(V,8)=D(V,3)+D(V,4):T=T+D(V,8)
360        D(V,9)=D(V,8)*D(V,6)*.01/D(V,2):T3=T3+D(V,9)
370        NEXT V
380     CLOSE #2
390     Z1$=LEFT$(A$,1):D(0,8)=T/T1:D(0,9)=T3/T1
400            '*** PICTOGRAPH
410     GOSUB 780   'GET PROMPTS
420            '*** DISPLAY
430            'HEADING
440     CLS
450     T$=STRING$(29,177):T1$=STRING$(2,177)
460     PRINT TAB(25);T$;TAB(58);FKEY$(7)
470     PRINT TAB(25);T1$;" SCATTER DIAGRAM Program ";T1$;
480     PRINT TAB(58);FKEY$(8);" to MANAGER"
490     PRINT TAB(25);T$;TAB(58);FKEY$(9)
500     PRINT
510            'KEY
520     X1=33
530     FOR Y=3 TO 15 STEP 3
540        LOCATE Y+2,X1:PRINT FKEY$(0)
550        LOCATE Y+3,X1:PRINT FKEY$(Y\3)
560        LOCATE Y+4,X1:PRINT FKEY$(6)
570        NEXT
580            'PROMPT
590     Y1=3
600     FOR Y=1 TO 5:Y1=Y1+3:FOR X=0 TO 1
610        FOR Q=0 TO 1:LOCATE Y1-Q,1+47*X:PRINT PROMPT$(Y,X,Q):NEXT
620        NEXT:NEXT
```

Appendix A-6   (Continued)

```
630          '*** SELECTION
640     LOCATE 20,39,0:PRINT " ";CHR$(29);
650     R$="":WHILE R$="":R$=INKEY$:WEND:PRINT CHR$(219);CHR$(29);
660     LOCATE ,,1
670     PRL=LEN(R$):R$=RIGHT$(R$,1)
680     IF PRL=1 THEN IF R$=CHR$(27) THEN 1570 ELSE 640
690     VR=ASC(RIGHT$(R$,1))-58:IF VR<1 THEN 640
700     ON VR GOTO 750,760,640,640,640,640,640,640,640,640
710     VR=VR-25:IF VR<1 THEN 640
720     ON VR GOTO 640
730     GOTO 640
740          'ACTION
750     CLS:GOSUB 1910:GOTO 440     'REVIEW DATA
760     GOTO 980
770          '***** GET PROMPTS   S
780     DIM PROMPT$(5,1,1)
790     T$=SPACE$(30):T1$=CHR$(24):RESTORE 870
800     FOR Y=1 TO 5:FOR X=0 TO 1:KEY Y+Y+X-1,"":FOR Z=0 TO 1:PROMPT$(Y,X,Z)=T$
810       READ N$:IF LEN(N$)=0 THEN 830
820       IF Z=1 THEN IF X=1 THEN N$=T1$+" "+N$ ELSE N$=N$+" "+T1$
830       IF X=0 THEN RSET PROMPT$(Y,X,Z)=N$ ELSE LSET PROMPT$(Y,X,Z)=N$
840       NEXT:NEXT:NEXT
850     RETURN
860          'DATA
870     DATA "Review data",""
880     DATA "Select parameters",""
890     DATA "",""
900     DATA "",""
910     DATA "",""
920     DATA "",""
930     DATA "",""
940     DATA "",""
950     DATA "",""
960     DATA "",""
970          '** INPUT PARAMETERS
980     CLS
990     GOSUB 2230     'NUM PAD TO DIGITS
1000    PRINT "Select the parameters to plot on the Y and X axes..."
1010    FOR V=0 TO NPROMPTS:PRINT P1$(V):NEXT V
1020    PRINT
1030    PARM$="Y":GOSUB 1650:IF PRM=0 THEN 440 ELSE Y5=PRM
1040    PARM$="X":GOSUB 1650:IF PRM=0 THEN 440 ELSE X5=PRM
1050    IF X5=Y5 THEN 440
1060    CLS
1070    LOCATE 25,1,1
1080    PRINT MID$(P1$(Y5),4);" (y-axis) VS ";MID$(P1$(X5),4);" (x-axis)";
1090    PRINT "   Esc to exit"
1100         '** LIMITS
1110    H=D(0,Y5):L=H:H1=D(0,X5):L1=H1
1120    FOR V=1 TO T1
1130      T2=D(V,Y5):IF T2>H THEN H=T2 ELSE IF T2<L THEN L=T2
1140      T2=D(V,X5):IF T2>H1 THEN H1=T2 ELSE IF T2<L1 THEN L1=T2
1150      NEXT V
1160    IF (H-L)=0 OR (H1-L1)=0 THEN 1550
1170    M=21/(H-L):M1=78/(H1-L1)
1180         '** BORDER
1190    USE$="#####.##"
1200    LOCATE 2,1:PRINT STRING$(79,177)
1210    LOCATE 23,1:PRINT STRING$(79,177)
1220    LOCATE 24,1:PRINT USING USE$;L1;
1230    LOCATE 24,30:PRINT USING USE$+" -";L;:PRINT USING USE$;H;
1240    LOCATE 24,70:PRINT USING USE$;H1;
```

Appendix A-6   (Continued)

```
1250   FOR Y=2 TO 23
1260     LOCATE Y,1:PRINT CHR$(177);
1270     LOCATE Y,79:PRINT CHR$(177);
1280     NEXT Y
1290   IF Z1$="R" THEN 1360
1300         '** AXES
1310   Y=INT((D(0,Y5)-L)*M)
1320   LOCATE 23-Y,2:PRINT STRING$(77,196)
1330   X=INT((D(0,X5)-L1)*M1):IF X=0 THEN X=1
1340   FOR Y=2 TO 23:LOCATE Y,X:PRINT CHR$(179);:NEXT Y
1350         '** PLOT & TAG DATA
1360   FOR V=1 TO T1
1370     GOSUB 1720:LOCATE 23-Y,X+1,1:PRINT C$(V);
1380     NEXT V
1390         '** AVERAGES & IDENTIFY
1400   LOCATE 1,1
1410   IF Z1$<>"R" THEN PRINT "Average";:PRINT USING USE$;D(0,Y5);D(0,X5)
1420   LOCATE 1,30,1
1430   PRINT "Letter: ";
1440   B$="":WHILE B$="":B$=INKEY$:WEND
1450   IF B$=CHR$(27) THEN 440
1460   V=0:WHILE (C$(V)<>B$) AND (V<=T1):V=V+1:WEND
1470   IF V>T1 THEN 1420
1480   PRINT B$;
1490         '** IDENTIFY DATA POINT
1500   LOCATE 1,45,1
1510   PRINT LEFT$(A1$(V),NL);:PRINT USING USE$;D(V,Y5);D(V,X5)
1520   GOSUB 1720:LOCATE 23-Y,X+1,1,7,7
1530   FOR Q=1 TO 2500:NEXT:GOTO 1420
1540         '** END PROGRAM
1550   PRINT "No data.  Initialize GRUPGRPH.SYD from STOCK INDEX program. ";
1560   PRINT "Press any key to exit to MANAGER ";:R$=INPUT$(1):PRINT
1570   GOSUB 2220:CLOSE:CHAIN PD$+"MANAGER",20
1580         '*****
1590         'TITLE   S
1600         '*****
1610   PRINT TAB(T9);"SCATTER DIAGRAM program":PRINT:RETURN
1620         '*************
1630         'GET PARAMETER   S
1640         '*************
1650   LOCATE ,1:PRINT PARM$;"-parameter= ";:LOCATE ,,1
1660   R$="":WHILE LEN(R$)<>1:R$=INKEY$:WEND
1670   PRM=VAL(R$)
1680   IF PRM<0 OR PRM>NPROMPTS THEN 1650 ELSE PRINT R$:RETURN
1690         '************
1700         'LOCATE POINT   S
1710         '************
1720   Y=INT((D(V,Y5)-L)*M):X=INT((D(V,X5)-L1)*M1):RETURN
1730         '******************
1740         'OPEN GRUPGRPH FILE   S
1750         '******************
1760   OPEN PD$+"GRUPGRPH.SYD" AS #2 LEN=W1
1770   FIELD #2,W2 AS SG$,4 AS PG$,4 AS VG$,4 AS GG$,4 AS RG$,4 AS BG$,4 AS QG$,4
AS MG$
1780   RETURN
1790         '***************************
1800         'ASSIGN FIELDS TO VARIABLES   S
1810         '***************************
1820   GET #2,V+1
1830   A1$(V)=SG$
1840   D(V,1)=CVS(PG$):D(V,2)=CVS(VG$):D(V,3)=CVS(GG$)
1850   D(V,4)=CVS(RG$):D(V,5)=CVS(BG$):D(V,6)=CVS(QG$):D(V,7)=CVS(MG$)
```

Appendix A-6   (Continued)

```
1860    RETURN
1870            '************
1880            'DISPLAY DATA   S
1890            '************
1900    CLS
1910    C5=0:GOSUB 1990    'HEADING
1920    FOR Z=1 TO T1:GOSUB 2050:NEXT   'LINE
1930            REM    PAUSE   S
1940    C5=0:PRINT "Press any key to continue ";:R$=INPUT$(1)
1950    R$="":CLS:RETURN
1960            '*******
1970            'HEADING   S
1980            '*******
1990    PRINT "    Name    Class Group Price ";
2000    PRINT "Val. Growth Yield  P/B Qual. Mkt V. Tot Ret  P/E"
2010    RETURN
2020            '************
2030            'DISPLAY LINE   S
2040            '************
2050    S$=A1$(Z)
2060    PRINT C$(Z);"   ";LEFT$(S$,NL);
2070    PRINT USING "#####";ASC(MID$(S$,NL+1,1));
2080    PRINT USING "#####";ASC(MID$(S$,NL+2,1));
2090    PRINT USING "####.##";D(Z,1);
2100    PRINT USING "###.##";D(Z,2);
2110    PRINT MID$(S$,NL+4,1);
2120    PRINT USING "####.##";D(Z,3);
2130    PRINT USING "###.##";D(Z,4);D(Z,5);
2140    PRINT USING "####";INT(D(Z,6));
2150    PRINT USING " ######";D(Z,7);
2160    PRINT USING " ###.##";D(Z,8);
2170    PRINT USING " ###.##";D(Z,9)
2180    C5=C5+1:IF C5>=20 THEN GOSUB 1940:GOTO 1990
2190    RETURN
2200            '**************************
2210            'SET NUM PAD TO LOWER/UPPER   S
2220    TESTBIT=&H20:R$="L":GOTO 2270
2230    TESTBIT=&H20:R$="U"
2240            '*********************
2250            'CHANGE KEYBOARD MODE   S
2260            'KBS=KEYBOARD STATUS, KBLA=KBS LOW ADDRESS, R$:LOWER/UPPER CASE
2270    DEF SEG=&H40:KBLA=&H17:KBS=PEEK(KBLA)
2280    STATE=(KBS AND TESTBIT)=TESTBIT
2290    IF NOT STATE AND R$="U" OR STATE AND R$="L" THEN POKE KBLA,KBS XOR TESTBIT
2300    DEF SEG:RETURN
2310    END 'PROGRAM
```

Appendix A-7

```
10      CHAIN 'STARTUP'
20  ''ESTIMATE'
30              'STOCK SELECTION SOFTWARE   VERSION 1.0   IBM PC
40              'ROBERT W JENKS  9/18/79  MOD 5/9/83
50              'STOCK EARNINGS PROJECTIONS
60              'USES FILES 'ESTIMATE.INX' AND THE ESTIMATE DATA FILES +'.EST'
70      CLOSE:GOSUB 4010   'OUTPUT TO SCREEN
80      SCREEN 0,0,0:CLS:KEY OFF
90      COMMON PD$,DD$
100     IF PD$='' THEN PD$='A:'  'PROGRAM DRIVE DEFAULT
110     IF DD$='' THEN DD$='B:'  'DATA DRIVE DEFAULT
120     L1=100            'INDEX SIZE,  MAX FILES PER DISK
130     EXT$='.EST'   'ESTIMATE FILE EXTENSION
140     T1=25             'TAB
150     NLB=&H20          'NUM LOCK MASK
160     DIM A(7,10),I$(L1+1)   'ARRAY, INDEX
170     E1$=SPACE$(6):EMPTY$=SPACE$(79)
180     DEF FNESC(I$)=I$=CHR$(27)
190             '**************
200             '** DATA DISK ON LINE?
210     ED$=DD$
220     CLS:GOSUB 3650    'NAME
230     GOSUB 3870   'SEARCH FOR INDEX
240     IF NOT F9 THEN 290
250     PRINT 'Mount Estimate data disk on drive ';ED$;' ';
260     GOSUB 3810   'KEY IN
270     GOSUB 3870   'SEARCH FOR INDEX
280     IF F9 THEN 320
290     PRINT 'ESTIMATE.INX found on drive ';ED$:GOSUB 3370:GOTO 560    'GET INDEX
300             '**************
310             '** DATA DISK NOT ON LINE
320     CLS:GOSUB 3650    'NAME
330     PRINT 'Estimate data disk not on line'
340     PRINT 'Drive for estimate data (A,B,C,D,E,F)= ';:GOSUB 3730   'CHAR IN
350     IF R$>='A' AND R$<='F' THEN ED$=R$+':' ELSE 340
360     PRINT '(E)stimate or (B)lank diskette to drive ';ED$;'? ';
370     GOSUB 3730   'CHAR IN
380     IF R$='E' THEN P=0:GOTO 220
390     IF R$='B' THEN 440
400     PRINT 'Esc  Exit to MANAGER? ';
410     GOSUB 3680   'CHAR IN
420     IF FNESC(R$) THEN 1140 ELSE 320
430             'CREATE DATA DISK
440     PRINT '(C)reate estimate data disk on drive ';ED$;'? ';
450     GOSUB 3730   'CHAR IN
460     IF R$<>'C' THEN 400
470     E$=ED$+'ESTIMATE.INX'
480     F9=0:ON ERROR GOTO 3840
490     OPEN E$ FOR OUTPUT AS #2:CLOSE #2
500     ON ERROR GOTO 0
510     IF F9 THEN PRINT 'Check drive ';ED$;' ';:GOSUB 3810:GOTO 320
520     FOR X=1 TO L1:I$(X)='          ':NEXT
530     GOSUB 3330   'WRITE BLANK INDEX
540             '**************
550             '*** MENU HANDLER
560     GOSUB 940   'GET PROMPTS
570             '*** DISPLAY
580             'HEADING
590     CLS
600     T$=STRING$(29,177):T1$=STRING$(2,177)
610     PRINT TAB(25);T$;TAB(58);FKEY$(7)
620     PRINT TAB(25);T1$;' STOCK ESTIMATES Program ';T1$;
```

Appendix A-7   (Continued)

```
630     PRINT TAB(58);FKEY$(8);" to MANAGER"
640     PRINT TAB(25);T$;TAB(58);FKEY$(9)
650     PRINT
660         'KEY
670     X1=33
680     FOR Y=3 TO 15 STEP 3
690       LOCATE Y+2,X1:PRINT FKEY$(0)
700       LOCATE Y+3,X1:PRINT FKEY$(Y\3)
710       LOCATE Y+4,X1:PRINT FKEY$(6)
720     NEXT
730         'PROMPT
740     Y1=3
750     FOR Y=1 TO 5:Y1=Y1+3:FOR X=0 TO 1
760       FOR Q=0 TO 1:LOCATE Y1-Q,1+47*X:PRINT PROMPT$(Y,X,Q):NEXT
770     NEXT:NEXT
780         '*** SELECTION
790     LOCATE 20,39,0:PRINT " ";CHR$(29);
800     R$="":WHILE R$="":R$=INKEY$:WEND:PRINT CHR$(219);CHR$(29);
810     LOCATE ,,1
820     PRL=LEN(R$):R$=RIGHT$(R$,1)
830     IF PRL=1 THEN IF R$=CHR$(27) THEN 1140 ELSE 790
840     VR=ASC(RIGHT$(R$,1))-58:IF VR<1 THEN 790
850     ON VR GOTO 900,910,920,790,790,790,790,790,790,790
860     VR=VR-25:IF VR<1 THEN 790
870     ON VR GOTO 790
880     GOTO 790
890         'ACTION
900     GOSUB 1170:GOTO 590     'DISPLAY INDEX
910     GOSUB 1340:GOTO 590     'NEW FILE
920     R$="R":CLS:GOSUB 1270:GOTO 590     'READ FILE
930         '***** GET PROMPTS  S
940     DIM PROMPT$(5,1,1)
950     T$=SPACE$(30):T1$=CHR$(24):RESTORE 1030
960     FOR Y=1 TO 5:FOR X=0 TO 1:KEY Y+Y+X-1,"":FOR Z=0 TO 1:PROMPT$(Y,X,Z)=T$
970       READ N$:IF LEN(N$)=0 THEN 990
980       IF Z=1 THEN IF X=1 THEN N$=T1$+" "+N$ ELSE N$=N$+" "+T1$
990       IF X=0 THEN RSET PROMPT$(Y,X,Z)=N$ ELSE LSET PROMPT$(Y,X,Z)=N$
1000      NEXT Z,X,Y
1010    RETURN
1020        'DATA
1030    DATA "Display index",""
1040    DATA "Set up new file",""
1050    DATA "Read file",""
1060    DATA "",""
1070    DATA "",""
1080    DATA "",""
1090    DATA "",""
1100    DATA "",""
1110    DATA "",""
1120    DATA "",""
1130        '** RETURN TO MANAGER
1140    CLOSE:CHAIN PD$+"MANAGER",20
1150        '**************
1160        'DISPLAY INDEX  MS
1170    CLS
1180    PRINT TAB(T1);"STOCK ESTIMATES INDEX"
1190    FOR Y=0 TO 19:FOR X=1 TO 5
1200      L=X+5*Y:IF L>L1 THEN PRINT:GOTO 1240
1210      PRINT USING "#### "+I$(L)+"  ";L;:NEXT X
1220    PRINT TAB(79):PRINT
1230    NEXT Y
1240    PRINT "(R) Read, or (D) Delete? ";
```

Appendix A-7   (Continued)

```
1250  GOSUB 3730
1260       ' S
1270  IF R$="R" OR R$="D" THEN INPUT "File name or #: ",N$
1280  IF N$="" THEN RETURN
1290  IF R$="R" THEN 2920
1300  IF R$="D" THEN 3180
1310  RETURN
1320       '**************
1330       'SET UP NEW FILE   MS
1340  PRINT
1350  INPUT "New file name: ",N$
1360  GOSUB 3580     'TEST FOR ALPHABETIC
1370  IF F9 THEN PT$="Not a valid name":GOTO 3800
1380  N1$=N$:GOSUB 3100   'SEARCH FOR FILE IN INDEX
1390  IF Z<=L1 THEN PT$="File already exists":GOTO 3800
1400  N1$=E1$:GOSUB 3100   'SEARCH FOR EMPTY INDEX SLOT
1410  IF Z>L1 THEN PT$="Index full":GOTO 3800
1420  GOSUB 3280     'WRITE NEW ENTRY TO DISK
1430  D=Z:N1$=N$
1440  FOR Y=1 TO 10:FOR X=1 TO 7:A(X,Y)=0:NEXT X:NEXT Y   'CLEAR DATA BUFFER
1450  INPUT "First year for data= ",Y
1460  FOR X=1 TO 10:A(1,X)=Y+X-1:NEXT X
1470  GOSUB 3020     'WRITE EMPTY FILE
1480  M=1    'MODE FLAG=SETUP
1490       '**************
1500       'DISPLAY AND MODIFY   S
1510  CLS:GOSUB 2460     'DISPLAY
1520  ROW=CSRLIN
1530  LOCATE ROW,1:PRINT EMPTY$:LOCATE ROW,1,1
1540  PRINT "(N)umeric, (Y)ear update, (S)tock split, (P)rintout? ";
1550  GOSUB 3730
1560  IF R$="N" THEN GOSUB 1690:GOTO 1510
1570  IF R$="Y" THEN GOSUB 2800:GOTO 1510
1580  IF R$="S" THEN GOSUB 2860:GOTO 1510
1590  IF R$="P" THEN GOSUB 4020:GOSUB 2460:GOTO 1510
1600       '
1610  LOCATE ROW,1:PRINT EMPTY$:LOCATE ROW,1,1
1620  PRINT "(W)rite to disk, Esc  Escape write? ";
1630  GOSUB 3730
1640  IF FNESC(R$) THEN M=0:RETURN
1650  IF R$="W" THEN GOSUB 3020
1660  GOTO 1530
1670       '**************
1680       'CHANGE NUMERIC   S
1690  LOCATE CSRLIN-2,1,1
1700  IF M=0 THEN T2=42:T3=52 ELSE T2=22:T3=62
1710  PRINT TAB(12);"⌐";TAB(T2);"⌐";TAB(T3);"⌐";TAB(78)
1720  IF M<>1 THEN 1750
1730  PRINT "Setup mode- ";
1740  PRINT "Enter back data in columns 2, 3 and 7 of rows 1 to 6.";
1750  IF M<>0 THEN 1780
1760  PRINT "Update mode- Enter new data or correct back data ";
1770  PRINT "in columns 2, 5 and 6.";
1780  PRINT TAB(79):PRINT
1790       '** INSTRUCTIONS
1800  PRINT "Esc to exit.";
1810  PRINT CHR$(24);" ";CHR$(25);" ";CHR$(26);" ";CHR$(27);
1820  PRINT ", Tab, Shift tab, Home, End and ";CHR$(17);CHR$(217);
1830  PRINT " move cursor. ";CHR$(17);" to delete."
1840  PRINT "Mode 1: Ins to accept data, Num pad numerics, ENTER to enter"
1850  PRINT "Mode 2: Upper row numerics, cursor control keys to enter.";
1860  LOCATE CSRLIN-1,,1:PRINT
```

Appendix A-7   (Continued)

```
1870    TESTBIT=NLB:R$="L":GOSUB 3950        'NUM PAD TO CC
1880    LOCATE 1,1,1:C=1:Y=1:NUM$=""
1890        '** MAP KEYSTROKES TO ACTIVITY
1900    B$="":WHILE B$="":B$=INKEY$:WEND
1910    B=ASC(RIGHT$(B$,1))
1920    ON LEN(B$) GOTO 1930,1990
1930    IF B=9 THEN 2160
1940    IF B=13 THEN 2150
1950    IF B=27 THEN 2110
1960    IF B=32 THEN IF C>78 THEN 1900 ELSE C=C+1:PRINT B$;:GOTO 1900
1970    IF B>47 AND B<58 OR B=45 OR B=46 THEN NUM$=CHR$(B):GOTO 2040
1980    GOTO 1900
1990    IF B>70 THEN ON B-70 GOTO 1870,2180,1900,1900,2190,1900,2200
2000    IF B>77 THEN ON B-77 GOTO 1900,2210,2220,1900,2030
2010    IF B=15 THEN 2170 ELSE 1900
2020        '** MAP SCREEN TO ARRAY
2030    NUM$=""
2040    IF Y<6 OR Y>15 OR C<6 OR C>65 THEN 1900
2050    X1=INT((C-6)/10)+2
2060    Y1=Y-5
2070    GOSUB 2250        'GET DATA
2080    A(X1,Y1)=U1
2090    GOTO 1900
2100        '** EXIT ROUTINE
2110    GOSUB 2650        'CALCULATIONS
2120    RETURN
2130        '******
2140        'MOVE CURSOR
2150    IF Y>23 THEN 1900 ELSE C=1:Y=Y+1:LOCATE Y,C,1:GOTO 1900      'CR
2160    IF C>74 THEN 1900 ELSE C=C+5:LOCATE ,C,1:GOTO 1900      'TAB = +5
2170    IF C<6 THEN 1900 ELSE C=C-5:LOCATE ,C,1:GOTO 1900      'SHIFT TAB = -5
2180    IF Y<2 THEN 1900 ELSE Y=Y-1:LOCATE Y,,1:GOTO 1900      'CSR UP
2190    IF C<2 THEN 1900 ELSE C=C-1:LOCATE ,C,1:GOTO 1900      'CSR LEFT
2200    IF C>78 THEN 1900 ELSE C=C+1:LOCATE ,C,1:GOTO 1900      'CSR RIGHT
2210    C=79:LOCATE ,C,1:GOTO 1900      'CSR TO END OF LINE
2220    IF Y>23 THEN 1900 ELSE Y=Y+1:LOCATE Y,,1:GOTO 1900      'CSR DOWN
2230        '******
2240        'GET DATA   S
2250    IF NUM$<>"" THEN 2320
2260        'MODE 1 INPUT
2270    TESTBIT=NLB:R$="U":GOSUB 3950        'SHIFT NUM PAD TO NUMERIC
2280    LOCATE ,POS(0)-1,1:INPUT "^",NUM$
2290    R$="L":GOSUB 3950        'SHIFT NUM PAD TO CC
2300    GOTO 2430
2310        'MODE 2 INPUT
2320    PRINT NUM$;
2330    B$="":WHILE B$="":B$=INKEY$:WEND
2340    B=ASC(RIGHT$(B$,1))
2350    IF LEN(B$)=2 THEN 2430
2360    IF B=46 OR B>47 AND B<58 THEN NUM$=NUM$+CHR$(B):PRINT CHR$(B);:GOTO 2330
2370    IF B<>8 THEN 2330
2380        'DELETE
2390    IF LEN(NUM$)>1 THEN NUM$=LEFT$(NUM$,LEN(NUM$)-1):GOTO 2410
2400    IF LEN(NUM$)=1 THEN NUM$="" ELSE 2330
2410    LOCATE ,POS(0)-1,1:PRINT " ";:LOCATE ,POS(0)-1,1:GOTO 2330
2420        'INPUT COMPLETE
2430    U1=VAL(NUM$):NUM$="":LOCATE Y,C,1:RETURN
2440        '**************
2450        'DISPLAY DATA   S
2460    PRINT #3,N$
2470    PRINT #3,
2480    PRINT #3," Year  Cap Exp/  Sales/ Inc in Sales/ Inc Sales/  ";
```

Appendix A-7   (Continued)

```
2490    PRINT #3,"PM %  Earnings/"
2500    PRINT #3,"        Share     Share        Share    prior yr Cap E      Share"
2510    PRINT #3,"-----------------------------------------------------------------------"
2520    FOR Y=1 TO 10
2530      FOR X=1 TO 7
2540        IF X=1 THEN PRINT #3,USING "#####";A(X,Y);:GOTO 2560
2550        PRINT #3,USING "#######.##";A(X,Y);
2560      NEXT X
2570      PRINT #3,
2580    NEXT Y
2590    PRINT #3,
2600    GOSUB 4010    'OUTPUT TO PRINTER
2610    RETURN
2620          '**************
2630          'CALCULATIONS  S
2640          'FROM SETUP DATA   2,3,7
2650    FOR Y=2 TO 6
2660      A(4,Y)=A(3,Y)-A(3,Y-1)
2670      IF A(2,Y-1)<>0 THEN A(5,Y)=A(4,Y)/A(2,Y-1)
2680      IF A(3,Y)<>0 THEN A(6,Y)=A(7,Y)/A(3,Y)*100
2690    NEXT Y
2700          'FROM UPDATE DATA  2,5,6
2710    FOR Y=6 TO 10
2720      A(4,Y)=A(5,Y)*A(2,Y-1)
2730      A(3,Y)=A(4,Y)+A(3,Y-1)
2740      A(7,Y)=A(3,Y)*A(6,Y)/100
2750    NEXT Y
2760    M=0
2770    RETURN
2780          '**************
2790          'YEAR UPDATE  S
2800    FOR Y=1 TO 9:FOR X=1 TO 7:A(X,Y)=A(X,Y+1):NEXT X:NEXT Y
2810    A(1,10)=A(1,10)+1
2820    FOR X=2 TO 7:A(X,10)=0:NEXT X
2830    RETURN
2840          '**************
2850          'STOCK SPLIT  S
2860    INPUT "New shares added (as a % of shares outstanding): ",Z
2870    Z=1+Z/100:IF Z=0 THEN 1510
2880    FOR Y=1 TO 10:FOR X=2 TO 4:A(X,Y)=A(X,Y)/Z:NEXT X:A(7,Y)=A(7,Y)/Z:NEXT Y
2890    RETURN
2900          '**************
2910          'READ FILE  S
2920    GOSUB 3530:IF F9 THEN PT$="Not a valid name/#":GOTO 3800
2930    OPEN ED$+N1$+EXT$ FOR INPUT AS #1
2940    INPUT #1,D
2950    IF D<1 OR D>L1 THEN PT$="Empty file":GOSUB 3800:GOTO 2980
2960    INPUT #1,N$
2970    FOR Y=1 TO 10:FOR X=1 TO 7:INPUT #1,A(X,Y):NEXT X:NEXT Y
2980    CLOSE #1
2990    GOTO 1510
3000          '**************
3010          'WRITE FILE  S
3020    GOSUB 3530:IF F9 THEN RETURN
3030    OPEN ED$+N1$+EXT$ FOR OUTPUT AS #1
3040    WRITE #1,D,N$
3050    FOR Y=1 TO 10:FOR X=1 TO 7:WRITE #1,A(X,Y):NEXT X:NEXT Y
3060    CLOSE #1
3070    RETURN
3080          '**************
3090          'SEARCH INDEX FOR FILE NAME  S
3100    N1$=N1$+E1$:N1$=LEFT$(N1$,6)
```

Appendix A-7   (Continued)

```
3110    IF N1$<"0" OR N1$>"999" THEN 3140
3120    Z=VAL(N1$):IF Z<1 OR Z>L1 THEN N1$="":Z=L1+1 ELSE N1$=I$(Z)
3130    RETURN
3140    Z=1:WHILE Z<=L1 AND N1$<>I$(Z):Z=Z+1:WEND
3150    RETURN
3160            '**************
3170            'DELETE FILE FROM INDEX  S
3180    IF N$="" THEN RETURN
3190    N1$=N$:GOSUB 3100    'SEARCH
3200    IF Z>L1 THEN PT$="File not found":GOTO 3800
3210    N$=E1$
3220    IF N1$=E1$ THEN RETURN
3230    GOSUB 3280:ON ERROR GOTO 3250:KILL ED$+N1$+EXT$:ON ERROR GOTO 0
3240    RETURN
3250    RESUME NEXT
3260            '**************
3270            'ENTRY TO INDEX  S
3280    I$(Z)=N$
3290    GOSUB 3410    'OPEN INDEX
3300    LSET EENTRY$=N$:PUT #2,Z:CLOSE #2:RETURN
3310            '**************
3320            'STORE INDEX  S
3330    GOSUB 3410    'OPEN INDEX
3340    FOR X=1 TO L1:LSET EENTRY$=I$(X):PUT #2,X:NEXT X:CLOSE #2:RETURN
3350            '**************
3360            'LOAD INDEX   S
3370    GOSUB 3410    'OPEN INDEX
3380    FOR X=1 TO L1:GET #2,X:I$(X)=EENTRY$:NEXT X:CLOSE #2:RETURN
3390            '**************
3400            'OPEN ESTIMATE INDEX  S
3410    OPEN E$ AS #2 LEN=6
3420    FIELD #2,6 AS EENTRY$
3430    RETURN
3440            '**************
3450            'SHORTEN TO VALID NAME OR EMPTY STRING  S
3460    X=INSTR(N1$," ")-1
3470    ON SGN(X)+2 GOTO 3490,3480,3500
3480    N1$=""
3490    RETURN
3500    N1$=LEFT$(N1$,X):RETURN
3510            '**************
3520            'CHECK FOR VALID FILE  S
3530    F9=0:N1$=N$:GOSUB 3100:IF Z>L1 THEN F9=-1:RETURN
3540    GOSUB 3460:IF N1$="" THEN F9=-1
3550    RETURN
3560            '**************
3570            'CHECK FOR ALPHABETIC FIRST CHARACTER IN NAME  S
3580    F9=-1:IF N$="" THEN RETURN
3590    F$=LEFT$(N$,1)
3600    IF (F$<"A" OR F$>"z") OR (F$>"Z" AND F$<"a") OR LEN(N$)>6 THEN 3620
3610    N$=N$+E1$:N$=LEFT$(N$,6):F9=0:RETURN
3620    N$="":RETURN
3630            '**************
3640            'TITLE   S
3650    PRINT TAB(T1);"STOCK ESTIMATES Program":PRINT:RETURN
3660            '**************
3670            'ONE CHAR INPUT S
3680    LOCATE ,,1:R$="":WHILE R$="":R$=INKEY$:WEND
3690    IF R$>" " THEN PRINT R$ ELSE PRINT
3700    RETURN
3710            '**************
3720            'ONE CHAR IN AND CONVERT TO UPPER CASE  S
```

Appendix A-7   (Continued)

```
3730    GOSUB 3680
3740        '**************
3750        'CONVERT TO UPPER CASE   S
3760    IF R$>="a" AND R$<="z" THEN R$=CHR$(ASC(R$)-32)
3770    RETURN
3780        '**************
3790        'PROMPT, PAUSE & RETURN
3800    PRINT PT$:PRINT "Press any key to continue ";
3810    LOCATE ,,1:R$=INPUT$(1):PRINT:RETURN
3820        '**************
3830        'ERROR TRAP ROUTINE   S
3840    F9=-1:RESUME NEXT
3850        '**************
3860        'SEARCH FOR ESTIMATE.INX   S
3870    E$=ED$+"ESTIMATE.INX"
3880    F9=0:ON ERROR GOTO 3840
3890    OPEN E$ FOR INPUT AS #2:CLOSE #2
3900    ON ERROR GOTO 0
3910    RETURN
3920        '********************
3930        'CHANGE KEYBOARD MODE   S
3940        'KBS=KEYBOARD STATUS, KBLA=KBS LOW ADDRESS, R$:LOWER/UPPER CASE
3950    DEF SEG=&H40:KBLA=&H17:KBS=PEEK(KBLA)
3960    STATE=(KBS AND TESTBIT)=TESTBIT
3970    IF NOT STATE AND R$="U" OR STATE AND R$="L" THEN POKE KBLA,KBS XOR TESTBIT
3980    DEF SEG:RETURN
3990        '**************
4000        'OUTPUT SELECT   S
4010    CLOSE #3:OPEN "SCRN:" FOR OUTPUT AS #3:RETURN    'TO SCREEN
4020    PRINT "Directing output to printer.  Please wait..."
4030    CLOSE #3:OPEN "LPT1:" FOR OUTPUT AS #3:RETURN    'TO PRINTER
4040    END 'PROGRAM
```

Appendix A-8

```
10  '"LOGTREND"
20           'STOCK SELECTION SOFTWARE   VERSION 1.0   IBM PC
30           'ROBERT W JENKS   1978   MOD 5/9/83
40           'CALCULATE THE GROWTH RATE OF YEARLY DATA
50  KEY OFF:CLS:WIDTH 80
60  COMMON PD$,DD$
70  L=50   'MAX # DATA POINTS
80  IF PD$="" THEN PD$="A:"   'PROGRAM DISK DRIVE
90  DIM D(L),Y(L)
100 GOTO 150
110 PRINT "Esc  Exit to MANAGER? ";
120 GOSUB 1060   'INPUT
130 IF R$=CHR$(27) THEN 640
140 CLS
150 GOSUB 980   'TITLE
160 INPUT "First year: ",V$
170 GOSUB 670:IF V<>0 THEN X5=V-1 ELSE X5=0
180 FOR X=1 TO L:D(X)=0:Y(X)=0:NEXT
190      '*** INPUT DATA
200 X=0
210   X=X+1
220   IF X>L THEN 250
230   PRINT X+X5;:INPUT " : ",V$:GOSUB 670:Y=V
240   IF Y>0 THEN D(X)=Y:Y(X)=LOG(Y):GOTO 210
250 N=X-1:IF N=0 THEN 110
260 IF N=1 THEN MSG$="An indeterminate case ":GOSUB 1030:GOTO 140
270 FIRST=D(1):TRIVIAL=-1
280 FOR Q=2 TO N:IF D(Q)<>FIRST THEN TRIVIAL=0
290 NEXT
300 IF TRIVIAL THEN MSG$="A trivial case ":GOSUB 1030:GOTO 140
310      '*** LINEAR REGRESSION
320 Y1=0:X1=0:S1=0:S2=0:S3=0
330 FOR X=1 TO N
340   Y1=Y1+Y(X):X1=X1+X:S1=S1+X*Y(X):S2=S2+X*X:S3=S3+Y(X)*Y(X)
350   NEXT X
360 IF (N-S1)=0 OR (N-S2)=0 OR N=0 THEN 110
370 M=(Y1*X1/N-S1)/(X1*X1/N-S2)
380 B=(Y1-M*X1)/N
390 R=ABS(M*(X1*Y1/N-S1)/(S3-Y1*Y1/N))
400      '*** RESULTS
410 GOSUB 710
420      '*** SUBSTITUTE X
430 X=1:Y=1
440 IF X+Y=0 THEN 550
450 INPUT "Find value for any time?   Enter time: ",V$
460 GOSUB 670:X=V:IF X<=0 THEN PRINT:GOTO 490
470 X=X-X5:PRINT TAB(25);"F(";X+X5;")=";INT(100*EXP(M*X+B))/100
480      '*** SUBSTITUTE Y
490 IF X+Y=0 THEN 550
500 INPUT "Find time for any value?  Enter value: ",V$
510 GOSUB 670:Y=V:IF Y<=0 THEN PRINT:GOTO 440
520 PRINT TAB(25);Y;"=F(";(LOG(Y)-B)/M+X5;")"
530 GOTO 440
540      '*** MENU
550 CLS
560 GOSUB 980:PRINT   'TITLE
570 PRINT TAB(30);"(R)  Review results"
580 PRINT TAB(30);"(N)  New series"
590 PRINT TAB(30);"Esc  Exit to MANAGER"
600 PRINT TAB(30);"? ";:GOSUB 1060   'INPUT
610 IF R$="N" OR R$="n" THEN 140
620 IF R$="R" OR R$="r" THEN 410
```

Appendix A-8 (Continued)

```
630   IF R$<>CHR$(27) THEN 550
640   CHAIN PD$+"MANAGER",20
650         '**********
660         'STRING VALID AS #?  S
670   IF V$="" THEN V=0 ELSE V=VAL(V$)
680   RETURN
690         '**********
700         'RESULTS  S
710   CLS
720   PRINT "Number of points:";N
730   E$="LN(Y) ="+STR$(M)+" * X ":IF B>=0 THEN E$=E$+"+"
740   E$=E$+STR$(B)
750   PRINT E$
760   PRINT "Zero year     =";X5
770   PRINT USING "Growth          =####.## _%";(EXP(2*M-B)/EXP(M-B)-1)*100
780   PRINT USING "Degree of fit=##.###";R
790   PRINT:PRINT "Press any key to continue ";:LOCATE ,,1
800   R$=INPUT$(1):PRINT
810         '**********
820         '*** REVIEW DATA  S
830   CLS
840   PRINT TAB(10);"Original";TAB(30);"Projected"
850   X=0:R$=""
860   WHILE R$<>CHR$(27) AND X<L
870    X=X+1
880    PRINT USING "####";X+X5;
890    IF X<=N THEN PRINT TAB(10);D(X);
900    PRINT TAB(25);:PRINT USING "#######.##";EXP(M*X+B);
910    IF X<=N THEN PRINT:GOTO 940
920    PRINT TAB(45);"   Esc  Exit? ";
930    GOSUB 1060
940    WEND
950   PRINT:RETURN
960         '**********
970         '*** TITLE  S
980   PRINT TAB(23);"LOGARITHMIC LINEAR REGRESSION program"
990   PRINT TAB(23);"To calculate the growth rate of yearly data"
1000  PRINT:RETURN
1010        '**********
1020        '*** PROMPT, PAUSE & RETURN  S
1030  PRINT MSG$;:R$=INPUT$(1):PRINT:RETURN
1040        '**********
1050        '*** CHARACTER INPUT  S
1060  LOCATE ,,1:R$="":WHILE R$="":R$=INKEY$:WEND:PRINT:RETURN
1070  END 'PROGRAM
```

Investment Analysis

Prior to World War II, the people who worked on the analysis of bonds, stocks, and other securities were generally referred to as statisticians since most of the work was statistical in nature. There was very little information available from invdividual companies, and it was not until well after the war that security analysts were able to get access to management and obtain sufficient information to sensibly analyze the company and its stock. Subsequently, the security analyst evolved into a financial analyst, and now many prefer the title *investment analyst*. This name implies a number of areas of expertise. First and fundamental is the analysis of the company's business in the context of its industry position and competitive strengths and weaknesses. From this the analyst develops the information from which he or she makes earnings estimates, projections of future growth, dividend-paying ability, and other fundamentals. This latter information is what we use in doing our valuations. As indicated previously, we do not advocate that the average investor attempt to make his or her own estimates. While a few may have access to sufficient information on one or two particular companies for various reasons, only the professional analyst who is concentrating on an industry will be able to assemble and analyze the information.

The purpose here, therefore, is not to encourage the average investor to do basic analysis, but rather to show the reader what is involved in recognizing good research. The methodology described here was derived from an approach used by the Boston Consulting Group, a management consulting firm; from the work of Shell International Chemical, part of Royal Dutch Shell; and other sources. This approach is used by some of the best analysts on Wall Street and is particularly applicable to complicated manufacturing industries such as the chemical industry.

Most large companies have a diversified product line. The products are usually related in a broad sense; that is, they may be food, chemical, petroleum or perhaps machinery products. We do not follow many companies referred to as conglomerates because it is so difficult to analyze them, and because we believe that there are very few managers who know how to run such concerns. However, even though a company's products may be all basically chemical, for example, they will still differ in a number of important respects. That is, they may be sold to very different markets, and these markets may have divergent cyclical or growth characteristics. Also, the products may have very different profitability potential because of competition or other factors. Basic chemicals may be very competitive and carry low margins, while specialty chemicals may have little or no competition because of patents or other factors, and therefore carry high margins. Also, a particular company may have lower costs than its competition because of superior processes, control of low-cost raw materials, or efficiencies of size. The analyst has to know enough about a company and its industry to know where it stands in terms of the competitive capabilities and share of market, as well as the product's prospects for profitability and growth. The following is a modification of an approach used by Shell, among others.

Competitive Position.

Market Position.

1. Percentage share? Largest score: three, second score: two, others: one.
2. Security of the share?

Production Capability.

1. Physical facilities.
   a. Capacity commensurate with the market share?
   b. Various plant locations that make sense in relation to raw materials, labor, and markets?
   c. Low-cost transportation?

2. Manufacturing economics.
   a. Are the processes or manufacturing methods modern? Are they owned or licensed?
   b. Is the company a research leader?

3. Do they own or control their materials? How do the costs compare with the competition?

4. Marketing.
   a. Do they have any special marketing advantages? How important are these in relation to the market share?
   b. Do they have any protection against a larger company entering the market? Patents?

(Each factor can be scored from one to three for every product that is presently or may become important in the future. If a factor is not important do not score.)

Product Attractiveness.

Market Growth.

1. Physical volume growth? Above 10% score three, 6%-10% score two.
2. How cyclical?

Market Quality.

1. Does the product enjoy high stable profitability?
2. Can margins be maintained when operations are below capacity?
3. Does the company control the price of the product?
4. Is the technology sufficiently restricted to deter new competition?
5. How many producers? If more than four, reduce the score.
6. Are there a large number of customers, or do only one or two represent a large share of the market? If the latter, reduce the score.
7. If it is a new product, will the market potential look so large that it will attract substantial new competition?
8. Can a customer easily adapt to a different supplier or a different material?
9. Are there substitution problems?

Industry Raw Materials.

Give a high rating if they are in limited supply, a low rating if they are byproducts whose supply depends on the demand for another product.

Environmental.

Is there pollution or other such problems?

Labor.

Are labor relations good? Are there unions? Are wage rates above or below the industry average?

Management.

1. Are the senior technical people likely to resign to form their own firms or join competitors?
2. Are management salaries and incentives adequate but not excessive?
3. Does management run a tight ship?

(The labor and management areas apply to the whole operation, but an effort should be made to look at these factors in terms of the product sector wherever meaningful. Score one to three)

Each product is scored and the information is entered in the appropriate box in the matrix below. For example, if product A represents $10 million of the company's sales and it scores the top rating of three in each category, then $10 is entered in box number nine. If the product scores a two in competitive position and product attractiveness, it goes in box number five. Once every product is entered in the proper box, the sums are added together in each box and expressed as a percent of total sales. A company with not more than 5% of sales in boxes one through five and not more than 15% in boxes four through six is in good shape. When over half the business is in box number nine, the company should do extremely well.

We have used this approach on companies we know well, and find it clarifies our judgments as to future earnings

PRODUCT ATTRACTIVENESS

		Unattractive (1)	Average (2)	Attractive (3)
COMPETITIVE POSITION	Weak (1)	Disinvest Box 1	Phased Withdrawal Box 2	Double or quit Box 3
	Average (2)	Phased Withdrawal Box 4	Custodial i. e., Watch it Box 5	Try Harder Box 6
	Strong (3)	Cash Generation Box 7	Growth/ Leader Box 8	Leader Box 9

prospects, growth rates, and, to a certain degree, helps in deciding whether the quality ratings are appropriate. One thing we are convinced of is that a report that purports to be a through, basic company analysis should go into considerable detail about the company's competitive position. The previous type of analysis may be more complete than necessary for many companies, but much less than this may prove inadequate. A good industry analyst will do this type of work on a company under review, then call on the company's competitors, in effect to check it out. However, some of this information is closely guarded by management, so it is not always easy to do an analysis that is this complete. We have to make our investment decisions on the basis of what we can learn. If the information is too sketchy and the management is entirely uncooperative, the best thing to do is forget the stock of that company. There are plenty of others.

Glossary

ALPHA: A term used in Modern Portfolio theory. The Alpha value expresses how much a stock would have appreciated or depreciated, on average each month over a period of years, assuming the market was unchanged.

ASSET VALUE PER SHARE: The company's assets less liabilities and any claims on the assets senior to the common stock, such as debt and preferred stock, divided by the number of shares. The same as book value per share.

BETA: A term used in Modern Portfolio theory. The Beta value defines a stock's sensitivity in either direction to changes in the market. It should be used as a measure of volatility, not as a measure of quality.

BREADTH: The number of issues that advance or decline on a given day, divided by the number of issues that trade.

CALL OPTION: A contract providing that one party to the transaction agrees to give the right to another party to buy 100 shares of a particular stock at a certain price, at any time prior to a fixed expiration date, in return for payment.

CASH FLOW: This is an analytical term that refers to the sum of earnings and noncash charges that have been deducted as an expense such as depreciation. A cash flow statement shows where the money comes from and what it is used for.

CONVERTIBLE: A bond or a preferred stock that may be exchanged into common stock on certain terms, frequently called "converts."

CURRENT ASSETS: These include cash and short-term investments, receivables from customers or others, and inventory. The latter assets may be expected to be converted to cash during the year.

CURRENT LIABILITIES: These are items payable within one year, such as accrued wages, trade accounts payable, taxes, and amounts due on long-term debt. The difference between current assets and liabilities, if positive, is called working capital.

DEPRECIATION: An expense item related to the wearing out or obsolesence of plant, machinery, and equipment. There are a variety of ways to calculate depreciation that are allowed for tax purposes, and some are more conservative than others. Because of inflation, the amount of depreciation charged off by most businesses has not been adequate in recent years to replace the facilities.

DEPLETION: An expense item related to the using up of assets in the ground such as oil, gas, or minerals. This is also a noncash charge in a cash flow analysis.

DIVIDEND YIELD: The dividend divided by the price of a stock.

EARNINGS YIELD: The earnings divided by the price of a stock.

EFFICIENT MARKET: A theorical condition in which the market immediately discounts all available information so that prices are in equilibrium. Markets are no more efficient than people, however.

INTANGIBLES: An accounting term refering to assets that are not physical property. They include patents, trademarks, the value of a franchise, or bookkeeping items such as goodwill, which is the excess of the cost of a business acquired, beyond the value shown on the books of the company. This latter is frequently referred to as "going concern value."

INVENTORIES: This includes raw materials, work in process, and finished goods. The usual ways of valuing inventories are FIFO (first in first out), LIFO (last in first out), and average cost. Retail trade businesses may use special variations of these methods.

KEOGH PLAN: A plan that permits individuals under certain conditions to set up retirement accounts with significant tax advantages. There are also Individual Retirement Accounts (IRAs) that have similar benefits. Consult your tax advisor or broker for details.

MARGIN: This refers to borrowing against securities from your bank or broker.

MUTUAL FUND: This is an investment company that sells stock to the investing public and invests the money in various kinds of securities. An open-end fund is constantly selling to investors and redeeming shares at asset value from investors. A closed-end fund is not selling or redeeming shares. There are various kinds of open-end funds. A "load" fund has a sales charge of usually 8% when you buy. A "no-load" fund does not have a sales charge when you buy , but it usually has a larger annual management charge. A money market fund invests in short-term debt instruments such as treasury bills, commercial paper, or certificates of deposit. As with anything else in investments, there are very large differences in funds, and one should pick those run by people with a good reputation and performance record.

PLOWBACK: The amount of earnings not paid out in dividends but reinvested in the business. Plowback is frequently expressed as a ratio to book value.

PRESENT VALUE: The value today of a payment, or several

payments, to be received in the future. It is calculated from compound interest tables.

PUT OPTION: The reverse of a call. Instead of contracting to sell a stock to a person at a price, you agree to buy a stock at a fixed price prior to an expiration date. The buyer of a put expects the stock to decline in price.

PRICE-EARNINGS RATIO (P/E):   The price of a stock divided by some earnings figure. The trailing P/E means the actual earnings for the most recent four quarters are used. However, P/E usually refers to the estimated earnings for the current year, unless otherwise specified.

PRIMARY EARNINGS: These are earnings calculated on the assumption of the conversion of convertible securities into common, and in some cases, the assumption that warrants to buy stock or options issued to management under incentive plans have been exercized. The term "fully diluted" earnings is also used.

PROSPECTUS: A summary of information that a company has to file with the Securities and Exchange Commission (SEC) when it sells new securities, or securities owned by management, or owners of the business to the public.

RANDOM WALK: A term referring to the theory that the price movement of a stock is not caused or affected by previous price changes; that is, it is random. This is contrary to the beliefs of technical analysts or chartists.

SHORT SELLING: Selling stock that you do not own, in the expectation that it will decline in price. You put up money or other securities as collateral, and borrow the stock you sell short. Short against the box is selling short when you own the stock, usually to postpone a sale into a different period for tax reasons.

SPECIALIST: A member of the stock exchange who keeps the book of orders to buy and sell a particular stock. He or she may act as a broker in some trades, or as a principal in others. There is a considerable body of opinion, which we share, that the specialist system is outmoded and adds unnecessarily to the cost of trading securities. Proposals have been advanced for setting up the specialist's book on a computer. There are various other kinds of members of the exchange who own a "seat," and who are entitled to go on to the floor of the exchange for the purpose of executing orders in securities.

TAX EXEMPT SECURITIES: These are securities sold by states, cities, or other organizations that are tax exempt such as water or sewer districts. They are frequently referred to as "municipals." The income is exempt from federal taxes and taxes imposed by the local government, but not necessarily from taxes imposed by some other state.

TOTAL RETURN: The capital gain or loss, plus the dividend or interest income received over one year, divided by the price.

YIELD: This is a bond term that means the interest to be recieved is expressed as a percent of the price, plus or minus a factor related to the difference in the current price and the amount to be recieved when the bond is paid off. For example, if you buy a bond at 99 due in one year at 100, that additional amount is added to the interest it pays in calculating the yield. On stocks, the term simply refers to the dividend divided by the price. Current return is a better term for stocks but is rarely used. In this book we use yield.

Bibliography

Altman, Edward I., *Financial Handbook*, 5th Ed., New York: Wiley, 1982.

Dreman, David, *Contrarian Investment Strategy*, New York: Random House, 1979.

Elton, Edwin J. and Martin J. Gruber, *Modern Portfolio Theory and Investment Analysis*, New York:, 1981.

Graham, Benjamin, *The Intelligent Investor*, 4th Ed., New York: Harper & Row, 1973.

Mader, Chris and Robert Hagin, *The Dow Jones—Irwin Guide to Common Stocks*, New York: Dow Jones—Irwin, 1973 and 1976.

Molodovsky, Nicholas, *Investment Values in a Dynamic World*, New York: Richard D. Irwin, 1974.

Nickerson, Clarence B., *Accounting Handbook for Non-Accountants*, 2nd Ed., CBI Publishers.

Seidler, Lee J. and D.R. Carmichael, *Accounting Handbook*, 6th Ed., New York: Wiley, 1982.

Teweles, Richard J. and Edward S. Bradley, *The Stock Market*, 4th Ed., New York: Wiley, 1982.

Tracy, John, *How to Read a Financial Report*, New York: Wiley, 1980.

Valentine, Jerome L. and Edmund A. Mennis, *Quantitative Techniques for Financial Analysis*, New York: Richard D. Irwin, 1971.

Index

Corrections to Appendix A, "Stock Selection Software," were received from the author and inadvertently omitted when the final pages were assembled. They are listed here, keyed to page number and program line.

```
       p.181
1300   DATA 1,1.058,1.151,1.258,1.323,1.401,1.504,1.634,1.786,1.955
1310   DATA 2.072,2.175,2.29,84

       p.189
2050   PRINT TAB(79):PRINT #3,:C5=C5+1:GOTO 1820
2390    IF R$="S" THEN INPUT "Symbol: ",R$:MID$(S$,NL+5,5)=R$+"       ":GOSUB 6320

       p.195
5970   PRINT "Run STORE SYMBOLS FOR PRICING routine and reprice by modem."
5980   GOSUB 6720:GOTO 5940

       p.196
6760   ON ERROR GOTO 6800
6770   CLOSE #3:OPEN "LPT1:" FOR OUTPUT AS 3    'TO PRINTER
6780   ON ERROR GOTO 0
6790   PRINT "Directing output to printer. Please wait...":RETURN
6800   RESUME 6810
6810   PRINT "Printer not available ";:R$=INPUT$(1):CLS
6820   ON ERROR GOTO 0:M1$="":M2$="":GOTO 6750
6830   END 'PROGRAM

       p.198
740    CLS:GOSUB 1000:GOTO 360   'NEW FILE
970             '* ENTER INITIAL STOCK DATA   MS
1010   INPUT "Stock code for new file: ",S$:IF S$="" THEN 1730
1090   CLOSE #2:GOSUB 8080:PRINT "Stock ";SF$;" not found in index":GOSUB 5960:
       GOTO 1730
1170   IF FNESC(R$) THEN 1730 ELSE 1250
1210   IF FNESC(R$) THEN RESUME 1730 ELSE RESUME 1130

       p.199
1270   PRINT H$;:LINE INPUT "",A1$
1610   PRINT "Footnotes (67 characters max.):":LINE INPUT "",A1$
1620   F$=LEFT$(A1$,67):PRINT
1730   RETURN

       p.202
3290   IF D$="D" THEN GOSUB 3380:GOTO 3170
3370            'CHANGE BACK EARNINGS   S
```

```
3400   INPUT "New base year for deflator calculations= ",R$:IF R$<>"" THEN Y1=
       VAL(R$)
3420   IF Y1<D1+D2 OR Y1>D1+D2+11 THEN PRINT "Not within range":GOTO 3400
3500   RETURN

       p.203
4070   WHILE X<15:INPUT "",R$:IF R$<>"" THEN D1(X)=VAL(R$):F2=-1

       p.207
6350   PRINT "Num pad for cursor control, top row digits for data.";
6360   LOCATE CSRLIN-1,,1:PRINT
6510   ON B-70 GOTO 6370,6610,6400,6400,6620,6400,6630,6400,6640,6650

       p.208
7140   IF LEN(B$)=2 OR B=13 THEN 7220

       p.210
8480   ON ERROR GOTO 8520
8490   CLOSE #3:OPEN "LPT1:" FOR OUTPUT AS 3    'TO PRINTER
8500   ON ERROR GOTO 0
8510   PRINT "Directing output to printer.  Please wait...":RETURN
8520   RESUME 8530
8530   PRINT "Printer not available ";:R$=INPUT$(1):CLS
8540   ON ERROR GOTO 0:D$="":GOTO 8470
8550   END 'PROGRAM

       p.217
1340   CLS
1840   PRINT "Num pad for cursor control, top row digits for data."
1850   PRINT

       p.218
2000   IF B>77 THEN ON B-77 GOTO 1900,2210,2220
2350   IF LEN(B$)=2 OR B=13 THEN 2430

       p.221
4020   ON ERROR GOTO 4060
4030   CLOSE #3:OPEN "LPT1:" FOR OUTPUT AS 3    'TO PRINTER
4040   ON ERROR GOTO 0
4050   PRINT "Directing output to printer.  Please wait...":RETURN
4060   RESUME 4070
4070   PRINT "Printer not available ";:R$=INPUT$(1):CLS
4080   ON ERROR GOTO 0:R$="":GOTO 4010
4090   END 'PROGRAM
```